FIRE FIGHTERS

STORIES OF SURVIVAL FROM THE
FRONT LINES OF FIREFIGHTING

FIRE FIGHTERS

STORIES OF SURVIVAL FROM THE
FRONT LINES OF FIREFIGHTING

EDITED BY CLINT WILLIS

Thunder's Mouth Press
New York

FIRE FIGHTERS: STORIES OF SURVIVAL FROM THE FRONT LINES OF FIREFIGHTING

Compilation copyright © 2002 by Clint Willis
Introductions copyright © 2002 by Clint Willis

Adrenaline ® and the Adrenaline® logo are trademarks of
Avalon Publishing Group Incorporated, New York, NY.

An Adrenaline Book®

Published by
Thunder's Mouth Press
An Imprint of Avalon Publishing Group Incorporated
161 William Street, 16th floor
New York, NY 10038

Book design: Sue Canavan

frontispiece photo: Fireman holding cup of tea, safety equipment on floor
© Alan Thornton/Stone

Library of Congress Cataloging-in-Publication Data.

Fire fighters: stories of survival from the front lines of firefighting / edited by
Clint Willis.
    p. cm
  ISBN 1-56025-402-5 (trade paper)
    1. Fire extinction 2. Survival after airplane accidents, shipwrecks, etc.
3. Fires. I. Willis, Clint.

TH9310.5.F54.2002
628.9'25--dc21   2002018147

Printed in the United States of America
Distributed by Publishers Group West

for Mark Klimek

with thanks, admiration and affection

c o n t e n t s

p h o t o g r a p h s

introduction

B ack in 1987, my wife and I took our baby to a concert in lower Manhattan's Battery Park City. When it was over, we left as part of a crowd of young families—parents pushing infants in strollers or holding hands with bigger kids. Amid all of these wheels and legs and feet, I spotted a twenty-dollar bill and quickly stooped to grab it; as I did so, the twenty-dollar bill moved.

I reached for the money again, and it kept moving. I looked up to follow its progress and saw that it was attached to a piece of twine or fishing line that was held by a crouching, grinning fireman. He peered out at me from the garage door of the neighborhood fire station with two of his colleagues—all three of them vastly amused at my expense.

I took their ribbing as graciously as I could, in part because it seemed to me that I had no choice. The fact that they were firemen—however obnoxious—meant that any complaint on my part would have amounted to a pip-squeak-ish display of bad grace; I'd have looked even more ridiculous. So I swallowed my tweaked pride and walked on; they'd had their laugh, but at least I didn't have to wear one of those ridiculous hats.

And I had to admit that it was kind of funny—for a moment, I'd believed that the money was running away from me. And after a while I had to admit, too, that they really had been having fun; that they were enjoying themselves in a way that I envied and admired, a kind of slightly reckless way that was rare among the neighborhood's buttoned-up hipsters—among people like me. I was mad at the firemen for picking on me, but I kind of liked them for it.

We envy and admire firemen as we envy and admire other risk-takers—mountain climbers, NASCAR drivers, polar explorers—in part because they seem to have discovered some pleasure or satisfaction worth staking their lives upon. Our admiration for firemen partly consists of gratitude, because we take it that their satisfaction comes in part from the service they perform: Firemen apparently believe that it's worth risking their lives to try and protect strangers' lives—our lives—and property. This belief they hold is not theoretical; they go to work prepared to act upon it at any given moment.

Our collective culture has decided that firemen are heroes; we apply the word to them again and again, like layers of paint. It's as though we fear the idea that their courage is an ordinary human quality; one we may lack. If firemen who rush into burning buildings are merely ordinary, what does that make the rest of us?

The layers of praise we lavish on firemen cover them up; so that it becomes harder to see them. The stories in this book help to uncover them; we begin to see where their behavior comes from and what constitutes that quality we rather glibly call courage. Often it derives from love. The love seems to grow in part from the conditions and nature of the work—firemen eat and sleep together; they face danger together; they rely on each other; they know that at any time they might lose each other.

Then again, most of us live under conditions that could be described in similar terms. Our work in the world involves high stakes and deep connections; to do our work well we must learn to love—the ultimate act of courage. And having learned to love, which of us wouldn't run into a burning building to save the object of that love?

Maybe what interests us most about firemen is that they do it for strangers—they do it for us. Those guys who made fun of me on the sidewalk in lower Manhattan loved us and so it feels fitting that fifteen years on we love them in retrospect and in return.

—*Clint Willis*

Blowup: What Went Wrong at Storm King Mountain

by Sebastian Junger

Sebastian Junger (born 1962) was in his late twenties when he saw photos of forest fire fighters and decided he wanted to be one of them. He began working for a tree company, figuring if he could climb and use a chainsaw he could fight wildfires. He became a writer instead. One of his best-known stories describes the tragic South Canyon Fire of 1994.

The main thing Brad Haugh remembers about his escape was the thunderous sound of his own heart. It was beating two hundred times a minute, and by the time he and the two smoke jumpers running with him had crested a steep ridge in Colorado, everyone behind them was dead.

Their coworkers on the slope at their backs had been overrun by flames that Haugh guessed were three hundred feet high. The fire raced a quarter mile up the mountain in about two minutes, hitting speeds of eighteen miles an hour. Tools dropped in its path were completely incinerated. Temperatures reached two thousand degrees—hot enough to melt gold or fire clay.

"The fire blew up behind a little ridge below me," Haugh said later. "People were yelling into their radios, 'Run! Run! Run!' I was roughly one hundred and fifty feet from the top of the hill, and the fire got there in ten or twelve seconds. I made it over the top and just tumbled and rolled down the other side, and when I turned around, there was just this incredible wall of flame."

Haugh was one of forty-nine firefighters caught in a wildfire that stunned the nation with its swiftness and its fury. Fourteen elite fire fighters perished on a spine of Storm King Mountain, seven miles west of Glenwood Springs, Colorado. They died on a steep, rocky slope in a fire initially so small that the crews had not taken it seriously. They died while cars passed within sight on the interstate below and people in the valley aimed their camcorders at the fire from garage roofs.

There were many other fire fighters on Storm King when Brad Haugh crested the ridge, yet he feared that he and the two men with him were the only ones on the mountain left alive. That thought—not the flames—caused him to panic. He ran blindly and nearly knocked himself unconscious against a tree. Fires were spotting all around him as the front of flames chased him. The roar was deafening; "a tornado on fire" was how he later described it. The light, he remembered, was a weird blood-red that fascinated him even as he ran.

The two smoke jumpers with him were Eric Hipke and Kevin Erickson. Hipke had been so badly burned the flesh was hanging off his hands in strips. Haugh paused briefly to collect himself, then led the two men about a hundred yards down the mountain, stopping only long enough to wrap Hipke's hands in wet T-shirts. As they started down again, the fire was spreading behind them at a thousand acres an hour, oak, pinyon, and juniper spontaneously combusting in the heat.

"I didn't have any nightmares about it later," said Haugh. "But I did keep waking up in the night very disoriented. Once I had to ask my girlfriend who she was."

The South Canyon fire, as it was called, ignited on Saturday, July 2, as a lightning strike in the steep hills outside Glenwood Springs. At first people paid it little mind because dry lightning had already triggered thirty or forty fires across the drought-plagued state that day; another wisp of smoke was no big deal. But this blaze continued to grow, prompting the Bureau of Land Management (BLM) district office in Grand Junction to dispatch a seven-member crew on the morning of July 5 to prepare a helicopter landing site, designated H-1, and start cutting a fire line along a ridge of Storm King. At this point the blaze was cooking slowly through the sparse pinyon and juniper covering the steep drainage below. Glenwood Springs was visible to the east, and a pricey development called Canyon Creek Estates was a mile to the west. Interstate 70 followed the Colorado River one thousand feet below, and occasionally the fire fighters could see rafters in brightly colored life jackets bumping through the rapids.

The BLM crew worked all day, until chain saw problems forced them to hike down to make repairs. Replacing them were eight smoke jumpers from Idaho and Montana (eight more would be added the next morning) who parachuted onto the ridgetop to continue cutting fire line. They worked until midnight and then claimed a few hours' sleep on the rocky ground.

Just before dawn, on the morning of July 6, Incident Commander Butch Blanco led the BLM crew back up the steep slope. Arriving at the top, Blanco discussed strategy with the smoke jumper in charge, Don Mackey. At about the same time, the BLM office in Grand Junction dispatched one additional crew to the fire, the twenty-member Prineville Hotshots, a crack interagency unit from Oregon whose helmet emblem is a coyote dancing over orange flame.

The smoke jumpers had cleared another landing spot, H-2, on the main ridge, and around twelve-thirty in the afternoon, a transport helicopter settled onto it. The first contingent of the Prineville crew ran through the rotor wash and crouched behind rocks as the chopper lifted off to pick up the rest of the unit from below. They'd been chosen alphabetically for the first flight in: Beck, Bickett, Blecha, Brinkley, Dunbar, Hagen, Holtby, Johnson, and Kelso. Rather than wait for their crew mates, these nine hotshots started downslope into the burning valley.

The layout of Storm King Mountain is roughly north-south, with a central spine running from the 8,793-foot summit to H-2. Another half mile south along this ridge was the larger site, H-1. The fire had started on a steep slope below these cleared safe areas and was spreading slowly.

The strategy was to cut a wide firebreak along the ridgetop and a smaller line down the slope to contain the blaze on the southwestern flank of the ridge. Flare-ups would be attacked with retardant drops from choppers. If there were problems, crews could easily reach H-1 in five or ten minutes and crawl under their fire shelters—light foil sheets that resemble space blankets and deflect heat of up to six hundred degrees.

"It was just an ugly little creeper," the BLM's Brad Haugh said of the early stages of the fire. Every summer, fire fighters like Haugh put out thousands of blazes like this one all over Colorado; at this point there was no reason to think South Canyon would be any different.

The second half of the Prineville crew dropped onto H-2 around 3:00 p.m. and began widening the primary fire line. Two hundred feet below, Haugh was clearing brush with his chain saw on a 33 percent slope. That meant the ground rose one foot for every yard climbed, roughly the steepness of a sand dune. The grade near the top was closer to 50 percent. He wore bulky Kevlar sawyer's chaps and a rucksack loaded with two gallons of water weighing fifteen pounds, a folding knife, freeze-dried rations, and some toilet articles. He also carried a folding fire shelter and a Stihl 056 chain saw that weighed ten or twelve pounds. Even loaded down as he was, Haugh could probably have reached the ridgetop in less than one minute if he had pushed it, and H-1 in five or ten minutes. Wildfires rarely spread faster than one or two miles an hour, and the vast majority of fire fighters are never compelled to outrun them—much less fight to survive them. By conventional fire evaluation standards, Haugh was considered safe.

About three-thirty Haugh took his second break of the day. It was so hot he had already consumed a gallon of the water he carried. The fire was burning slowly in the drainage floor, and the crews fighting it— nine from the Prineville unit and twelve smoke jumpers—were several hundred feet below him in thick Gambel oak, some of the most flammable wood in the West.

Around 3:50 Haugh and his swamper—a sawyer's helper who flings the cut brush off the fire line—were finishing their break when their crew boss announced they were pulling out. Winds were picking up from a cold front that had moved in a half hour earlier, and the fire was snapping to life. They were ordered to climb to the ridgetop and wait it out.

It's rare for an entire mountainside to ignite suddenly, but it's not unheard of. If you stand near H-2 and look several miles to the west, you can see a mountain called Battlement Mesa. In 1976, three men died there in a wildfire later re-created in a training video called *Situation #8*. Every crew member on Storm King would certainly have seen it. In *Situation #8*, a crew is working upslope of a small fire in extremely dry conditions. Flames ignite Gambel oak and race up the hill, encouraged by winds. The steep terrain funnels the flames upward, and fire intensity careens off the chart, a classic blowup. Four men are overrun, three die. The survivor, who suffered horrible burns, says they were never alerted to the critical wind shift—an accusation the BLM denied at the time. "It's a hell zone, really," said one Forest Service expert on Colorado's oak- and pinyon-covered hills. "It's one dangerous son of a bitch."

At about 4:00 p.m. high winds hit the mountain and pushed a wall of flames north, up the west side of the drainage. Along the ridge, the BLM crew and the upper Prineville unit began moving to the safety of H-1. Below them, Don Mackey ordered his eight jumpers to retreat up to a burned-over area beneath H-1. He then started cross-slope to join three other smoke jumpers deployed with the Prineville nine. Apparently, no one had advised them that the situation was becoming desperate. In the few minutes it took Mackey to join the twelve fire fighters, the fire jumped east across the drainage. "I radioed that in," said Haugh. "And then another order came to evacuate." That order came from Butch Blanco on the ridgeline, who was hurriedly conducting the evacuation. "This was a much stronger warning than the previous one," recalled Haugh. "I sent my swamper to the ridgetop with the saw and radioed that as soon as the lower Prineville contingent came into sight below me, I would bump up to the safe zone."

Suddenly, fierce westerly winds drove the fire dangerously close—though still hidden behind the thick brush—to the unsuspecting fire fighters. "The crew was unaware of what was behind them," said Haugh. "They were walking at a slow pace, tools still in hand and packs in place." As Haugh watched them, a smoke jumper appeared at his side. "He said that his brother-in-law was down in the drainage, and he wanted to take his picture."

That fellow was Kevin Erickson, and Don Mackey was his brother-in-law, now in serious trouble below. As Erickson aimed his camera, everything below him seemed to explode. "Through the viewfinder, I saw them beginning to run, with fire everywhere behind them," Erickson said. "As I took the picture, Brad grabbed me and turned me around. I took one more look back and saw a wall of fire coming uphill." Closing in on Haugh and Erickson were smoke jumper James Thrash and the twelve other fire fighters in a ragged line behind him. Though Blanco and others were now screaming, "Run! Run! Run!" on the radio, Thrash chose to stop and deploy the fire shelter he would die in. Eric Hipke ran around him and followed Haugh and Erickson up the hill. The three-hundred-foot-high flames chasing them sounded like a river thundering over a waterfall.

In his book *Young Men and Fire*, Norman Maclean writes that dying in a forest fire is actually like experiencing three deaths: first the failure of your legs as you run, then the scorching of your lungs, finally the burning of your body. That, roughly, is what happens to wood when it burns. Water is driven out by the heat; then gases are super-heated inside the wood and ignited; finally, the cellulose is consumed. In the end nothing is left but carbon.

This process is usually a slow one, and fires that burn more than a few acres per hour are rare. The South Canyon fire, for example, only burned fifty acres in the first three days. So why did it suddenly rip through two thousand acres in a couple of hours? Why did one hillside explode in a chain reaction that was fast enough to catch birds in midair?

Fire typically spreads by slowly heating the fuel in front of it—first drying it, then igniting it. Usually, a walking pace will easily keep fire fighters ahead of this process. But sometimes a combination of wind, fuel, and terrain conspires to produce a blowup in which the fire explodes out of control. One explanation for why South Canyon blew up—and the one most popular in Glenwood Springs—was that it was just so damn steep and dry up there and the wind blew so hard that the mountain was swept with flame. That's plausible; similar conditions in other fires have certainly produced extreme fire behavior. The other explanation turns on a rare phenomenon called superheating.

Normally, radiant heat drives volatile gases—called turpines—out of the pinyon and juniper just minutes before they are consumed. But sometimes hot air rises up a steep slope from a blaze and drives turpines out of a whole hillside full of timber. The gases lie heavily along the contours of the slopes, and when the right combination of wind and flame reaches them, they explode. It's like leaving your gas stove burners on for a few hours and then setting a match to your kitchen.

A mountainside on the verge of combustion is a subtle but not necessarily undetectable thing; there are stories of crews pulling out of a creepy-feeling canyon and then watching it blow up behind them. Turpines have an odor, and that's possibly why some of the Prineville survivors said that something had "seemed wrong." The westward-facing hillside had been drying all afternoon in the summer sun. Hot air was sucked up the drainage as if it were an open flue. The powerful winds that hit around 4:00 p.m. blew the fire up the drainage at the hottest time of day. And turpines, having baked for hours, could conceivably have lit the whole hillside practically at once.

When Storm King blew, Haugh had to run 150 feet straight up a fire line with poor footing. Despite rigorous conditioning—he is a runner and a bodybuilder—his heart rate shot through the roof and his adrenal glands dumped enough epinephrine into his system to kill a

house cat. Behind him, sheets of flame were laid flat against the hillside by 50 mph winds. The inferno roared through inherently combustible vegetation that had been desiccated, first by drought, then by
hot-air convection, finally by a small grass fire that flashed through a
few days earlier. The moisture content of the fine dead fuels was later
estimated to be as low as 2 or 3 percent—absolutely explosive. As
Haugh ran, panicked shouts came over the tiny radio clipped to his
vest for people to drop their equipment and flee. One brief thought
flashed through his mind—"So this is what it's like to run for your
life"—and he didn't think again until he'd reached the ridgetop.

Above him, the BLM and upper Prineville crews had abandoned
hope of reaching H-1 and scrambled north toward H-2. When that
route too was blocked, they turned and plunged over the ridge. Due
south, one hundred feet below H-1, the eight smoke jumpers who had
been ordered out by Don Mackey fifteen minutes earlier were crawling
under their foil shelters to wait out the approaching fire storm. At
Canyon Creek far below, a crew of fresh smoke jumpers who were
preparing to hike in watched in horror as eight little silver squares
appeared on the mountainside. Meanwhile, hidden from view by
smoke, Mackey, the Prineville nine, and the three smoke jumpers were
running a race only one of them, Hipke, would win.

In the end twelve of the dead were found along the lower fire line.
Prineville hotshot Scott Blecha had also run past Thrash but lost his
race a hundred feet from the ridgeline. The rest were in two main groups
below a tree—*the* tree, as it came to be known, where Haugh had started
his run—a few clumped so close together that their bodies were actually
touching. Only smoke jumpers Thrash and Roger Roth had deployed
their shelters, but the blistering heat disintegrated the foil. Kathi Beck
died alongside Thrash, partly under his shelter. It seemed that in his last
agony, Thrash may have tried to pull her in. In addition, Richard Tyler
and Robert Browning, two fire fighters deployed earlier to direct helicopter operations, perished just north of H-2, only a few hundred feet
from a rocky area that might have saved them.

The Prineville nine's dash for safety ended after three hundred feet.

They were caught just three or four seconds before Haugh himself cleared the ridgetop, and he could hear their screams over his radio. Reconstructing the details of the victims' agonized last seconds would occupy many hours of professional counseling for the survivors.

Dying in a fire is often less a process of burning than of asphyxiation. Their suffering was probably intense but short-lived. Pathologists looked for carbon in their lungs and upper airways and found none, which meant the victims weren't breathing when the fire passed over them. Their lungs were filled with fluid, their throats were closed in laryngeal spasms—responses to superheated air—and their blood contained toxic levels of carbon monoxide. This gas, given off during incomplete combustion, displaces oxygen in the blood and kills very quickly.

"They died after a few breaths at most," said Rob Kurtzman, a pathologist at the Grand Junction Community Hospital, "probably in less than thirty seconds. All the body changes—the charring, the muscle contractions, the bone fractures—happened after they were dead."

About four-thirty Haugh, Erickson, and Hipke staggered onto Interstate 70. Just an hour before, they had enjoyed a well-earned break on the mountain; now fourteen people were dead. But all they knew at that point was that Blanco, the incident commander, was calling out names on the radio and a lot of people weren't answering.

Haugh and Erickson laid Hipke in the shade of a police cruiser and doused him with water to lower his body temperature and prevent him from going into shock. Blanco climbed back up toward the fire to look for more survivors but found none. The eight smoke jumpers who'd deployed their shelters below H-1 emerged, shaken but unhurt. They were saved not by their shelters but by having deployed them on previously burned ground. The fire was still pumping at this point, and Glenwood Springs was now in danger. Flames were racing eastward along the upper ridges, and the BLM command post at nearby Canyon Creek had begun ordering residents to evacuate.

Haugh's BLM crew had survived. The other Prineville Hotshots—the upper placements—made it out as well. They had snaked their way down the east side of the ridge through a hellish maze of spot fires and exploding trees. Two of them had tried to deploy their shelters but were dragged onward by friends.

Word quickly filtered back to BLM officials in Grand Junction that something terrible had happened on Storm King. Mike Mottice, the agency's area manager, had driven past the blowup and arrived at his Glenwood Springs office around 5:00 p.m. Minutes later crews began arriving from the mountain, and Mottice realized for the first time that there were people unaccounted for. "I hoped that the fire shelters would save them," he said. "But that evening some smoke jumpers confirmed that there were deaths."

The surviving Prineville crew members suspected that some had died, but they didn't know for sure until later that night. They were shuttled first to the Glenwood Springs office, then to Two Rivers Park at the center of town. An open-air concert was in progress, and they sat in their fire clothes while the mountains burned and local youths took in the music. Finally, around nine, a social worker named Carol Kramer arrived with Prineville crew boss Brian Scholz. Kramer was to take the crew back to the Ramada Inn. A conference room was quickly prepared where she could tell them privately that nine of their friends had died.

"When we reached the hotel, they started falling apart," said Kramer. "At that point, they knew. They were begging us to tell them, to just get it over with. I told them it was bad, that twelve were dead and five were missing."

The survivors' reaction was quick and violent. Some sobbed; others pounded tables. One fire fighter fled the room and threw up. Two crew members quickly left, followed by Scholz, who wanted to keep an eye on them. As a crew boss Scholz considered himself still on duty, and he refused to lose control in front of his men. Gradually a list of survivors was compiled.

"For a while there was a lot of being out of control," said Kramer. "Then for a few hours the sobbing was only intermittent; finally, there were a lot of thousand-yard stares. They'd just sit together silently. The next morning they ate a little food. It was a small thing, but that's what you look for."

Some of the most traumatized accepted individual counseling. One thing they needed was to describe the things they had experienced. One man relayed in excruciating detail the sounds of screams and shouts he had heard as he escaped over the hill. Within thirty-six hours, the eleven Prineville survivors were flown home to Oregon—in part to reunite them with their families, in part to protect them from being hounded by the national press corps. The Ramada Inn had become a shark pool of competing journalists, and the last thing survivors needed was TV cameras panning their faces for tears and anguish.

On Monday, July 11, a memorial service was held in Glenwood Springs. While Storm King Mountain smoldered in the background, helicopters flew in formation overhead and people wept to the strains of "Amazing Grace." President Clinton called Governor Roy Romer from Air Force One, and flags on government buildings throughout the country were at half-mast. At dawn the next day, the bodies of the Prineville nine were driven to Walker Field in Grand Junction and then flown home in a Forest Service DC-3. The remains were delivered to four different airfields in Oregon while honor guards played taps and next of kin received the caskets on the tarmac.

Before the embers were even cold on Storm King Mountain, a ten-member investigation team was convened and given forty-five days to examine the site and deliver its findings. The team was composed of former fire fighters and experts in fire behavior, meteorology, and safety equipment. The question of specific blame, however, was not supposed to arise; it was to be a strictly analytical study of what had happened and when.

The preferred view among most federal fire personnel and even most South Canyon survivors was that the West was apocalyptically dry and huge fires were bound to happen. On such fires, people sometimes die; indeed, there are a few fatalities every year. "I would go out on a fire line again with any person who was there," insisted the BLM's Mike Hayes. "We were doing the best we could with the resources we had. I mean, there were fifty fires in our district at the time."

A siege mentality developed in Glenwood Springs. Questions of specific culpability were construed as lack of respect for the fire fighters and even for the dead. On Monday, July 11, the *Glenwood Post* ran an article titled "Glenwood Incident Commander: Plans for Escape Worked," a daring stance to adopt concerning a fire in which fourteen people died. Butch Blanco had told the *Grand Junction Daily Sentinel* the day before that one smoke jumper (Hipke) who'd escaped had started his run behind the ill-fated Prineville crew. That suggested to him that there had been sufficient time to reach a safe area ahead of the fire. "Whether they [the Prineville nine] didn't take it seriously, I don't know," he said.

The first people to see the dead were the smoke jumpers who had deployed fire shelters below H-1. "I walked straight to the lower group of bodies and called for a helicopter," said smoke jumper Anthony Petrilli. "They asked if we needed medevac. I told him it was too late for that, and then I walked up the hill and found six more."

An hour later twenty-six smoke jumpers helicoptered in to investigate further. It was an early, unnatural dusk on the mountain as they picked their way past the charred bodies. They reported eleven dead and three missing. Within an hour, Governor Romer was on the scene; he told the smoke jumpers he wanted to remove the bodies as quickly as possible. The jumpers objected, saying that this was no different from a crime scene and the bodies should be left until someone examined them. Romer abided by their wishes. The next morning investigators began to measure things, ponder the dynamics of the mountain, and coax secrets from the dead.

The first question was how fast the fire had moved, and Haugh's estimate—that the last three hundred feet were covered in about twelve seconds—turned out to be close. In the end, the investigators confirmed that the fire had covered the quarter-mile slope in about two minutes, hitting its top speed of 18 mph in the dried-out Gambel oak.

The next question was why it had done that. Fire behavior is determined by an incredibly complicated interaction of fuel, terrain, and wind, and there are mathematical models describing the interaction. (The models are programmed into hand-held calculators carried by most incident commanders these days.) The deadly hillside faced west at a 33 to 50 percent slope, and the vegetation on it possessed burning characteristics described in a formula called Fuel Model Number Four. The moisture content of the small dead fuels on Storm King Mountain was around 3 percent. And the live Gambel oak (which had only been partly burned earlier) was several times drier than normal. In a light wind, according to this model, those conditions would produce twenty-three-foot flames spreading at a maximum of seven hundred feet an hour.

That's a manageable fire, or at least one that can be outrun, but an increase in wind speed can change the situation dramatically. At 7:20 p.m. on Tuesday (less than twenty-four hours before the blowup), the National Weather Service issued a "Red Flag" fire warning for the area around Glenwood Springs. Dry thunderstorms were expected the following morning, followed by southwest winds gusting up to 30 mph. A cold front would come through sometime that afternoon, swinging the winds to the northwest.

Gusts of 35 mph, plugged into Fuel Model Number Four, produce sixty-four-foot flames racing up the mountain at up to fifteen feet per second. In the superdry Gambel oak, the rate of spread would have been almost twice that—much faster than any human can run. The lessons of the Battlement Mesa fire (detailed in the *Situation #8* video) had not been learned: A small fire on steep ground covered with extremely dry vegetation had once more exploded in a mathematically predictable way—again, with tragic results.

The 226-page federal investigators' report concluded that just about everyone involved had been negligent in some way. Ground crews had been arrogant about the fire danger; supervisors had ignored local fuel and drought conditions; and the Western Slope Fire Coordination Center had failed to relay crucial weather information to the fire crews in the field. "Extreme fire behavior could have been predicted by using weather forecasts and information readily obtainable at the BLM Grand Junction District Office," read one of many such findings.

The most horrifying conclusion of the report was that twelve of the victims could have easily escaped from the valley if they had started running when evidence of extreme danger first emerged. Instead, they began a slow walk, some of them dying with their tools in their hands. This meant two things: The order for an all-out retreat was given far too late, and the victims had an inherent reluctance to acknowledge the seriousness of their situation. "Putting down the saw jacked the pucker factor up one notch," said smoke jumper Petrilli, who himself had not accepted the fact that he was running for his life until he put down his tools. The last thing fire fighters are supposed to do is give up a saw or shovel, so they are understandably loath to do so, since it means they are in a life-threatening situation.

"I know in my heart," said Haugh, "that the twelve persons who died in that part of the fire were unaware of what was happening." By the time the Prineville nine and the three smoke jumpers with them saw the horror coming—by the time great sheets of flame hit the dry Gambel oak and frantic voices over the radio screamed at them to run—they had only twenty seconds to live. They must have died in a state of bewilderment almost as great as their fear.

Which Way Did He Run?
by David Grann

Fire fighter Kevin Shea had three broken vertebrae and a case of amnesia when rescue workers picked him out of the World Trade Center rubble on the evening of September 11. Journalist David Grann recorded Shea's painful attempts to find out what really happened that day.

Firemen have a culture of death. There are rituals, carefully constructed for the living, to process the dead. And so on Sept. 11, when members of Engine Company 40, Ladder Company 35 discovered that every man from their house who responded to the World Trade Center attack—12, including a captain and a lieutenant—had disappeared, they descended on the site in droves, prepared, at the very least, to perform the rite of carrying out their own. Several who had been on vacation in Maryland barreled into their cars and raced up the Interstate, arriving within hours. Others, who got to the firehouse only to find there were no more vehicles, commandeered anything with wheels—taxis, Red Cross vans, buses.

Eventually, they located their engine and ladder trucks, covered in soot, near ground zero, and tried to "visualize," as one of them later put it, what had happened: where the men had gone, what their last movements might have been. By the rigs, they found some of the missing firefighters' extra shoes, a discarded shirt, a pair of sunglasses.

Slowly, in makeshift teams, they fanned out into the rubble, trying to retrace their steps, searching for air pockets. But there was nothing to be found. It was as if the fire had consumed not just the living but the rites of the dead as well.

Then, that evening, as the number of the missing grew into the thousands, word spread that rescue workers had found someone—a member of Engine 40, Ladder 35. He had been buried under rubble. What's more, he was alive. The men hurried to the hospital, hoping he could tell them where the others might still be trapped. "If there was one," said Steve Kelly, a veteran member of the house, "we were hopeful he could lead us to the others."

When they got there he was lying in bed awake. He had fractured his neck in three places and severed his thumb, but he seemed alert and happy to see them. After they embraced, they began to pepper him with questions. Do you remember where you were? they asked. "No," he said. Do you know where the others were before the towers came down? He looked at them utterly perplexed. "The towers came down?" he asked.

I first heard the story of the survivor who couldn't remember what no one else could forget as I went from house to house reporting on the Fire Department's recovery. Initially, I assumed it was one of the many myths that had begun to circulate, but when I visited Engine 40, Ladder 35 one afternoon, a firefighter told me that there was in fact one survivor in their company—a man named Kevin Shea—who had some kind of amnesia. He said Shea was still in the hospital, but I left him my number, and a few days later the phone rang and a peculiar voice said: "This is Firefighter Kevin Shea. How can I help you?"

The next morning I went to meet Shea at his firehouse on Amsterdam Avenue and 66th Street. It was only two weeks after the attack, and he had just gotten out of the hospital. "Technically, I'm not supposed to be working," he said, "but I can still answer phones, and I thought it might help to be near the guys." He wore a thick neck brace that pressed against his chin, thrusting his face forward. He is a handsome mix of

Italian and Irish, with intense brown eyes; but the doctors had shaved his head, making his features seem disconcertingly stark, and as he bent to answer the phone I could see curving along his scalp a long gash flecked with dried blood. "I fractured the fifth vertebra in my neck," he said. Although his doctors were still skeptical, he said he was determined to make it back as a fireman. "I don't want to be a pencil pusher," he said.

Outside the firehouse, people were gathering to light candles. As word spread that Shea was there, more and more of them came inside. He had become, in a strange way, a shrine for the living—the hero who had made it out. At one point a little girl walked in with her mother and handed him a donation for the company. "Thank you so much for what you did," she said. He smiled awkwardly and extended his good hand to take the check. But as each person streamed in, approaching him and shaking his hand, he grew more and more uncomfortable. "This isn't about me," he told one man who praised his courage. And while he had agreed to let me document his recovery over the next several months, after the last person had trickled out, he turned to me, his face ashen, and said, "Please don't make me out to be a hero."

As he glanced around the room, taking in all the emblems of the dead—photos of the missing men, piles of donations, a notice for a memorial—he started to fidget nervously. He said he had no way of knowing what he had done in those crucial moments. "Maybe I panicked and . . . " He closed his eyes as if trying to conjure something out of the blankness. He seemed haunted not just by the gaps in his past but also by a single question that they prevented him from answering: had he survived because he was a hero, as everyone treated him, or because, as he feared, he was somehow a "coward," someone who had abandoned his men? "I like to think I was the type of person who was trying to push someone out of the way to save them . . . and not the type who ran in fear," he said. "But I can't remember anything, no matter how hard I try. It's like my memory collapsed with the building, and now I have to piece the whole thing back together again."

There are some things he does remember. He remembers Mike

D'Auria, a 25-year-old rookie with a bright Mayan tattoo on his leg. He remembers Frank Callahan, his captain, and Mike Lynch, another fire-fighter who was about to get married. He remembers what they carried: a Halligan, a maul, an ax, a Rabbit Tool, 8-penny nails, utility ropes, wire cutters, chucks and a screwdriver. He remembers waking on Sept. 11 and the alarm sounding at the firehouse at 9:13. He remembers them getting on the rigs. He remembers the rigs. He remembers asking the lieutenant if he thought it was a terrorist attack and the lieutenant saying yes and them riding in silence.

There are other things he remembers, too. He remembers his nick-name, Ric-o-Shea. He remembers his age, 34, and his favorite color, yellow. He remembers growing up on Long Island and hiding from the other kids in a giant cardboard box. He remembers his parents fighting and his mother moving out when he was 13. He remembers some things even if he doesn't want to—things that refuse to dissolve, along with all the insignificant memories, with the passage of time.

Memory is a code to who we are, a collection of not just dates and facts but also of epic emotional struggles, epiphanies, transformations. "Memory is absolutely critical to our identity," says Daniel L. Schacter, a psychologist and expert in the field of memory research. And in the wake of tragedy, it is vital to recovery. After a traumatic event people tend to store a series of memories and arrange them into a meaningful narrative. They remember exactly where they were and to whom they were talking. But what does one do when the narrative is shattered, when some—or most—of the pieces of the puzzle are missing?

In the last week of September, I went with Shea to visit the St. Charles Hospital and Rehabilitation Center in Long Island. The doctors still didn't know if he was blocking out what had happened as a result of physical or psychological blows or both. A neuropsychologist named Mark Sandberg greeted Shea in the lobby and led him into a small, cluttered office. "I know very little about you," Sandberg said, closing the door as Shea sat nervously crossing and uncrossing his legs. "So what do you remember?"

Shea said: "I can tell you what I remember and what I was told. I remember responding to the scene. I'm in Ladder 35, but they have an engine in there as well and they had a free seat. I wasn't working that day, and I said, 'Can I jump on?' "

The doctor seemed surprised. "You were off-duty that day?"

Shea explained that he was buffing, or volunteering, which was "the right thing to do." Then he added: "So the officer gave me permission, and I . . . went down the West Side Highway. . . . We noticed car fires and debris falling everywhere—like big falling carpets. There were pieces of metal and glass. And people were falling—"

"Do you recall that or did someone tell you that?"

Shea closed his eyes. "I recall that."

Sandberg made several notes, then asked Shea to go on. On the way to the scene, Shea said, he pulled out the video camera that he sometimes used to document fire scenes for training. "I remember putting it in the plastic bag and putting it back in my coat," he said. "I knew I couldn't be filming that long." He then prepared to go into the chaos. "I don't remember anything after that, except waking up in the hospital."

"Are your memories back after that?"

"Yes, they started to come back. They were in and out. They were drugging me at the time, with morphine, I think. They said I was conscious, but I don't know."

"You can be conscious and have no memory. It's called post-traumatic amnesia."

"That's what this is?"

"That's what I'm trying to understand."

Shea fidgeted with his bandages. "Some say it's better not to remember. Maybe the fact that I don't know if I was trying to save someone, maybe that's helping me deal with the post-stress . . . or whatever you call it."

Sandberg asked how many men from his house were lost. For the first time, Shea looked up from the bandages he'd been fidgeting with. "All of them," he said. "All of them but me."

• • •

He had never intended to become a fireman. Though he came from a long line of firefighters—his grandfather and uncle and father and older brother Brian were all firemen—he didn't fit the stereotype. He wasn't, as he put it, "a typical macho." He was smaller and more bookish than the other men; he didn't drink or like sports. Initially, he embarked on a career in computer software, at which he excelled, but by 1998 he felt compelled to follow in the family tradition.

When he was first assigned to Engine 40, Ladder 35, last summer, he showed up at 3 in the morning. The men were going out on a call, and when they returned, he was standing there with piles of eggs and French toast and chocolate-covered strawberries. "They were looking at me, like, who is this freakin' guy?" Shea recalled.

"A lot of the guys didn't know what to make of Kev," Kelly says. But he displayed an almost monkish devotion to the job, until he gradually found his place as the guy who was always willing to help out, speaking in frenetic bursts, saying, "Yes, sir," and "Negative K, sir," and answering the phone with the refrain: "Firefighter Kevin Shea. How can I help you?"

"When I got on the job, I loved it," Shea said. "It was like a big freakin' family. Even when they bust on you, it's direct. When they'd say, 'You're one freaky kid,' I'd have no problem with it. It was all done with love and to my face."

After the disaster, many in the house assumed Shea would retire, given the severity of his injuries. But within days he vowed he'd be back on the job by Christmas. "I have my family," he said, "but this is my family, too."

Yet even as he tried to move forward—eating only protein, gingerly strengthening his legs—he seemed trapped in the past. Unlike some amnesiacs, he could not forget that he had forgotten. He was reminded of the gaps in his memory at every turn, when he flipped on the television or saw the relatives of the missing men, staring at him, too afraid to ask what he knew. "He needs to figure it out," his brother Brian told me. "I don't want him 30 years from now walking around angry at the world and not knowing why. I don't want him to be like one of these guys who comes back from Vietnam and loses his mind."

When one of Shea's colleagues mentioned offhandedly a news clip of a lone rescue worker who, instead of carrying out victims, was standing in front of the towers paralyzed with fear, Shea worried that the other men in the house suspected he was that guy. Worse, he dreaded they might be right. "I hope that wasn't me," he said. "I hope I wasn't that kind of person."

His brother was right, he said; he needed to figure it out—"no matter what I discover." And so, with his body still in bandages, he set out on his search, sifting through names and pictures like a detective, trying to find clues.

He started with only a scrap of paper, a note from the hospital that read: "Patient is a 34-year-old white male firefighter . . . who was knocked unconscious by falling debris just outside the trade center."

He soon tracked down the neurosurgeon who treated him on Sept. 11 and beseeched him for something more. The doctor said all he knew was that he was carried in on a stretcher and that the injuries to his neck were consistent with being hit by something from the front. "Is there anything else?" Shea asked. "Anything at all?"

The doctor thought for a moment. "Well, I remember one thing," he finally offered. "You said you crawled 200 feet toward light."

Shea didn't remember crawling or even saying that he had crawled. It was common in patients with amnesia, the doctor explained, to continue, shortly after the trauma, to forget. Still, Shea seemed stunned. "How the hell could I have crawled 200 feet with a broken neck?" he asked.

He tried to be scientific. First, he interviewed his closest friends and family for other things he might have said in the hospital, things he had subsequently forgotten. He discovered that he had mentioned grabbing a Purple K extinguisher, which was used to put out airplane fires.

He now had three clues, one of which—because of the image of the frozen lone rescue worker that was now embedded in his mind—filled him with dread: "If I was hit from the front," he said, "then I was most likely facing the building, like that guy, as it came down."

As more people learned of Shea's search, he was inundated with tips from strangers. One morning he flipped on his computer and showed me a list of individuals who claimed to have information. "People keep calling, saying, 'Yeah, I was there, I pulled you out.' It's hard to know what to believe."

One person who called was Joe Patriciello, a lieutenant whom he had known for years and who recalled for Shea the moment they saw each other just before the first tower came down. "You embraced me in the command center," Patriciello said. "Don't you remember?"

"What command center?"

"In the south tower."

Shea felt something jarring loose in his mind, a fragment: a room full of people. They were standing in the lobby of the south tower, which was decimated only a moment later. Oh, my God, Shea thought. "I remember that," he later told me. "I'm sure of it."

While he tried to free other recollections—"It's possible other things could come back," he said excitedly—he received a call from a doctor who had seen him at the scene and who told him he had been found on Albany Street. Shea frantically searched his house for a map and measured the distance from the lobby of the south tower, where he had hugged Patriciello, to Albany, trying to imagine how he had gotten there. He made several notes: Saw Patriciello 10 minutes before the first tower came down. Tower came down in nine seconds. Albany Street about one block distance.

Though he tried not to make guesses, he slowly began to construct fragments of his story: "I was found on Albany Street," he started to tell people matter-of-factly. "I was in the lobby command center and hugged Lieutenant Patriciello."

Then, on Oct. 17, more than a month after the attack, he visited his firehouse for the first time in a while and saw pinned to the wall a *Daily News* article about several firefighters who had rescued two men lying in the street after the first tower collapsed. One of them was badly injured, his face covered in ash. His name, the article said, was Kevin Shea. "I'm looking at it, going, 'What the hell, that's me!' " He carefully wrote down the name of each person in the article and asked other firefighters to help him find them.

A few days later, he parked his car outside a station on the Upper East Side near his apartment. As he was walking home, a man on the street yelled out, "Oh, my goodness, Kevin Shea?" Shea looked at the man's face but didn't recognize him. "Don't tell me you don't remember?"

"Remember what?"

"We went in the ambulance together."

He recalled a detail from the *Daily News* story, that he was rescued along with another bloodied firefighter. "You're the other guy?" Shea asked.

The stranger smiled. "That's me. Rich Boeri."

They shook hands, as if they were meeting for the first time. Shea took out a piece of paper and pen and began to pepper him with questions. Boeri said they were transported in an ambulance to a police boat and taken to New Jersey. "Did I say anything about the other guys from my company?" Shea asked.

Boeri shook his head. "You just kept saying: 'Did the towers collapse? Did the towers collapse?' "

Days later, he still seemed overcome. "I'm just walking down the street and out of nowhere he starts telling me what happened to me." Perhaps because of his own miraculous survival, he began to believe in accidents of fate. "Guess what the name of the firefighter who was injured on the first attack on the World Trade Center—in 1993—was," he said to me one day. "Kevin Shea. Pretty freaky, huh?"

As Shea sensed the puzzle inexorably coming together, he found the phone number of one of the people *The Daily News* said had saved him, Capt. Hank Cerasoli, and asked him to meet him at a diner on the Upper East Side. "I hope I can handle it," he told me earlier. As he walked in on a Saturday morning, he spotted a small, muscular man wearing a fireman's coat.

Cerasoli had brought his wife with him, and Shea had brought his girlfriend, Stacy Hope Herman. Over eggs and French toast, Cerasoli, a modest man in his 50's with a bald head and silver mustache, described how he was struggling with his own memory loss. He had also been hit on the head and initially could not recall the location of the firehouse he had worked at for 17 years. But his memories had gradually come back, he said, and he recalled stumbling upon Shea in the middle of the street just after the first tower collapsed. "I thought you were dead," he said. "You weren't moving at all."

The color drained from Shea's face, and Cerasoli asked if he was sure he wanted him to continue. When Shea nodded, Cerasoli explained how he and several others, including another firefighter, Gerard Pirraglia, carried him on a backboard when they heard the second tower rumble. "We lifted you in the air and ran with you on the board, down an alleyway and into a garage. It suddenly got all black and dark." He drew a map on a napkin, showing where the garage was on the corner of West Street and Albany Street.

"Was I conscious?" Shea asked.

Cerasoli thought for a long moment. "I don't remember. There are some details I still can't remember."

Shea asked what happened next. Cerasoli said the Fire Department doctor, Kerry Kelly, opened Shea's shirt and pants. "I was holding your hand. You kept asking me: 'Where are the others? Are they O.K.?' I said, 'Yeah, sure, they're O.K., they're out there laughing.' I didn't really have any idea, but I wanted you to feel O.K." Cerasoli paused, then asked, "So were they O.K.?"

Shea shook his head. "No, none of them made it," he said.

"I'm sorry," Cerasoli said. "I had no idea."

After they finished eating, Cerasoli's wife took a picture of them sitting together. "I know he doesn't want to forget this," she said.

Cerasoli reached over and put his arm around Shea. "God was with you that day," he said.

While he wasn't searching for his past, Shea went from memorial to memorial. One out of every 10 people who died that day was a fire-fighter. Thirty-three died in Shea's battalion alone, and 11 in his house, including his captain, Frank Callahan, and Bruce Gary, a veteran whom Shea worshiped. "Bruce Gary was a senior man with over 20 years," Shea told me. "He was like Yoda in the house. He was very wise. I wanted to hang out with him all the time. I'm asking: 'Why you? You would have been a resource for everyone. Me? I'm a positive guy, but when people have enough of positive they can't come to me.' "

He tried to attend as many memorials as he could. But there were so many that he had to do what everyone in the department had to—choose between friends. In late October, as another service was taking place in the city, I accompanied him to a Mass in upstate New York for his lieutenant, John Ginley. Shea still couldn't drive, and Steve Kelly picked us up. Kelly and Shea both wore their Class A uniforms—navy blue suits and white gloves—and as we made our way along the highway, they both spoke of the dead.

But as they talked about Sept. 11, Shea seemed detached from his own words, as if he were reading from a piece of paper. Several people close to him had noticed that rather than seem depressed, he seemed increasingly numb. "I don't know what's wrong with me," Shea told me at one point. "I'm not sad enough. I should be sadder."

While the other men spent more and more time together—searching at ground zero, eating all their meals at the firehouse, drinking at P.D. O'Hurley's nearby—Shea spent less and less time at the house.

As we rode toward the service, he stared out the window at the changing leaves. "Look at them," he said. "They're all orange and purple."

Kelly watched him peering out the window. "You sure you're O.K., Kev?"

Shea lowered his window and let the wind wash over him. "Ten-four."

By the time we arrived at the church, scores of firemen were already lined up. There was still no body, and in place of a casket a helmet rested at the foot of the altar. "I will never forget those memories," one of Ginley's brothers said in his eulogy. "I believe in time this pain will become bearable because all our memories will be alive in our mind."

I glanced at Shea. Unlike the other men who had begun to weep, his face was utterly blank.

By the end of October, Shea began losing interest in his search. "What's the point?" he asked me one day. "What am I going to figure out? They're all dead."

Even though he now knew how he was rescued, the part that had always mattered most to him—what he was doing in the moments before the tower collapsed—remained a mystery. Indeed, the closer he got, the more impenetrable it seemed. One day a *Daily News* photographer named Todd Maisel who had been searching for Shea for weeks showed up at his apartment. He had seen him at the scene and was the one who had originally gone for help. As if to prove his story, Maisel pulled out a photo he had taken of Shea lying on the ground, covered in mounds of debris, blood trickling down his forehead. Shea stared at the image. But even after he had looked at it for hours on end, studying every detail, every nick and cut, nothing came back to him.

And even before then, those close to Shea said he had started to get angry for the first time. He lashed out at his doctor and at his girlfriend, Stacy. "I don't even realize I'm doing it," he said.

Then one day he found, through the relatives of one of the dead in his house, a news clip from Sept. 11 that showed the men from Engine 40, his truck, going into the towers. At last it was over, he thought, as he prepared to watch the clip. On the grainy film he could see each of the men from his company going inside, their faces grim and determined, heroic. But he wasn't there. Everyone was there but him. "I don't know where the heck I was," Shea said. "I don't know what the hell happened to me."

Finally, he just stopped looking. Rather than track down leads or scour the paper or search for "cues" that might trigger his recollections, throughout the rest of the fall he went from fund-raiser to fund-raiser, trying to raise money for the families of the dead. He often wouldn't stop, would keep going even when he hadn't slept or his body ached.

He had increasing pain in his hand and leg, where the contusions were, and in his groin, where the doctors had removed 90 percent of the tissue in one of his testicles. At a fund-raiser in Buffalo in November, after having appeared only a few days earlier at another in California, he was wan and exhausted. "He's not letting himself heal," Stacy said. "He's in so much pain but he won't say anything."

As he stared off into space, strangers surrounded him as if he were a rock star; one even asked for his autograph. "I'm not a hero," he snapped. "This isn't about me."

The next morning, after Flight 587 crashed near Kennedy Airport, reporters, believing it was another terrorist attack, tried to track Shea down for comment. Rather than speak to them, he went to the hotel gym and got on the StairMaster, climbing up and down with his neck brace, watching the fire burn on TV. "How do you feel, Mr. Shea?" he said over and over, parodying their questions. "How do you feel? How do you feel?"

"He's starting to have nightmares," Stacy said. "He's kicking and thrashing." One dream involved the ark of the covenant. People had gathered all around it to peer inside. He told them not to, to look away, but they didn't, and in an instant, a ray of light appeared, disintegrating everyone but him.

He woke up sweating; he turned on the light and began to write down what he had seen. "I remember the dreams," he said.

Emotions that once seemed nonexistent now overwhelmed him. One minute he was numb, unable to feel anything, and the next he began to cry without warning. "I don't know what's happening," he said.

He found an article about post-traumatic stress that he began to read obsessively: "It is O.K. to be in pain. That is the first principle of recovery."

By the beginning of December, many in the house were showing their own signs of trauma. "You see signs," Kelly told me. "Guys are getting hurt, pulling muscles from the stress. Marriages are starting to come under fire more than usual. I don't know if there is more drinking, but there is plenty of it."

But while the rest of the men relied on the familial nature of the fire-house as a refuge, Shea had drifted further away over the last several months, and he now felt cut off. Many of the new men who had replaced the missing barely recognized him. And so in early December he tried for the first time to reintegrate himself back into the fabric of the force. "Being with the guys," he said. "That's the most important thing to me right now."

He went with them to Roosevelt Island for courses on antiterrorism. "He was so excited," Stacy said. "He got to wear his uniform again."

His physical injuries were gradually healing, and in mid-December the doctors removed his brace. It would still take another year for the bone to completely fuse, but it was possible that he could then return to active duty.

Yet even as he drew closer to his goal of making it back full time, he still seemed caught in a strange netherworld. In the kitchen, where the men gathered to eat and reminisce, he sensed that they were shying away from him. Sometimes when he showed up in the morning they barely acknowledged him, he said, and when he tried to engage them in conversation, they seemed uninterested. "A lot of the guys are reluctant to even look at me," Shea told me one day, sitting in his car. "As odd as it may sound, I think I remind them of the others."

Once he told me that one of the other firefighters had come up to him and said there was a rumor going around the house about why he alone had survived. "People are saying you were out there at the site, just taking pictures with your camera."

"That's not true," Shea said. "I put it back in my pocket. I wouldn't do that." In early December, at another wake, Shea seemed to stand off by himself. "I sometimes think it would've been easier if I had died with the rest of the guys," he said.

"It's hard to watch," Kelly said. "Every time I talk to him he's not the same guy who walked into the firehouse" five months earlier. "First thing he needs to do is simply heal physically," Kelly went on.

"Hopefully, then he can come back and be a full-duty fireman, because he lived for that and he was going to move up in the department. He was brilliant in the books."

Just before the three-month anniversary of the attack, Shea showed up early for the Christmas holiday party to help with preparation. Many of the relatives of the dead were there, and he served them hot dogs and sauerkraut. He worked alongside the other men, saying, "Yes, sir," and "Negative K, sir," as if he were still on active duty. "More of the guys are talking to me," he said. "Maybe in time it will get easier."

Hanging on the wall at the firehouse was the riding list from the morning of Sept. 11, a chalkboard that had the names of each member who had hopped on the rig and died. The men had put a piece of Plexiglas up to preserve it as a memorial. On the bottom, scribbled almost as an afterthought, were the words Kevin Shea.

"I need to go down," Shea finally said.

He had called me at home one night, his voice agitated, and it took me a moment to realize he meant ground zero. He said someone in the Fire Department would pick us up tomorrow afternoon in Chelsea.

It was a cold day, and Shea wore a sweatshirt and mountain-climbing boots. Stacy stood beside him, holding his hand. He had never gone down since that day and had consciously avoided pictures of it in the newspaper and on TV. A member of Rescue 4—a hulking fellow named Liam Flaherty—showed up in a Fire Department van. He had trained Shea at the academy and had been down at the site, digging for his men since Sept. 11, leaving only long enough to sleep. "I saw guys at their absolute best that day," he said as he drove. "Guys just kept running in. They went up as it came down. They didn't turn and run."

As we passed through several checkpoints, trying to follow the route in which Shea had come with his own company, Shea stared silently out the window. He seemed nervous, pressing his face against the glass. We could see the tops of the cranes rising out of the debris and, farther on, two huge metal beams, molded together in the shape of a cross.

"Look at that," Shea said, suddenly pointing out the opposite window. "That's Engine 40. That's the rig we drove in on." On the side of the road was a huge red truck, the number 40 painted on the side. "It must've been moved," Shea said. "We weren't parked there." He looked at me for reassurance. "Right?"

As we passed through the final checkpoint, Flaherty said: "This is it. You're in."

"There's the south tower," said Stacy.

"Where?"

"There. By the crane."

"Oh, my God," Shea said.

All we could see was a giant hole in the sky. We parked the car and climbed out. Flaherty got us hard hats and yelled at us to be careful as we approached the debris.

"Where's the lobby command post?" asked Shea.

"Ten stories underground," Flaherty said. "It's still burning."

Shea opened and closed his eyes. He began to recall all the pieces that he had strung together, his words flowing out faster and faster. "I grabbed a Purple K," he said. "I was going to look for my men in Ladder 35. There were bodies falling. I remember them hitting the ground. I remember the sound. I went to put out car fires. Then I went into the command post. I saw Patriciello." He closed his eyes. "I hugged him. I told him to be careful."

He stopped. How could he have gotten from the lobby command post to Albany Street? He couldn't run that fast. "Maybe you were blown out," Flaherty said. "A lot of guys were picked up and blown out from the concussion."

"Where's Albany?" Shea asked.

"It's over here," Flaherty said. We started to run, mud splattering on our shoes. We turned down a small street. There were cars still covered in ash, their windows shattered. Shea said the doctor told him he had crawled 200 feet toward light, and now he walked several paces, then stopped and turned around. "This is where they found me," he said. "Right here." He looked back at the tower, surveying the distance. "Is there a garage around here?" There was one up the road, Liam said, and we ran again, past a burned-out building and several men in surgical masks. "This must be it," Shea said.

The garage was small and dank. We waited a moment, then an instant later we were rushing out into the street again, down one alley and another—over here, over here—until we arrived at the edge of the water. "This is where they lowered me down on a stretcher."

As he finished his story, drawing new theories from Flaherty about being blown out, estimating the wind speed and the power of the concussion, we were all cold and exhausted. By the time we got back to the site, it was dark, and the workers had turned on their spotlights. While the others wandered off, Shea walked toward what was left of the south tower.

He stood in silence, listening to the cranes. I watched him for several minutes, not saying anything. Finally I said, "Are you O.K.?"

"Yeah."

He finally seemed aware, after months of searching, of calling strangers, of waking up in the middle of the night trying to interpret his dreams, that he might never know everything, that there was no way to piece together a logical story for that day. "I'm so tired," he said. He wiped his eyes. No matter what happened, I offered, he'd done his job, and at some point he needed to let go of the rest.

Shea stepped closer to the hole, his feet now resting on the edge. "I just wish I had learned one thing today," he said, "anything that showed I was trying to save someone other than myself."

from The Fire Inside: Firefighters
Talk About Their Lives
by Steve Delsohn

Oral historian Steve Delsohn's book about American fire fighters includes these four accounts by firemen from Boston, Chicago, and New York City.

've been on the Boston Fire Department for twenty-five years. In that period, I've experienced quite a few gruesome deaths and real bad accidents. In time, you get over it. Maybe you go out after work that night and have a few beers.

It stiffens your lip a little. In the months and years to come, you learn to let it go.

That's usually how it works, but not every time. We had a tragedy here this June I'll never forget. We lost one of our own, and I was involved in that. In fact, I had gotten lost in the building myself.

It was a warehouse on top of a pier in the Charlestown section of Boston. A little after midnight, we received a call for a building fire there. I happened to be driving Rescue 1 that night. Going over the top of the North Washington State Bridge, I could see we had a small fire at the end of a pier. I said to myself: *Oh. We'll be out of here in fifteen or twenty minutes. It's no big deal.*

So we got out of the truck and grabbed our tools and masks. Engine 8 and Ladder 1 were already there. As they started to stretch a line inside the warehouse, we followed them in. Even though we knew we had a fire, from that vantage point we still saw no indication. We were standing right in the middle of the warehouse. It was as clear as my kitchen.

Without any warning whatsoever, this whole place turned to thick black smoke. The smoke came down from the ceiling. It was so thick you couldn't see the hand in front of your face. I dropped to the floor, trying to get on my face piece. I got it on and turned on my air supply. Otherwise, I'd be choking.

It was so dark you couldn't see anyone now. Nobody from the Ladder, the Engine, the Rescue. There was probably thirteen of us, but you couldn't even see one. All you could hear was mumbling and grumbling and groaning. I was still down on my hands and knees. When I looked underneath me, I saw the fire coming up from the floorboards. That was when we determined to leave the building. Anything that turns sour that fast, there is something definitely wrong.

When I turned around and yelled for the rest of them, they were gone. I got no reply at all. Everybody was already on their way out.

Normally, your training and experience always tells you: If you bring a hose line into a building, you follow that hose line right back out the door you came in. So I started scrambling around the floor, searching for the hose. I knew it was off to my right, but I didn't know where. So I go off to the right and, geez, there's the line. I start to follow it back, and meantime this place is really turning rotten. The fire is up through the floor, and I'm following the hose, and suddenly it hits me: I'm going in circles.

I thought, *I'm in real trouble here. I should be going in a straight line, and I'm going round in a circle.*

Then I thought, *Stop! Get your head together and try something else.*

So I got another plan. I'd follow the hose line the other way, back to the nozzle, and start all over again. But in the next split second, I realized that I had no time to do this. I didn't know how far back the nozzle was, and this place was burning up. That's when I got worried I might get trapped. Because I still couldn't find anyone.

I thought, *I'm lost. I'm trapped in here. I'm gonna die in this place. All the rotten, lousy, friggin' vacant warehouses there are, I'm gonna die in here.*

That was the last thing I remember going through my mind. Then one of the fellows I work with grabbed my shoulder.

He said, "Come on, you stupid son of a bitch. You're going the wrong way."

We turned around, hand in hand, followed the line, and went out the front door. Outside the building, I turned around and looked back and started shaking my head. I couldn't believe it took off the way it did. Even to this day, they haven't found the cause. But I think it still seems suspicious. How does a pier take off like that, at midnight, if there aren't any combustibles involved?

Assuming now that everybody was out, we went back to the Rescue to get the K-12 saws. We had seen an overhead door, and thought we could make another entry there. But as I went to start the saw, the deputy chief's driver came running up to us. He said the deputy chief wanted us right away. Two men from Engine 8 were reported missing.

Once we got the order to go back in, we put down our saws and grabbed our steel cables. They have hooks on the end, for hooking to outsides of buildings. You use them for guidelines when you go inside. You keep your hand on the cable and never let go. That way, if you gotta leave, you know you're coming back out.

The cables are about fifty feet in length; I think we grabbed a couple hundred feet of them. A building this deep in size, we figured we needed that much. Then we went back to make another entry. The entire pier, not just the warehouse, was burning at this point. Underneath the pier, also, was fully involved. It had gotten some wind, and that wind was like gasoline. It just went up like, *poof.*

We didn't know what to expect once we got inside. We didn't know if the fire had penetrated the floor entirely. But we were going in there anyway. We had to make an attempt to find the two guys. Anybody on this fire department would do it. This is a ballsy department in my opinion.

Five of us went inside from the Rescue Company, but there was an instant problem. The fire was overlapping the door we just came in. An engine company tried to knock it down, but there was too much fire. So now we had fire behind us, and we knew we'd soon have heavy fire in front. It was determined that we could not stay inside.

We were informed outside that both men from Engine 8 had just been found. They were located in another part of the building. Both men were still alive and on their way to the hospital.

We were also informed at this time about Lieutenant Minehan. They said he was missing. His entire company, Ladder 15, had gone in the same door we had, to look for the two missing members of Engine 8. Like us, they had encountered great fire and heat and determined they had to leave. But as they turned to go, the lieutenant got separated from his crew. And he got lost in there.

I looked at the warehouse burning. I prayed he wasn't inside. Maybe he'd gotten out some way we didn't know.

Then they asked our Rescue if we could get in there again.

If they got a couple of lines in that front door, we said we would give it our best shot.

So they got some lines in there, and they started hitting the fire and knocking some of it down. We took the cables again and in we went. But we were not able to penetrate very deep. The fire by then had burned right through the floor. For the third time that night, we were driven out of the building. That's when I looked at the water.

I said, "Maybe he was able to get out a window. Maybe he jumped in the harbor. He could be hanging on to a pier. A piling or something."

Right away, we had divers in the water. It was probably 2:00 a.m., but with that amount of fire beneath the pier, the water was all lit up. You could see pretty well. There was no sign of Stevie Minehan.

We ended up there until first daylight. By then, it had already been determined that he was lost. But then, around 7:00 a.m., the commissioner asked if we could get in there again. So we went in again and took a look. Most of the fire was pretty much knocked down, but the walls had collapsed. Sections of the roof had dropped on top of the pier. Parts of the pier had dropped into the water. There was scattered debris all over, pieces of roofs and walls. We lifted the debris, looking everywhere. We were in there two hours when one of the Rescue members hollered to me.

He said, "Hey, I found him."

I went over and looked and there was Stevie. He was the farthest point in the warehouse that you could possibly be. It meant we would never have found him anyway. That made us feel a little bit better. If we had found him right inside the front door, we would have felt terrible. This way at least we didn't miss him, you know?

Before we had gone in to find him, we had been told not to touch him if we did. Because if Stevie's own company wanted to remove him, with our assistance, they would have that option. *Only* if they didn't feel up to it, would we bring him out ourselves.

The commissioner and the chaplain came in. The chaplain gave Stevie his last rites. Then the commissioner called in Ladder 15.

He said, "You guys want to take him out?"

They said, "Yeah, we do."

So they took him out and we gave them a hand. He was later pronounced dead.

It turned into a very big story. Not only in the city of Boston, but in all the surrounding cities and towns. His funeral was carried on all the TV stations here, and the public was extremely sympathetic. They raised quite a bit of money for his family. The outpouring was unbelievable. I think it was because of the way he died. If Stevie was inside there to save a civilian, or if he died because his fire truck flipped, it wouldn't have been the same. But he died trying to save two other firemen. He knew they needed help and he went in.

Stevie's death hit close to home for me. We are a very tight family in this department. Even to this day, if we go on a rescue call and run into Ladder 15, I stand there and look at their truck. I look at the front seat. I still think, *Where's Stevie? He should be there.*

* * *

It was a Sunday morning. It was summertime, so we had our windows open. I was sleeping at home, about to wake up and go in to the firehouse. A few minutes before six, I heard someone screaming outside our bedroom window.

I recognized the voice and stuck my head out the window. My next-door neighbor was yelling to me for help.

There was fire in her house and her mom was in there. I knew her mom and she was eighty years old.

I yelled, "I'm coming down!"

I didn't have a shirt on, but I had slept that night in some cut-off sweats. So I bolted out of the room, told my wife to call 911, threw on my work shoes and ran downstairs. By the time I got outside, I could see smoke seeping out their windows.

I asked her, "Where's your mother's bedroom at?"

She said it was in the front part of the house. I asked if the front door was open. She said yes, so I ran to the front door. It all happened fast. I didn't think about getting hurt. I just ran into the building. I know how fire is and time is a major factor.

Smoke was starting to push out the front doorway, so I got in the crawl position and crawled inside the front entrance. Then I crawled up five or six steps to their first-floor apartment. Once I crawled in their door, I could feel the heat and smoke building up.

About eight feet inside their apartment, I saw another doorway. That's where the fire was concentrated at. As I went through that doorway, I kind of stood halfway up.

All I could see was the woman on the bed. Even though she was unconscious, I knew she was alive. I could see her body twitching, still reacting to the flame.

As I made my way toward her, the flames were already starting to jump up the sides of her mattress. She was right in the center, so at first I tried to put my arms around her, in a bear hug position, and pull her off the bed that way. But with the flames now coming through the mattress, my hands and arms were starting to burn. She was slipping out of my hands, because my skin was melting.

So I tried something different. I pulled her arms toward me and got a lock on her wrists. With that grip, I started dragging her off the bed. At one point she slipped from my hands and we both fell into the curtains. They were on fire, and I felt the burning sensation right on my buttocks. When I stood back up, I started feeling woozy from the heat. It was almost as if I was in a drunken state. But I wasn't going to stop. We were already halfway out.

I grabbed her wrists again. I kept dragging her body across the floor. The room was becoming more involved in flames, but there was more fire than smoke, so I could see enough to spot her bedroom door. Just before we got there, her hip hit a chair that was sitting by the door. She got jammed between the chair and the doorway. The doorway, by that time, was on fire, and that did some damage to me. I got burned on my back, my upper arm and my shoulder.

I pried loose the chair and untangled the woman, then I continued dragging her through the apartment. I was close to passing out when I got through her front door, so I just took her out to the hallway steps, jumped over her body and ran downstairs. By then, there were people assembled down there.

I said, "Come on! Help me get her down the stairs!" No one came up, so I went back up myself. I dragged her down the steps, then a couple guys helped me drag her out to the lawn.

First, I opened her airway. Her breathing was barely there, and I didn't want it to stop. Her tongue was black from smoke. I mean black like shoe polish. Then I did some compressions on her chest, a couple respirations into her mouth. She started breathing at more of a normal pace. Then my wife ran up with the woman who lived below us. Together, they started peeling off her burnt clothing. By that point she was breathing on her own, even though she was unconscious. That was a good sign. Firefighters were already showing up, and I thought she could hold on until paramedics arrived.

I stood up at this point and walked back and forth. That's when I started feeling extremely hot. I actually felt like I was on fire, so I asked my next-door neighbor to hose me down. But when my neighbor hit me with his garden hose, I screamed for him to stop. The water was hitting my burns and it hurt like hell. So I yelled out to my wife. I told her to run upstairs and call 911 again.

I said, "Tell them we're going to need a second ambulance."

While we waited for the ambulance to come, I realized that I was in pretty bad shape. The adrenaline had worn off and the pain was sinking in. My body started shaking uncontrollably. I was going into shock.

The firemen told me to sit down on the sidewalk. Once I did, I saw the damage I'd done. The skin on my left arm was hanging off and melted. On my left hand, the skin melted there had fused together my fingers. My fingernails had also fallen off.

I thought that was pretty much it—I thought my left arm and hand were burned up. But it turned out I had burns over 30 percent of my body. Actually, I had burns almost everywhere, but only 30 percent were third-degree. Most of that was sustained by my upper body, because I went into there without a shirt.

The first thing they did at the hospital was put in a catheter. Then they tried hooking me up to the IV, but my arms were so burnt they couldn't get into the veins. Instead, they stuck two IVs into my femoral artery. So I had these two big needles going in next to my groin.

They then proceeded to take me into the scrub room, which is just a steel bed with hoses all around it. They started washing and scrubbing off my burnt skin, probably the worst thing I've ever felt in my life. I think I can take most pain pretty well, but I screamed at the top of my lungs when they took me in there. Everybody screamed. You could hear each person they brought in. You have to scream. You have to let it out.

After I was scrubbed, they rubbed this cream called Silvadine all over me. Over the cream, they wrapped me up like a mummy. They told me I would swell up, and I swelled up like a balloon. One eye was completely shut. The other one, I could barely see out of. The swelling came from the burns, and also all that intravenous fluid.

They listed me in critical condition.

For the next three days, they did their scrubbings two or three times a day. After my fourth day there, they took me in for my skin graft operation. The doctor said since I was young and in real good shape, they would try and do the whole thing in one operation. It lasted somewhere between eight and twelve hours. They stripped the good skin off my legs and lower back, and they grafted it onto the places where I had third-degree burns. Then they stapled the skin so it would remain in place. When I came out of surgery the next morning, I had about fifteen hundred staples on my left side.

When I woke up from that, the guys I work with were there. So was my wife. I couldn't talk with this tube going in my throat, so I just scribbled notes. I told them I was fine, but I wanted to know when this doctor was taking this tube from my throat. I really wasn't fine, though. There were areas on my left arm where the skin grafts didn't take. Those areas had formed large open wounds. I couldn't sleep that night or several nights after. Not only from the burns, but all that sweating you do when you're all bandaged up. I have to tell you, some nights it felt like torture. There were some moments, you know, I wished I was dead.

I was also dealing with the psychological thing. I mean about my burns, the way I looked. I kept thinking about that day when they'd let my children see me. Our oldest daughter was nine, our son was almost five, and our little girl was two. I had already dropped about forty pounds, and I had been gone three weeks. I was afraid our two-year-old wouldn't know me. All that stuff was playing on my mind.

Finally, about three or four days before I got released, they let the children come. My smallest child ran right up to me. I picked her up and she knew it was her dad. Wow, did that feel great.

At first, with those open wounds, it didn't look like I'd be going home too quickly. The doctor said he was guessing about six weeks. I couldn't wait that long. After twenty-two days, I said, "I want to go home. I've shown you people that I can walk. I can exercise. I can handle it. Let me go home."

So they gave my wife some lessons on how to treat me at home. She was just wonderful. She would change my bandages and bathe me. She would help me eat. We hung in there together, but it got hard sometimes for both of us. I was off work for nine months—a real up-and-down time, emotionally. I was still self-conscious about my looks. There were times I doubted why my wife was with me. I didn't want her to be with me out of pity. When you get burned like that, all those crazy things go through your mind.

It took awhile for my head to get straight. Sometimes out of frustration, I'd go off the deep end and punch a wall. It was pretty bad, but my wife just stuck with me the whole way through. I needed that from her. I needed that sense of security.

The rescue effort I made was actually successful: the elderly woman survived. She stayed in the hospital for about six months, then her family put her in a nursing home. Unfortunately, she died in the nursing home about four months later. This entire time, there was never a knock at our door from her daughter and son. They never said one word. Never even, "Is everything okay?"

At first, that was hard to deal with. Especially for my wife. She saw her husband get burned, and this family was so cold.

I told my wife, "I understand how you feel, but you should stop being upset. I don't regret what I did."

I never have regretted it. It doesn't matter who was inside that building, how old the person was, or how the family was afterwards. What I did was right. I took the extra step. I'll always be proud of that.

For that particular rescue, I wound up winning several big awards. I got first prize that year from *Firehouse* magazine. I received the Lambert Tree Award, the highest award from the city of Chicago. There were state awards and national awards, and an international award from the International Association of Fire Chiefs. For that ceremony, they flew my wife and myself to California. They took us to Disneyland and Universal Studios. They put us up at a nice hotel.

It was great. All of that kind of recognition was. We have a real good fire department here in Chicago. I felt honored to carry on that tradition.

• • •

I was assigned to Rescue 3 in upper Manhattan. It covers the Bronx and Harlem, and it also responds to any major emergency in New York City. One evening in September, almost at midnight, we got a call on a plane crash at La Guardia Airport.

It wasn't my first one. Before I was a firefighter, I was a New York City police officer. We went on a plane crash then at Kennedy Airport. The plane came short of the runway and crashed on landing. Every passenger died; I think about 60 people. So this time, I wasn't sure what we would encounter. We were advised on the way that people were in the water, but we didn't know their condition.

On Rescue 3, we have a small lifesaving boat. We also have exposure suits, for the elements in the New York City water. In this specific area where the plane was, the currents are swift. As a matter of fact, there is a part they call Hell's Gate. It's a notorious place where they lose a lot of boats.

That was the kind of stuff that was going through my mind, because I already knew I was going into the water. That's how we do it here. We have six firefighters on the rig. The officer and the driver sit up front, and four men sit in back. So right away in the back of the rig, we make up the assignments. Two guys will go into the water. They are the entry team. The other two guys will stay nearby and watch you. They're the safety people. This way everyone knows the plan, so we can jump off the rig and go into action.

We were one of the first pieces of apparatus there. But when we got to the end of the runway, there was a twenty-foot drop into the water. There was also a pier. The plane was crashed in the water near the pier. It was a Boeing 737, a pretty big plane. The pilot had tried taking off, but he didn't think they had enough power. Once they tried to abort, it was too late. They couldn't stop the plane. It skidded off the runway and into the East River.

Naturally, there was a lot of hysteria. Passengers were screaming. There were passengers on the wings and in the water. The plane had torn in half. It looked like a bent piece of pipe, with the tail section bending down into the water. The main fuselage was separated from that, and the only thing holding the plane up was some pilings. They looked like telephone poles stuck in the water. Fortunately, that's what the plane fell on. Otherwise, many more people would have been killed.

Our particular unit does not have scuba gear. We more or less do surface-water rescues. So with this twenty-foot drop, we lowered a portable ladder and climbed down that to the water. I didn't feel the cold with my exposure suit on, but I could smell fuel. Everyone could. That was a fear for our supervisors there: they thought the fuel could ignite.

But they were worried about it more than us. We had victims. We had to take the risk.

I swam right to the tail section, while another firefighter went to the wing. The tail-section door was partially open. I opened it up the rest and went inside the cabin. I started searching the rubble with my flashlight. It was a wreck, a mass of mangled steel and mangled chairs. The tail section was also submerged in water, so the cabin had maybe a foot of water inside.

The lower part of the tail was in the water. That's where I was, so I had to walk up. Going up what used to be the aisle, I called out for victims and searched with my flashlight. When I got near the top I saw two people. A mother and daughter. Obviously both dead.

I thought that was it. I thought nobody else was in there. But I yelled again anyway. And I heard a faint cry for help.

I held up my flashlight and I could just see a face. The closest I could get was seven or eight feet away, but I could see it was a woman. She couldn't move. The floor of the plane had actually met the ceiling, and she was totally pinned inside her chair. As it turned out later on, she had a broken arm and a broken shoulder, broken ribs and a broken leg.

Her name was Mrs. Crews. She was about sixty years old.

I said to her, "I see you. We're gonna get you out of here."

Then I got on my handie-talkie. I told my lieutenant out on the pier, "I have a victim pinned in the rear of the plane."

I said I was going to need a lot of tools. For sure the Jaws of Life.

Within ten minutes, Chris Blackwell, another fireman, joined me from Rescue 3. So did Mike Milner from Rescue 4. Standing inside together, the three of us decided we wouldn't leave her. We told her that. Because now there was all this talk on the handie-talkie. The officers thought the tail section might break off, then sink in the water with all of us inside. The woman could hear those radio transmissions.

So we told her not to worry. We weren't going anywhere without her. She said, "Oh, thank God. Thank God."

As the rescue went on, the tail section kept taking more and more water. Our chiefs were telling us to abandon the rescue. We kept telling them we weren't giving up; it was just a matter of time before we would have her out.

It turned into quite a bit of time. Even though we got the Jaws of Life, there was no way we could operate it inside. The Jaws run on gasoline and there were too many fumes. It would have been a disaster. So what they wound up doing was pretty smart. They shot a tower ladder over the water, with this power unit on it, so they could power the Jaws from outside.

As we started cutting debris to get to Mrs. Crews, we were also administering psychological first-aid. And she was very good with that part, too. She never panicked. She kept her wits. She told us she had a son in the marines. He was a drill instructor. I told her he would be proud of the way she was acting.

I said, "You're the one who's keeping us calm. It's supposed to be the other way around."

We just kept working and teasing her like that.

In reality, it was tense for everyone. For one thing, she was sitting behind where the mother and daughter died. She could see them, too. One time, she asked me how they were doing. I told her not too good, only because I thought she already knew. She was one seat below them, and their blood was dripping down in her direction.

Though I kept it to myself, by then some doubt was creeping into my own mind. The plane kept taking more water. There was still a maze of metal between her and us. The chief officers kept screaming that we should abort the rescue, and we kept stalling them. We kept saying "one more minute," and it would turn into another fifteen. It was becoming a race against time. So we just kept cutting away with the Jaws of Life.

When we finally got close enough, we switched to the Ram Tool. We used it to push the bulkhead off of her, then we used it to cut the back of her seat. But even then, she wasn't free. When we tried pulling her out, her foot was caught in a twisted sheet of heavy aluminum. I had to crawl down in there and use a hacksaw.

Once we had her completely loose, we knew our position was still precarious. To get her off the plane, we only had a two-foot clearance to work in. The rest of the cabin was filled with water; it was up to our chest now. So we held her over our heads, the three of us, and we were able to carry her like that.

When we got her to the door, next we had to get her onto a raft. And we were in a pretty swift current here.

So I told the other guys, "Whatever we do, we cannot drop her."

She was all broken up and she was older, too. We didn't want to drop her in twenty-five feet of water.

We got her on the raft with Lieutenant Tom Williams' help. By then we were exhausted, dripping with diesel fuel. So other people took care of her from then on.

It was a great day for all the rescuers there. In a Boeing 737, the only two deaths were that mother and daughter. But much of that credit must go to the passengers. They didn't panic and jump into the water. They waited in the plane until help arrived. Had more people jumped in with the current so fast, you're looking at multiple drownings.

The next time I saw Mrs. Crews was later that afternoon. Chris Blackwell and myself went to visit her at the hospital. Usually when you save someone, you never get to see them again. But this was really nice. She had asked to see the guys who got her out of the plane.

That was probably the high point of the whole thing. She kissed us and hugged us. She said she didn't think she was gonna make it, until she heard my voice. And once we told her we wouldn't leave, she said she knew for sure she'd get out alive. This is what she told myself and Chris. It was real emotional for us.

Later that year, I received the highest award in the New York City Fire Department. It's called the Gordon Bennett Medal. They only give one a year, and who do you think showed up on Medal Day? Mrs. Crews came all the way from Virginia. She was the one who called me up onstage, then she gave a little talk about what happened. That was really something. Nobody even told me she was coming.

We still exchange Christmas cards. Sometimes she'll call our house when I'm at work, and she and my wife will talk. When her son the drill instructor was in the Gulf War, my kids wrote letters to him and he wrote them back. One time he sent my young daughter a Marine Corps patch, and she was all excited. He also wrote her a letter saying what a good job we'd done in helping his mom. I'm very proud of that letter. This is an instructor in the marines.

Firefighters aren't in it for the glory. When you go on a call, your goal is not to get thanked or win an award. You just want the people out safely. You just want to do a professional job.

But looking back on it, this was the ultimate experience I could have. The rescue was successful. The woman and her family were wonderful to us. I was awarded by the New York Fire Department, the biggest and, I think, the best department there is. I was just very fortunate, I feel.

It was about ten at night. We had just finished dinner when we got called to an explosion at the Consolidated Edison plant. The plant runs along the west side of Manhattan. It's three or four blocks long and it generates electricity. The by-product is this superheated steam—about five hundred degrees—which they pipe throughout the city and heat the skyscrapers with. On this night, they had an explosion in one of their steam lines. They had a major steam leak and still had workers inside.

I was the captain of Rescue 4 in Queens, so the plant was just a few minutes from our quarters. It was eerie when we arrived. The escaping steam was making this ear-piercing noise. It sounded like a 747 with all of its engines going at one time.

As a rescue squad, we are normally sent to emergencies of this kind. We search for victims and then try to remove them. This time we followed some Con Ed employees into the plant, to an area where some people had last been seen working. One man was already dead, but we didn't know that yet.

The area we went into was large and open. It looked like the boiler room of a very, very big ship. Obviously, from conditions, this was also where the steam had been released. Initially, I didn't think we could get in there. It seemed beyond our capabilities. But once we worked our way in, we felt we could handle it.

There were six of us in the Rescue. I took one firefighter with me to conduct the search. I told the other fellows to stay in the safe area outside. They'd be our safety team if anything went wrong.

The two of us searched the first level and didn't find anyone. So we climbed the staircase up to the second level. The firefighter with me went searching around the far end of this second level. Visibility was very poor. There was nothing there but open grating, so there was nothing stopping the steam from going from level to level. As he continued walking, it was like he disappeared into a steam cloud.

Right about then, I realized something had changed. Conditions had gotten much worse. If I stayed there much longer, I would start burning up. Everything in my body was telling me to leave.

The only problem was, our firefighter was still inside the steam cloud. If I went to try and find him, it would be like going into a fog bank; I could very well miss him. So I decided to stay right where I was. That firefighter was my responsibility.

It seemed like eternity, but he returned maybe thirty seconds later. He must have felt the same increase in heat: As he hit the open area where I was, he actually turned around to go back the way he came.

That wasn't good. It was like a blast furnace in there now. He needed to get to the exit.

He couldn't hear me with the noise in there, so I kept motioning with my arms. When he realized I was pointing to the exit, he just ran and went diving down the stairs.

Once I knew he went down, I ran for the stairs and dove down also. There was no hesitation at that point. I had to get out of there. I was burning up.

The other firefighter had also gotten burned, but he landed at the bottom of the stairs, which was probably the best spot. That's where the other fellows from our squad were. So all they had to do was reach in and drag him out.

Then they looked up the stairs to see about me. I was halfway down the stairs on a metal landing. According to their accounts, I'd only made it that far when I dove down the stairs. Then the air pack on my back had somehow got jammed in the railing.

All I know myself is that I dove for the stairs. And the next thing, I was stuck. I was struggling to move forward but something was caught. I could move my arms and legs, but I could not progress.

I thought I was dead. There was no two ways about it. I was being baked alive by the heat coming up beneath me. All I could think was, *Dear God, please take me.* When you're being cooked, you don't want to hang around for very long.

Fortunately, I passed out at that point.

As I found out later on, the firefighters were trying to rescue me. They came up the stairs to get me, but they were being burnt also in these conditions. So one firefighter would make a mad dash in, pull me a little, and have to get back out. They did it like a relay, all three of them rotating, trying to get a hand on me and grab me. Finally, with this action, they managed to free me. Once I was freed up they pulled me out of the heat.

Right outside the steam area, I regained consciousness immediately. But I couldn't breathe. I was going into shock. My mind was still functioning, but I was piercingly hurt. I couldn't help myself, or even stand. So they had to pick me up and carry me out of there, and that turned into a tragedy of errors. We were buried inside this huge complex, and there was nobody there to give us directions. Our guys couldn't make any contact on their radio. Not with that roaring steam drowning everything out.

It took a long time to find our way outside. But once we did, the air temperature was in the upper thirties, and I could feel the cooling effect on my body. They brought me into an ambulance. The EMS people started working on me.

They cut away my clothing and they poured water on me. I must have still been in some kind of shock; everything seemed to be moving in slow motion.

We ended up at New York Hospital's burn center. They put me on a respirator and started the intravenous. Then people started coming to visit me there. The fire commissioner, the police commissioner, Mayor Dinkins—all the dignitaries came in. When *they* all start showing up, it means you're in a bad way.

I remember being conscious while they were there. I remember writing down notes to all their questions. But all this time in the back of my mind, I was saying to myself, *Where are the drugs? I wish they would give me something to knock me out.*

Some good friends of mine had gotten the word what happened. They brought in my wife. When she walked into the emergency room, there was nothing but firefighters in there, even a few she recognized. Nobody would look at her. She said it was the worst feeling in her life. They couldn't look her in the eyes. They all thought I was dead, or about to be.

It seemed like a long time before they could give me drugs. First they had to do all the initial care, and they don't want to do that with any drugs in you. Finally, after hours and hours, they gave me morphine and I drifted off. For the next two weeks, I was in something like a drug-induced coma.

Morphine does the job. You don't feel the pain. But I wouldn't recommend it to anybody. While I was taking the morphine those two weeks, I created a whole world inside my head. It was part reality and part hallucination. Some parts were terribly frightening. At one point I was certain this one nurse was trying to kill me. It was horrible, absolutely horrible. Like I say, it killed the physical pain. But what was happening in my head wasn't pleasant at all.

It turned out my entire body was burned. But the serious, third-degree burns were from my knees to my buttocks. Also, both my wrists were burned all the way around. From the top of my head to my eyebrows had to be grafted. A section of my neck had to be grafted. I lost pieces of both my ears. I lost part of my nose. They had to rebuild my eyelids. That's just a fast rundown of the burns on the outside. Plus, there was some damage to my throat and lungs. That was actually the main concern—the respiratory part. How much steam I inhaled.

Psychologically, it was very difficult. For twenty years, you are in the position of helping other people. Suddenly, you are the victim. Now you have to rely on everyone else, and that took quite some time for me to adjust to. The toughest part was the burden I put on my family. I remember crying in the hospital, just thinking about what I had done to them. I didn't want them to worry, and I knew they were. I kept trying to communicate to my wife, "Don't worry. I'll be all right. It doesn't look good, but I'll be all right." It was a hard thing to get through. I couldn't help myself, let alone anyone else.

It took me a long time to even look in the mirror. And up until the first time I did, I never realized the extent of my injuries. I mean, I knew they'd done operations on my eyes. I knew they'd grafted my forehead and the top of my head. I knew all that, but somehow I still thought I looked exactly the same. It was my mind, obviously, protecting me in some way. When I finally looked in the mirror, it was very shocking to see the change.

You know what got me through? The support I got.

I got letters from people I'd gone to grammar school with. I got letters from people I'd never met. Firefighters from all over the country were sending me their fire department T-shirts, or these gorgeous baskets of fruit. In the neighborhood we live, they actually organized to show their concern. They delivered a meal to my house every day. Outstanding, delicious meal, but my wife finally said, "Please, only make it a few times a week. There is just so much food!"

If there was even one inch of snow on the ground, the local volunteer firemen would come and shovel my driveway. The support I got was amazing. Unbelievable. Especially from my family. Every day at the hospital, my wife and four daughters were there for me. Every time they came in, they had smiles on their faces.

I even asked my wife, "What did you tell the kids? They were always so upbeat, joking around. It's just what I needed."

My wife said, "I never said a word to them. They figured it out themselves."

I ended up at the burn center for twelve weeks. During this time, I had eight operations. The final one they did was a skin graft on my head. I received that skin from a fireman on Long Island who had died. Either his family or himself, before he died, chose to donate his skin for other burn victims. That made me feel good. While this man was alive, he tried to protect people from fire. Even after he was done, he was still helping others.

In some way, I also felt that things had come full circle. I was a donor myself in 1990. About six years before that, my daughter Mary came down with a rare form of kidney disease. She was treated by drugs through 1990. But over the years, the disease progressed to the point where Mary would have two choices: go on dialysis or have a kidney transplant. Knowing how hard it is to live a normal life on dialysis, both my wife and I were happy to donate a kidney. So we went in and got checked out and both of us matched. But when the time came up in 1990, I told my wife I wanted it to be me. All I could think about was how much I wanted to do this.

So I went in and did it, and there's no describing the feeling. This was the little girl you cradled in your arms. You held her and tried to protect her. Now she is grown up, and you have a chance to improve her life.

So that's why I felt things had come full circle. I did my share as a donor, for my daughter, and now this dead fireman was helping me.

I'll never forget the day I left the hospital. The president never got better treatment than I did. They had news media outside. A couple of fire trucks. A good crowd of people. There were bagpipes and speeches. Then the fire department presented a plaque to myself and a fireman friend of mine, a guy who had helped me tremendously during my stay. So he also got recognition and I thought that was great.

I assumed that was the end of it. The next thing I know, there's a white stretch limousine waiting to take us home. With a full police escort leading us, they closed down the FDR Drive, closed down the tunnel, closed down the parkways, and we just sped along. When we got one block from where we live, we passed the nursery school where two of my daughters had gone. All these little kids were standing outside. They had one of these banners that said, "Welcome Back."

When I saw that—all these little preschoolers out there—I really got emotional.

I said, "Gee whiz, they're making this into like I'm a hero or something."

The kids took me by surprise. They really made me feel special. Everyone did that day, and it made me realize something. What all those people were doing was celebrating life.

Because everyone knew I could very well have died. But I didn't die. I was on my way home, ready to go on.

That was the celebration, the exuberance, the excitement. We are all still here. We can go on.

from Fire Line: Summer Battles
of the West
by Michael Thoele

Michael Thoele's book about fighting forest fires includes this account of a hard day's work for the Wyoming Hotshots, by reputation the toughest crew of fire fighters in the U.S. Forest Service.

Beisler felt it first. Something still, heavy, ominous. Something speaking to him from that place where experience lives, distilled to intuition. Something filtering to him through a dozen years of chasing big fire across the West. Something left with him from the chaparral of California and the big timber of Oregon and the piney slopes of the Rockies. But something that the diggers and the sawyers, sweating, panting, pushing, yellow shirts sticking to their backs, still didn't feel in the waning hours of this 104-degree day.

They were the Wyoming Hotshots, best damn fire crew in the Forest Service if you cared to ask them, and they'd been at it for days, pounding in line and touching off roaring burnouts on first one Eastern Montana fire and then another. It was Thursday now, and they'd stolen maybe twelve hours sleep since Monday. With fire on their flank, they were at it again, shovels and pulaski tools clinking, chainsaws screaming, heads down, elbows pumping.

The dragon seemed complacent today. He crept downhill on their right, close enough that his glow beat back the twilight and his breath cooked the sweat from their faces as they worked the toe of the slope. But his march was slow and his teeth were short, no more than two feet tall as they gnawed through dry grass and the duff blanket of needles beneath the towering ponderosas. Still, it was odd, aggressive behavior for a fire this late in the day.

Bad stuff, maybe, for a rookie crew shanghaied away from painting picnic benches in some national forest. But they were hotshots, this Wyoming bunch—wildfire professionals who ranked up there with the smokejumpers and the best of the West's helicopter rappel crews. They had seen the dragon in worse moods. What was a ground crawler with two-foot flames easing downhill against the wind to them? They were drawing their line in the dirt, stealing the grass and needles and trees that the dragon needed to live, fighting fire with fire by touching off the duff with their long, red fuses, and burning out any sustenance that he might find as he stalked toward their thin trail of bare soil. And behind them were two crack crews of Cheyenne Indians, the seasoned fire-fighters of Western legend, reinforcing the line, chasing down hot spots.

But in that moment, Beisler's foreboding grew.

Forest fires, like new ships and new babies, are christened. If a fire survives its first day, it gets a name, drawn usually from a geographic feature but occasionally tugged from a creative vein hidden in the psyche of some fire bureaucrat. The great campaign fires of the West have had names as poetic as Sleeping Child and as rude as Hog. The Wyoming Hotshots had drawn the fire named Brewer, after a spring that burbled a few miles away.

They were a good crew on that June day in 1988, twenty strong and fresh from spring training. In a season that was off to an eerily early start, they could already claim three fires. Rogers, the ramrod of the Wyoming Hotshots, thought of his crews the way high school coaches talk of their teams. This one was younger and a bit less experienced than some he'd had, but strong and smart, and jelling in a way that pleased him. Officially, in the fashion that hotshot seasonal crews are organized in the nation's wildfire agencies, he was the unit's superintendent.

Figuratively, he was captain of an elite little infantry platoon, one of the sixty-six outfits that fire bosses scream for each summer when the dragon goes thundering through the forests. Beisler, the foreman, the crew's nominal top sergeant, had chased the dragon through every state in the West.

In the paramilitary world of wildland fire, smokejumpers are the Special Forces, dropping deep behind the lines, risking that long step between airplane door and rocky landing to catch the enemy when he is small, insurgent, and least expecting opposition. And hotshots are the Marines, gung-ho groundpounders charging up the beach against stacked odds. Hotshots, who number only 1,360 in all of America, go where the big fires walk.

From their base in the Wyoming town of Greybull, Rogers and Beisler had crafted this crew around a nucleus of veterans, returnees such as the squad bosses, Graham and Meier, and the sawyers, Mader and Halvorsen. They'd stirred in a batch of recruits, all new to the hot-shot business, but most of them bumping up from lower echelons of the wild land fire game. They were a diverse bunch, with three Crow Indians, a Chicago black, and two women in their ranks. They were as old as thirty-six, as young as eighteen. Among them marched athletes, ranch kids, college students, ex–oil field workers, world-traveled adventurers, locals from Bighorn County, and Easterners from as far away as New Jersey.

Today, the twenty had become nineteen. The fire bosses, sequestered back at camp with their maps and radios, had pulled Rogers off the crew and made him a division superintendent. He'd turned the crew over to Beisler—they'd done it before—and moved up to oversee a five-mile section of the Brewer fire's north flank, a piece of the battle that included his own crew, the Cheyenne, a pair of off-road pumper engines, and a bulldozer. The shots had seen Rogers occasionally that evening as he came through their sector and heard him talking on the radio with Beisler.

The engines had never caught up with them. And they'd lost the bulldozer around eight o'clock. It had been easy going until then.

Rogers had relayed a helicopter pilot's message to Beisler. Ahead of the crew lay a meadow, an open island of an acre or so, surrounded by trees. It ran just a bit below the slow-moving line of fire, opposite a small draw at the bottom of the slope they were working. A gift. With a bit of a detour, Beisler could get the crew onto kinder terrain just above the meadow. Beisler had passed the word to Graham, his squad boss at the front of the crew. They'd bent the line and headed north, moving well, with the sawyers sprinting out ahead and knocking down trees, the dozer peeling a ten-foot swath, the diggers cleaning up behind and firing out, creating a blackened line to stop the approaching flames.

But the 'dozer jockey was a flatlander, not like the ones they'd seen on so many other fires, the sure-handed artists who spurred their diesel steeds into action like tank commanders in warfare. This one was a grader of subdivision lots, a new hire seeing action he hadn't contemplated. Craning over his shoulder at the approaching fire, he'd pulled up short at the top of a modest sixty-foot grade. Too steep, he'd said. Graham, decisive and always a bit impatient, had argued. Nothing to it, he'd said, the regular fire dozer guys do it all the time. But, face pale and hands shaking, the flatlander had spun his iron monster in its tracks and gone clanking back the way he'd come.

There was nothing for it after that but to dig. Digging, after all, is the quintessential work of forest fire. Birds sing, fires burn, hotshots dig. So they'd set off, tools swinging hard, taking out trees to break the forest canopy and cutting fire line, gouging their two-foot trail through the dirt beneath the ponderosas as if digging were an Olympic event. They'd expected to don their helmet headlamps after dark and to punch in maybe two or three miles of line before their shift ended at six the next morning. Killer work. The hardest work there was. Their work. Beisler had trotted off to ribbon a stretch of the new course with bits of plastic tape. His path took him down across the small draw, then up again to the edge of the tree-rimmed meadow. In minutes he was back.

It was then he felt the strangeness.

The temperature was climbing paradoxically as twilight deepened. It was up maybe fifteen degrees since he'd hiked down the trail. Odd. The uphill wind was dropping, disappearing. The humidity was skittering downward, the air becoming a desiccant that sucked the moisture off his skin. And there was the stillness, the dead calm, the heaviness. The fire still crept at ground level. But up the line, two or three trees torched off in a momentary seventy-foot tongue of flame, as if the dragon had cleared his throat and spit into the sky.

In war stories told by the old hands of Western forest fire, the spooky calm before the monumental blowup is standard fare. The stuff of rustic mythology, the academics used to say, like the business of moss growing only on the north side of trees. But no more. Now the meteorologists and the fire behaviorists know it's so. They can explain how the dragon holds his breath just before he breathes fire across the land in an explosion that comes faster than the fastest runner. They can chart it and graph it, though they can never predict its precise time or place. And they can detail the incidents, tragedies often, where no one read the signals, no one felt.

But Beisler felt it now. He moved to Graham. They shut down the saws, told the diggers to take a break. They listened. Beisler turned and trotted the two hundred yards ahead to the meadow, wondering if it could be a safety zone if things went sour. By the time he returned, Graham, too, had picked up the drop in the wind, the faintest hint of some new vigor in the fire.

A few airborne embers, now without the uphill wind to hold them off, flitted down across the line, dropped into the parched grass on the crew's left, and blossomed instantly into tulips of fire. Graham set the diggers to chasing them. Farther back along the line, toward the Cheyenne, more embers drifted over, more fires erupted. Another tree torched off, then another, momentary Roman candles rising above the ground fire, their resinous needles sizzling like bacon. Spectacular but hardly urgent. The Wyoming crew plunged to the task at hand willingly, chasing down the spots even as more ignited.

Beisler watched for a minute or two, thinking and feeling. Logic battled instinct. Then he turned to Graham: "Get 'em out. Let's get 'em out now. Up to the meadow." In the years that Graham and Beisler had worked together, they had gone toe to toe with fire vastly more threatening. This was not a fire to make a hotshot crew turn tail. But there was a trust between the two of them. Not questioning, Graham began rounding up his spot chasers. The rookies responded quickly. A couple of the sawyers balked for just a moment, reluctant to leave a fray they were certain could be won. Graham moved them out.

The dragon was stirring now. The wind, no longer neutral, blew lightly downhill. Beisler ran back down the line. Below, spot fires were picking up on his right, and up the hill the main fire began to drive down on his left. Graham was leading the crew out of the trees, counting heads. Beisler turned and trotted after them. Behind him, the embers were falling in earnest, like bits of hot, red snow.

The oral history of every Western hotshot crew has a chapter for tales of being chased out. A crew boss makes a decision and the troops retreat to a burned out black zone, a rock field, a meadow. Like freight cars on a siding, they sit it out and let the fire go highballing past. It is often searing and uncomfortable, so hot that firefighters hide their faces behind hard hats or backpacks. But it always plays well in the retelling: "Fire all around us, three-hundred sixty degrees, and we had our cameras out and were eating lunch." As Graham pushed them toward the draw that separated them from the meadow, the veterans on the crew saw one of those forced respites coming. The meadow would be safe.

But the dragon was growing. More embers were falling. Farther up the ridge in the trees behind them, an insistent roar was building. Kulow, a rookie less than a month out of Greybull High School, picked up his pace as the crew broke from a walk to a jog. He felt the growing urgency but had no perspective in which to place it. This was why he'd joined. It was exciting. It was great.

They broke out of the trees, rushed to the bottom of the draw and hit the upslope on the opposite side. As they reached the meadow, a stand of trees torched off down the line, between them and the

Cheyenne. The fire was working harder, growing faster. It had become a crescent pushing toward them, its tips beginning to hook around the meadow. Beisler caught up with them. He and Graham conferred. Their message rippled through the crew. Start preparing shelter sites. Just a precaution.

Across the West, those who head off to do business with wildfire carry a yellow pouch, not much larger than a box of chocolates. It is worn always at the ready, usually at the waist. It seems almost too small to yield what it contains—a tiny, man-sized, aluminum foil pup tent, a floorless, frameless, poleless, doorless pop-up shelter that a trained firefighter should be able to deploy in twenty seconds. A bonded inner lining of heat resistant glass fiber lends the foil strength, so it will not tear like a chewing gum wrapper. Even so, the aluminum pup tent's walls are thinner than a firefighter's shirt, and the whole improbable structure weighs less than four pounds.

The Wyoming Hotshots had renewed acquaintances with the shelter only three weeks before. In a ritual of spring training that plays out across the West, the thousands of seasonals who hire on for fire duty practice with old shelters, like toddlers climbing under cardboard boxes. They learn about the corner straps for hands and feet, the narrow flaps that tuck under the tent's perimeter to be held down by elbows and knees. They are told that the shelter could save them from flames as hot as a thousand degrees. They are also told that they do not ever want to prove the point. There is no fun in facing the dragon in his foulest mood with only a handful of tinfoil. And across the years very few firefighters have—some minuscule fraction of one percent.

So, even as they began to clear spots in the meadow, few of the hotshots expected to pull their aluminum tents. To the most jaded of the veterans the digging was just another Forest Service safety precaution, part of life in an outfit that could sometimes seem more preoccupied with abating risk than with fighting fire. Beisler started back toward the draw, wanting to make a last check on the line. He raised Meier, his second squad boss, on the radio. Just before the crew had pulled off the line, Meier had dropped back to touch base with the Cheyenne.

Beisler never made it to the draw. From above it, he could see fire surging over the line where the crew had labored moments earlier. The wind clearly had reversed. It was pushing strongly downhill now. Barely a quarter mile away, up behind the line, a thickening column of black smoke climbed into the sky, and fire romped on the crowns of the trees. The dragon, having spent the afternoon preheating and drying the forest canopy above, was coming after it hungrily. And out just a few hundred yards, the crescent of fire was becoming a horseshoe, its two sides driving down to flank the meadow. Meier could not possibly rejoin them. Beisler radioed him to stay with the reservation crews and to fall back. In the meadow, they would be eighteen.

Even before Beisler turned back to the meadow, the pace there quickened. There was an earnestness now to the digging but little progress. Their haven was no grass savannah. It was covered instead with a thick, knee-high, vinelike brush that resisted their tools. Worse, the six sawyers had no hand tools at all; they could only stand and wait. Hamilton, strong and capable from years of work in the oil fields, had cleared only a one-foot square. She found the going almost impossible. She handed off her pulaski to McWilliams, the geology major from Michigan. Kulow stood, watching fire build on the ridge and hearing a new sound, a huffing like a locomotive building speed. Sembach, one of the veterans, heard it too. He shouted at Kulow, "C'mon Kevin, you gotta dig, you gotta dig!" Somewhere in those moments, Graham told them they would deploy shelters. Not all of them believed. It was a possibility too rare. The digging went on.

But it was hopeless work. The strongest among them had hacked out barely two feet. Embers, larger now, fell in the meadow. Momentarily, Graham was gone. Now he was returning. "Up here, up here!" he yelled. "There's a road. It's more open." Nearer to them now, the fire rose in the trees. It was still beyond the closest trees, the thick wall of pine that ringed the edges of the meadow. But its smoke darkened the twilight sky, and in the near distance flames marched across the roof of the forest.

Some of the veterans shed yellow backpacks. They dug out the metal gasoline and oil bottles they each carried to feed the saws, and the flarelike fusees they used to touch off burn-outs, and they began flinging them away. Others took the time to dig the flammables off the backs of the rookies still carrying packs. Through it all they walked, stumbled, ran toward the road. Beisler, returning to the meadow as they were moving out, trailed them. It was a few minutes before nine o'clock. Daylight was waning. Barely fifteen minutes had passed since they left the fire line.

The meadow was not much of a meadow and the road that ran along its north edge was not much of a road. A two-track, really, a pair of wheel lines pounded into the dirt by hunters' pickup trucks. But it was brush-free, covered at its shoulders and center with dry grass. The crew arrived in a rush. The wind whipped their yellow shirts and tore away their words. In the rising noise, the ember shower became a storm. Bits of branches and fist-sized ponderosa cones, resinous firebrands that had been swept hundreds of feet into the air and ignited by the fire's updraft, tumbled from the sky.

Graham sensed time getting away. In the crew, he saw disbelief. The never-never moment was at hand, but most of them still wore shelters at their belts. He stepped to the head of the line, the approaching fire over his shoulder and the crew before him. He ripped his shelter from his pouch and flipped it open into the wind. He shook out the last folds and hooked his boots into the foot straps. Then he looked down the line and saw with satisfaction that shelters were coming out.

Beisler reached the road as his crew wrestled their foil tents in the wind, like Kansas farm wives trying to clean off the washline before an approaching tornado. Hamilton had her tent unfolded. She looked fearfully at Beisler. "You can handle it," he yelled. "You'll be okay." As he tucked into his shelter, Antos, the recruit from New Jersey, saw spot fires dancing downwind in the meadow and the trees beyond. The horseshoe was closing. They were encircled. The seconds raced. Beisler turned to see Mader, the sawyer, with a shadow of resigned doom on his face. His hand protruded through a huge seam split in his shelter. "No, no, you're okay," Beisler yelled. "Remember the training film. Grab the rip. Tuck it under you."

As he rushed to throw his own shelter down, Beisler stole a glance at the fire. He had watched fire race across grassy hills faster than an antelope could run, and he had seen it thunder up the chaparral canyons of California, eating houses like popcorn. But he was seeing something different now. He looked into a firestorm, a panorama of flame. Down low, sheets of fire danced beyond the trees at the meadow's edge. Farther up the ridge they whipped above the forest and licked at the sky. The smoke column boiled ten thousand feet into the air. The embers and ash blew so fiercely that he lowered his head and squinted his eyes against them. Down the line to the south, a stand of trees was crowned in fire. To the north, like an image in a mirror, a second batch raged. Pillars of fire, to the right and left.

And then, in the second that Beisler watched, the pillars connected and became a wall. As if marinated in gasoline, the trees at meadow's edge, the last barrier between the hotshots and fire, crowned out in an eighth-mile sheet of flame. Like it was driven by a bellows in a forge, the ground fire had simply lifted, vaulting to the canopy above. It matched nothing in Beisler's experience. And it roared and seethed now, a giant red-orange picket fence, with flames spiking 150 feet above the treetops and bending before the wind, stretching toward the meadow. The dragon was at the door.

Beisler was in trouble. Along the line of shelters, elbows and knees poked and bumped behind the foil, hands reached out to pull in flaps and tuck down tight. The fire was close now, and waves of heat rolled over him. Near the spot Beisler had chosen for himself, Bates, the recruit from Colorado, stood alone, gloved hands fumbling with his still-folded shelter. Beisler ripped it away, shook it out in the rising wind and handed it back. "Get in! Get in!" he yelled.

Out of time now, Beisler spun to his spot, shaking out his shelter, falling to the ground. As he went down, pulling the shelter over his shoulders like a cape, a sheet of flame rolled out of the trees and swept horizontally over the meadow. The grass at his feet ignited. He pulled the shelter in around him, hurrying, hurrying. He stole a final look at the meadow and took into the tent with him a vision of surrealist hell.

Before a backdrop of orange flame, giant maroon and purple balls of unburned gases rolled toward them. They coursed two feet above the meadow, like an armada of great, malevolent, sinuous, airborne steam-rollers, seeking oxygen so they could explode into flame, while white vapor streamed off their tops like foam off an ocean curler.

And then the fire was on them.

The shelters were arrayed across the road in rows of two and three, packed in so tightly that some of them touched. They were boulders now in a river of flame, and the rapids eddied and curled and broke over each of them differently, with a venomous sort of whimsy. At the head, Graham felt the superheated wind buffet his shelter and push it down against his back. Beneath the edges he saw a thin line of flickering light, like a racing dynamite fuse, as the grass outside his tent erupted and the fire swept over him. On his right, he could hear Beisler struggling, still working to secure the edges of his tent and coping with tiny grass fires inside. Beisler had been caught with gloves off and sleeves rolled up. But he had a plastic water bottle in each hand and, as he secured the edges of his shelter, he used the canteens to beat out fire and to hold down the front corners.

The fire's first wave was the curtain of flame sweeping off the trees, igniting the volatile gases ahead of it. It was a flash flood, a stampede of flame that filled the meadow and swept over the road. It buffeted the tents and lifted their corners. Into most, it drove heavy smoke and into some, fire. Stewart, one of the Crows, was in the tallest grass along the road. He took fire inside the back of his tent and then in the front. He beat the flames out with his legs and hands, taking more searing air beneath the edges of his tent, choking on smoke. He fought the urge to do what he had been taught would be instantly fatal—to stand and run.

McWilliams had fire. Old Horn had fire. Bates had fire. Red Horn had fire, and in his tent he lifted himself to his fingers and toes, and watched little tongues of flame run beneath his body. Kulow saw that the shelter had pinholes, tiny openings that glowed red-orange, just as the training film had promised. The walls of his tent were too hot to touch, and the temperature inside was climbing. But, with an eighteen-year-old's sense of immortality, he was still fascinated and excited. Then the corner of his tent lifted. He took fire and smoke. In the next moments, he thought about dying. And he heard the screaming begin.

It came first from Trummer. The shortest member of the crew, she had struggled with the long stretch between the foot and hand straps of her shelter. Now wind lifted the back of her tent and for the briefest moment a wave of fire washed inside. Even as she screamed she fought the flaps back into place. Beside her, McWilliams cursed in frustration and shouted above the wind, "Don't panic, Lori! Don't run!" She beat flames out with her hands and rolled onto her side to smother a patch that was searing her leg. As Trummer's cries died, they could hear others. Long, tortured, repeated. Sembach. Those closest to the back could hear him screaming, thrashing in his tent, then screaming again.

Among the tents there was talk. Names were called out, and people checked in with each other even as they fought their interior fires and struggled for breath. They could hear McWilliams swearing colorfully at each new scream, voicing for them all the frustration of being able to do nothing for the others. Up front, Beisler and Graham talked over hand-held radios. They had heard the screams, too. They were certain that some had stood and run, entering the race that could not be won. Graham narrated each moment into his radio, not knowing if his transmission was reaching outside the meadow, wondering if his words would be the only record of what happened there. Kulow had heard nothing from the four crew members between his tent and Sembach's, and he counted them for dead.

Some in the crew sensed the briefest of pauses. The flame front from the trees roared past them, into the forest downwind from the meadow. It had been a prelude, an airborne attack that passed so quickly and claimed so much oxygen that it had burned only the lightest fuels around them. Now the dragon would send an army of towering flame marching at ground level through the brush of the meadow. It came with a volcano of sound, as if they were standing in the afterblast of a battalion of jet engines. It was on them with winds that approached sixty miles an hour. The tents filled with smoke, much thicker than before, and new fingers of fire crept under their edges.

They had heard of the noise and the wind that came with big fire. Some had experienced it before, from a distance. But mere humans were not meant to be at its epicenter, with breakers of flame washing over their tinfoil tents. The shelters shook and flattened and flapped and filled with thick smoke. Inside, as the temperatures rose toward two hundred degrees, the hotshots fought fire with water from their canteens and pressed their mouths close to the dirt, cupping their arms around their faces and struggling for breath. In the enveloping noise, each was alone.

In her tent, Hamilton thought over and over, "Some of us are dying." Bates had weathered the first blast of fire, but he was suffocating now, wrestling with the impulse to run. Hearing nothing but the roar, Kulow began to think that he was the only survivor. Alone in his shelter, Antos had a crystalline vision of the faraway New Jersey girl named Donna and wondered if he would make their wedding, just two months off. McWilliams took a shallow, searing breath. He ripped the earth with his fingers, trying to create a hole for his mouth and nose. There was little oxygen in the smoky air he had drawn; he held it perhaps twenty seconds, then let it go and pulled in another breath. Worse, much worse. Now he was frantic, digging the ground with his fingers, and finally with his teeth, as if some reservoir of sweet air could be chewed from the earth beneath him. He could hold the second breath only thirty seconds. Face in the dirt, he let it go and drew a third. He was dizzy now, choking, losing concentration.

And then, in all the tents, the smoke was gone. Some curious passing eddy of the fire drafted it out as quickly as it had come. A few on the crew felt the smallest whiff of cool air as the smoke exited, though the fire still raged around them. At the rear of the formation, Sembach no longer screamed. But they heard his moans, heard him calling out, heard him thrashing in his shelter. Up front, Graham and Beisler still talked. They listened for a while, felt the foil walls cool slightly. Briefly, they raised the edges of their tents and peered out. Still too hot. Beisler waited another minute, then rose to his knees. A fifty-mile-an-hour wind pulled his shelter from his hands and rolled it back. But it was wind without fire, and he called to Graham as he rose to his feet.

Beisler turned, and he was sickened. Twilight had given way to the first edge of night. He noted vaguely that the racing flame front was gone, already out of sight beyond the next ridge. The meadow had become a blackened moonscape, with clouds of ash and smoke whipping across it. On its edges, as far as he could see, the seared skeletons of pines stood, their branches fingering the night without a single needle. Here and there, small fires burned in the gloom, and several of them were very close-burning clumps of yellow. Yellow, the color of fire shirts. For the briefest moment Beisler saw bodies that had fallen where they'd run. The nearest of the fires was on the road and he went to it. It was a backpack, a piece of fire gear discarded in the headlong dash into the shelters. And so, he realized, were the other yellow lumps, because the tents, battered and misshapen, were shining there before him, row on row.

He and Graham went down the line, shaking shelters, softly calling names and hearing answers in smoke-rasped voices, bringing people out into the darkness and the wind. They found Sembach, rolled in his shelter, delirious from pain. He was burned, seriously, and he had inhaled superheated air. He had deployed at the edge of the road. The fire winds had swirled most cruelly around his shelter. The brush and fuel next to it were heavy, and they had burned with extreme heat. For long moments, as he fought his solitary battle, the winds had curled back both ends of the shelter. His legs, arms, and face were burned. But he would live, they would all live.

They would be alone for almost an hour in the dark before help arrived. Beisler and Graham, sensing the shakiness of the moment, spun the crew into action—gathering packs, counting heads, inventorying equipment, digging out first-aid gear and canteens. The medics, Antos and Bates, treated Sembach. They gave him water, swathed his burns in gauze, and talked him through the pain. The first van into the meadow carried him away, starting him toward a Montana hospital two hundred miles distant.

The crew was alone for most of another hour, treating its minor burns, talking, sharing food salvaged from the packs, waiting for transport. They swapped stories. Mader, the sawyer with the huge rip in his shelter, had survived unscathed. McWilliams had risen from the ground to see his silhouette etched in burned grass, like the police outline of a murder victim chalked onto pavement. Their sense of family was heightened. In the spirit of their moment, they posed for a group photograph, facing the retreating fire and mocking it with the universal one-finger salute. The T-shirt committee conducted its first meeting. Though they didn't know it that June night, they had survived the opening round of the fire siege of 1988, the season like no other. The blazes that would burn until November already were up and running in Yellowstone Park. The grapevine would do its work, and in the fire camps that never seemed to close in that endless summer of drought and flame, others would nod knowingly when they saw the shirts that read, "Been to hell and lived to tell. Brewer Fire."

At dawn they walked through medical checkups. Hamilton called her parents in Wyoming. Like so many other young people who wander onto fire crews, she was a second generation firefighter. Decades before, her father had cut line on Western fire. He had supported his daughter's decision to chase the dragon. He listened knowingly to her story. His memories of other fires in other times were keen. So was his fire camp humor. "See," he said, "I told you it wasn't dangerous."

When the doctors and the training counselors were done with them, the Wyoming Hotshots faced a choice. They knew that Sembach would live. And they knew that, most often, crews that have survived an entrapment go home, take a week off, regroup. The choice was theirs. It was no choice at all. They went back to the Brewer Fire.

from Working

by Studs Terkel

Studs Terkel (born 1912) talked to people about their jobs for his 1972 book Working. *Here former cop Tom Patrick discusses life as a New York City fireman.*

Know why I switched to fireman? I liked people, but sometimes I'd feel hate comin' into me. I hated it, to get me like that. I caught these three guys drinkin' wine, three young Spanish guys. I said, "Fellas, if you're gonna drink, do it in some apartment." 'Cause they were spillin' the wine and they'd piss right in front of the house, in the lobby. I came back in a half-hour and they had another bottle out. They were pissin' around. I'm sayin' to myself, I'm tryin' to be nice. I walked over. There was two guys facin' me and one guy had his back to me. So he says, "What the fuck's the mick breakin' our balls for?" He's callin' me a mick. He's changing roles, you know? He's acting like they say a cop does. So I said, "You fuckin' spic." So I took the night stick and I swung it hard to hit him in the head. He ducked and it hit the pillar. He turned white and they all took off. It scared me that I could get this hatred so fast. I was fuckin' shakin'.

A few times I pulled my gun on guys. One time I went to the roof of this project and there's this big black guy about six seven on top of the stairs. He had his back to me. I said, "Hey, fella, turn around." He said,

"Yeah, wait a minute, man." His elbows were movin' around his belt. I was halfway up. I said "Turn around, put your hands up against the wall." He said, "Yeah, yeah, wait a minute." It dawned on me he had a gun caught in his belt and he was tryin' to take it out. I said, "Holy shit." So I took my gun out and said, "You fucker, I'm gonna shoot." He threw his hands against the wall. He had his dick out and he was tryin' to zip up his fly, and there was a girl standin' in the corner, which I couldn't see. So here was a guy gettin' a hand job and maybe a lot of guys might have killed him. I said, "Holy shit, I coulda killed ya." He started shaking and my gun in my hand was shaking like a bastard. I said—I musta been cryin'—I said, "Just get the hell outa here, don't . . ."

I took the fire department test in '68 and got called in '70. I always wanted to be a fireman. My other brother was a fireman eleven years. He had a fire and the floor gave way, he was tellin' me the story. He thought it was just a one-floor drop. But the guys grabbed him by the arms. They said, "If you go, we all go." He couldn't believe this kind of comradeship. They pulled him out. He went down to get his helmet and it was two floors down. He really woulda got busted up.

I like everybody workin' together. You chip in for a meal together. One guy goes to the store, one guy cooks, one guy washes the dishes. A common goal. We got a lieutenant there, he says the fire department is the closest thing to socialism there is.

The officer is the first one into the fire. When you get to captain or lieutenant, you get more work not less. That's why I look up to these guys. We go to a fire, the lieutenant is the first one in. If he leaves, he takes you out. One lieutenant I know got heart trouble. When he takes a beatin' at a fire he should go down to the hospital and get oxygen or go on sick. He don't want to go on sick. I used to go into a fire, it was dark and I'd feel a leg and I'd look up and see the lieutenants standing there in the fire and smoke takin' beatings.

When I was in the army I didn't respect the officers, because the men did all the work. That goes for the police department, too. Cops get killed. You never see a lieutenant get shot. Ten battalion chiefs got killed in fires in the last ten years in the city. The last three guys in the fire department were lieutenants that got killed. 'Cause they're the first ones in there. I respect that. I want to respect an officer. I want to see somebody higher up that I can follow.

You go to some firehouses, these fuckin' guys are supermen. I'm not a superman, I want to live. These guys are not gonna live. Every day orders come down, guys are dyin', retirement. I don't think these guys get their pensions too long. I never heard a fireman livin' to sixty-five.

When you get smoke in your lungs, these guys are spittin' out this shit for two days. A fireman's life is nine years shorter than the average workingman because of the beating they take on their lungs and their heart. More hazardous than a coal miner. The guy don't think nothing's wrong with him. You don't think until you get an x-ray and your name's on it. We got this lieutenant and when he takes a beating he can't go to a hospital because they'll find something wrong with him. He was trapped in a room and he jumped out of the second-story window. He broke both his ankles, ran back into the building, and he collapsed.

There's more firemen get killed than cops, five to one. Yet there's only one-third of the amount of men on the job. We get the same pay as policemen. These politicians start to put a split between the departments. I'd like to take some of these politicians right into the fuckin' fire and put their head in the smoke and hold it there. They wouldn't believe it. They don't give a shit for the people. Just because they wave the flag they think they're the greatest.

The first fire I went to was a ship fire. I jumped off the engine, my legs got weak. I nearly fell to the ground, shakin', right? It was the first and only time I got nerves. But we have to go in there. It's thrilling and its scary. Like three o'clock in the morning. I was in the ladder company, it's one of the busiest in the city, like six thousand runs a year.[*]

---

[*] "You go on false alarms, especially two or three in the afternoon, kids comin' home from school. And four in the morning when the bars are closed. Drunks. Sometimes I get mad. It's ten, eleven at night and you see ten, twenty teen-agers on the corner and there's a false alarm on that corner, you know one of 'em pulled it. The kids say, 'What's the matter, man? What're ya doin' here?' and they laugh. You wanna say, 'You stupid fuck, you might have a fire in your house and it could be your mother.' "

The sky is lit up with an orange. You get back to the firehouse, you're up there, talkin', talkin' about it.

I was in a fire one night, we had an all-hands. An all-hands is you got a workin' fire and you're the first in there, and the first guy in there is gonna take the worst beatin'. You got the nozzle, the hose, you're takin' a beating. If another company comes up behind you, you don't give up that nozzle. It's pride. To put out the fire. We go over this with oxygen and tell the guy, "Get out, get oxygen." They won't leave. I think guys want to be heroes. You can't be a hero on Wall Street.

There's guys with black shit comin' out of their ears. You got smoke in your hair. You take a shower, you put water on your hair, and you can still smell the smoke. It never leaves you. You're coughin' up this black shit. But you go back and you have coffee, maybe a couple of beers, you're psyched up.

You get a fire at two, three in the morning. The lights go on, you get up. I yelled, "Jesus, whatsa matter?" It dawned on me: Where else could we be goin'? All the lights goin' on and it's dark. It's fuckin' exciting. Guys are tellin', "Come on, we go. First Due." That means you gotta be the first engine company there. You really gotta move. It's a pride. You gotta show you're the best. But what they're fightin' over is good. What they're fightin' over is savin' lives.

You go in there and it's dark. All of a sudden smoke's pourin' outa the goddamn building. It's really fast. Everybody's got their assign-ments. A guy hooks up a hydrant. A guy on the nozzle, I'm on the nozzle. A guy's up to back me up. A guy's puttin' a Scott Air Pack on. It's a breathing apparatus. It lasts twenty minutes.

Two weeks ago we pulled up to this housing project. On the eighth floor the flames were leaping out the window. We jumped out, your fuckin' heart jumps. We ran into the elevator. Four of us, we rolled up the hose, each guy had fifty feet. We got off on the seventh floor, the floor below the fire. We got on the staircase and hook into the stand-pipe. The guys were screamin' for water and smoke was backin' up. You're supposed to have a wheel to turn on the water and the wheel was missin'! Someone stole it in the project. You get these junkies, they steal brass, anything. They steal the shittin' life. A guy with a truck company came with a claw tool and the water came shootin' out.

They started yellin' for a Scott. It weighs about thirty pounds, got the face mask and cylinder. I couldn't get the damn thing tight. There's three straps, I tied one. They need me upstairs. They push you into the room. (Laughs.) This is it. One guy's layin' on the floor and I'm crawlin', feeling along the hose. The second company comes in with Scotts on. One guy's got his face piece knocked to the side, so he's gotta get out because the smoke is gettin' him. The other guy yells, "Give me the nozzle." It started whippin' around, fifty, sixty pounds of pressure. Knocked my helmet off. I grabbed the nozzle. I looked up and saw this orange glow. I start hittin' it. The damn thing wouldn't go out. It was a fuckin' light bulb. (Laughs.) A bulb in the bathroom.

I felt this tremendous heat to my left. I turn around and this whole fuckin' room was orange, yellow. You can't see clear through the plastic face piece. You can just see orange and feel the heat. So I open up with this shittin' nozzle to bank back the smoke. The guys came in and ventilated, knocked out the windows. A seven-room apartment, with six beds and a crib. That's how many kids were living there. Nobody was hurt, they all got out.

There was a lot of smoke. When you have two minutes left on the Scott, a bell starts ringin'. It means get out, you got no oxygen. The thing I don't like about it, with the piece on your face, you feel confined. But as I went to more fires, I loved the thing because I know that thing's life. Ninety percent of the people die from smoke inhalation, not from burns.

You got oxygen, it's beautiful, but you can't see. It's a shitty feeling when you can't see. Sometimes a Scott's bad because it gives you a false sense of security. You go into a room where you're not supposed to be. You'd be walkin' into a pizzeria oven and you wouldn't know it. You can't see, you feel your way with the hose. You straddle the hose as you get out. You gotta talk to yourself. Your mind's actually talkin'. I'm sayin' things like: It's beautiful, I can breathe, the fire's over.

In 1958 there was a fire across the street from where I live. It was about one o'clock in the morning. There's flames on the second floor. I ran up the stairs and grabbed this little girl. She was burnt on the arm. I ran down the street and yelled to the firemen, "I got a girl here got burnt." They went right past me. I hated the bastards. Now I understand. You gotta put the fire out. There's more life up there you gotta save. This girl's outside . . . It's real . . .

When you're with the police, it wasn't real. I heard guys makin' arrests, they found a gun in the apartment. In the paper they say the guy fought with the guy over the gun. When you know the truth, the story's bullshit. But in the fire department there's no bullshit. You gotta get into that fire—to be able to save somebody's life.

About two years ago a young girl ran to the firehouse. She's yellin' that her father had a heart attack. The guy was layin' in the kitchen, right? He pissed in his pants. That's a sign of death. The fella was layin' there with his eyes open. Angie pushes the guy three times in the chest, 'cause you gotta shock his heart. The son was standin' in the room, just starin' down. I got down on his mouth. You keep goin' and goin' and the guy threw up. You clean out his mouth. I was on a few minutes and then Ed Corrigan jumped on the guy's mouth. The captain bent down and said, "The guy's dead. Keep goin' for the family." We took over for ten minutes, but it was a dead man. The son looked down at me and I looked up. He said, "Man, you tried everything. You tried." You know what I mean? I was proud of myself. I would get on a stranger, on his mouth. It's a great feeling.

We had this fire down the block. A Puerto Rican social club. The captain, the lieutenant, and the other firemen took the ladder up and saved two people. But downstairs there was a guy tryin' to get out the door. They had bolts on the door. He was burnt dead. Know what the lieutenant said? "We lost a guy, we lost a guy." I said, "You saved two people. How would you know at six in the morning a guy's in the social club sleeping on a pool table?" He said, "Yeah, but we lost a guy." And the lieutenant's a conservative guy.

You get guys that talk about niggers, spics, and they're the first guys into the fire to save 'em. Of course we got guys with long hair and beards. One guy's an artist. His brother got killed in Vietnam, that's why he's against the war. And these guys are all super firemen. It's you that takes the beating and you won't give up. Everybody dies . . .

My wife sees television, guys get killed. She tells me, "Be careful." Sometimes she'll call up the firehouse. I tell her we had a bad job, sometimes I don't . . . They got a saying in the firehouse: "Tonight could be the night." But nobody thinks of dying. You can't take it seriously, because you'd get sick. We had some fires, I said, "We're not gettin' out of this." Like I say, everybody dies.

A lotta guys wanna be firemen. It's like kids. Guys forty years old are kids. They try to be a hard guy. There's no big thing when you leave boyhood for manhood. It seems like I talked the same at fifteen as I talk now. Everybody's still a kid. They just lose their hair or they don't fuck that much.

When I was a kid I was scared of heights. In the fire department you gotta go up a five-story building with a rope around you. You gotta jump off a building. You know the rope can hold sixteen hundred pounds. As long as you got confidence in your body and you know the guy's holding you, you got nothing to be scared of. I think you perform with people lookin' at you. You're in the limelight. You're out there with the people and kids. Kids wave at you. When I was a kid we waved at firemen. It's like a place in the sun.

Last month there was a second alarm. I was off duty. I ran over there. I'm a bystander. I see these firemen on the roof, with the smoke pouring out around them, and the flames, and they go in. It fascinated me. Jesus Christ, that's what *I* do! I was fascinated by the people's faces. You could see the pride that they were seein'. The fuckin' world's so fucked up, the country's fucked up. But the firemen, you actually see them produce. You see them put out a fire. You see them come out with babies in their hands. You see them give mouth-to-mouth when a guy's dying. You can't get around that shit. That's real. To me, that's what I want to be.

I worked in a bank. You know, it's just paper. It's not real. Nine to five and it's shit. You're lookin' at numbers. But I can look back and say, "I helped put out a fire. I helped save somebody." It shows something I did on this earth.

from Will the Circle Be Unbroken?
by Studs Terkel

His own advancing years prompted Studs Terkel

(born 1912) to write a book based on conver-

sations about death. Here he catches up with

Tom, the retired New York City fireman he

spoke with almost 30 years earlier for a book

about working.

L et's talk about firefighters. January, 1976. I was on vacation when Charlie Sanchez and nine guys from my firehouse went into the basement of an A&P. Charlie Sanchez got killed, and they thought the other eight were dead. They heard the firemen crying for their mothers on the walkie-talkies and the guys outside were crying, too. The fire commissioner come down and said to give up, they were dead, turn off the walkie-talkies. They told the fire commissioner to get the fuck out of there. They're doing their job. They breached the wall with a battering ram, sixteen inches of brick. In the 1800s it had been a prison room for slaves. They grabbed the eight firemen and dragged them through the hole.

I went to the hospital and I remember Paul Matula, a big Polish guy—senior man, Ladder 131. Tremendous hands. I said to him, "Paul, did you talk to God?" I don't believe really in churches. To me, churches is business—but there could be somebody out there. Paul said, "Listen, I thought I was dying, so I gave God a couple of shouts." You couldn't do better than that.

Gordon Sepper, the carbon monoxide was getting to him, and the smoke, he was falling asleep, his head down, knowing he was going. Just then, he says, a twenty-four-foot portable ladder appeared and he knew he could be saved. So he started reaching up, climbing up the rungs, and when he got to the top rung, his brain told his hand to grab the floor of the A&P there, because he was all carbon-monoxide-to-the-brain disorientated, right? Just then two firemen grabbed him by the coat and pulled him out. Another guy was Joe Pennington. When the A&P was collapsing into the basement, Joe counted eighteen steps to the street—he knew enough to count the steps. They went down eighteen steps in the basement next door and breached the wall. I look up to those men. It was the greatest job you can ever have, a fireman . . .

Most firemen die after they retire, eight to ten years earlier than the general population. Cancer, emphysema, stuff like that. Smoke inhalation—it's cumulative. The chemicals, the plastics burn. My brother Billy was thirty-five years a firefighter—he's got a disability. He can't breathe. He's got asthma, emphysema—he never smoked. He was a marathon runner, twenty-six miles.

It's even worse than with the miners, who get everything, black lung, cave-ins, everything. I'm going with a woman whose father was a coal miner in Scranton, Pennsylvania. When she was a little girl, she remembers her father coming home with one finger chopped off from a mine accident. He took the finger, still in his glove, and threw it into the fireplace. A few days later, he went back to work . . . We've come a long way since then, but they're still my heroes, working-class people. My father instilled that in me.

I remember August 2nd, 1978. Six firemen got killed in Brooklyn. Louise O'Connor, with three kids, went to see her husband at the firehouse near Sheepshead Bay. They were going for a weekend down to the Jersey Shore . . . Just a routine fire. Her husband was on the roof of the Ward Bond grocery—he waved to her as the roof caved in.

I was on vacation walking on a country road. My father came running down. "Six firemen just got killed." It's like being at war and you're home. I said, "I gotta go in. I gotta go in." My wife says, "Why do you gotta go in?" Because, I told her, this is my family, my second family. She said, "You gotta stay here." I said, "No, I gotta go in." I went in the shower. I didn't want her to see me cry. I put the water on and started screaming, *"Fuck! Fuck! Fuck!"* I went in and was missing for three days. I went to as many funerals as I could—'cause it was two, three different churches. That was twenty-two years ago.

I ran into Louise O'Connor again in 1988 at the American Legion Post where another guy killed in a fire was being honored. She introduces me to her son, who's now a New York City cop. I said, "That kid was a couple of years old when your husband got killed." So the beat goes on. It never ends.

I hate guns. I wasn't a good cop because I used to walk around with no bullets in the chamber. I used to have them in my pocket and kid around saying if somebody starts in, I'll just throw the bullets real hard. *[Laughs]*

A few times I pulled my gun on guys. One time I went on the roof of this project and there's this big black guy, about six-seven, on top of the stairs. He had his back to me. I said, "Hey, fella, turn around." He said, "Yeah, wait a minute, man." I said, *"Turn around* and put your hands against the wall." He said, "Yeah, yeah, wait a minute." It dawned on me he had a gun caught in his belt and was tryin' to take it out. I said, "Holy shit . . ." So I took my gun out and said, "You fucker, I'm gonna shoot." He threw his hands up against the wall. He had his dick out and was tryin' to zip up his fly, and there was a girl standing in the corner, which I couldn't see. So here was a guy gettin' a hand job and maybe a lot of guys would have *killed* him. I said, "Holy shit, I coulda killed ya." He started shaking and the gun in my hand was shaking like a bastard. I said—I musta been cryin'—I said, "Just get the hell outa here . . ." That's when I decided to quit the force and become a fireman.

My brother Billy was a fireman five years before me. He said, "It's a different quality of life—it's great." He was in a fire in a high-rise, knocking out windows in the bathroom. The bathtub gave way and he fell through the floor. They teach you when you fall to put your elbows out to your side. He caught on to the floor and the firemen come in and grabbed him. He said, "No, let me go, I'll fall to the next floor and

I don't want to take you with me." The two firemen said, "If you go, we all go"—that's the job.

I retired from the fire department in '88 and as a fire safety director in '95. Now it's just a memory. I just sit back and watch the world go by. Talk about dying—it affects everything I do. I feel life is like the twenty-four-second clock in a basketball game. I got the ball now and I gotta score. By scoring, I mean I want to travel, see the world more. I got twenty-four seconds left and I want to stretch it out. But if they hook up tubes to you and you're on a monitor and unconscious for months, they gotta be kidding. I'm outa here. Twenty-four seconds ran out.

We had a great fire captain, Bill Huber. When he passed away, I went to his wake, his funeral. He had a simple pine box, closed, with a picture on top of him in a fire uniform. That's what I want. In red pajamas, fire red. Then I want to be cremated. I want my ashes to be thrown into a beautiful pond in Jersey. I want somebody to sing "I'll Be Seeing You." [*Sings*]

> *In all the old familiar places*
> *that this heart of mine embraces*
> *all night through*
> *I'll see you . . .*

Isn't that wonderful? All the old girlfriends, the old neighborhood . . .

I remember years ago, a Laurel and Hardy movie, they're in the First World War. Hardy says, "If we get killed, what do you want to come back as?" Laurel says, "I want to come back as myself." Hardy gets mad: "You stupid, you can't come back as yourself, you have to come back as something else. You're gonna come back as a donkey." They both get killed and Hardy comes back as a donkey.

I always said I'd like to come back as myself but with a great voice like Johnny Mathis or Tony Bennett. Well, this one time, I got off the subway train at Seventy-ninth by mistake, and there's a black man about fifty, in rags, with a bag to put money in, singing "My Funny

Valentine." He sounded like Sammy Davis, Jr., a beautiful voice—unbelievable. I'm saying, *Holy Jesus*—I just wanted to come back as myself with a great voice and you can end up on the goddamn IRT, penniless.

Right now, I'm OK. My hearing's going, I got a ringing. My eyesight's going. The thing I still got left is my taste buds—I still love food.

These days I get out of a car like my father used to get out: grab the roof and pull yourself out. I got a bad back. My father passed the baton on to me, and I'm passing it on to my kids.

I'm not going to worry about any hereafter. A few months ago, my sister got a call at one in the morning. The police told her that they found her husband dead in bed. They were divorced, but they still loved each other and called each other up every day on the phone. I drove her in about two in the morning. My sister told me she had a dream a couple of days before that there was a hand coming out to her. I went into the bedroom where her husband was laying and he had his arm outstretched. My sister is strong, they got two sons. He was a young man, fifty-five. Like I said, it's a spaceship and we gotta keep going on.

So, here I am, a retired firefighter who almost died from drowning in the ocean. It was 1994, I was down in Bermuda, walking along this beach, hardly anyone in the water. It was a beautiful day. I went in. I'm not a good swimmer. Before I knew it, I was dragged out in the tide. It was up to my chest. The lifeguard was on a hill, couldn't hear me scream. I figured this was it, I'm going to die in Bermuda. Everything went through my head, the kids, memories—it's all over. The water was way past my chest and dragging me out. So I took a deep breath and dived toward the beach. My legs were kicking, hands moving, hoping when I came down I wasn't stepping on water, and when I got to the beach, I was like . . . *[gasps]* . . . heavy breathing. Barely made it. That was 1994. I'm sixty years old and I have a second chance. Yeah, I think about death more and more, but I can't do nothing about it. It's gonna come. Suppose somebody said, "You can be alive forever, but you gotta drive through the Holland Tunnel for the rest of your life"? What would you do? Would you want to live forever driving through the Holland Tunnel?

from Report from Engine Co. 82
by Dennis Smith

Fire fighter Dennis Smith's (born 1940) South Bronx firehouse averaged 700 calls per month, making his company the busiest in New York City. Smith had been a fire fighter for eight years when he wrote Report from Engine Co. 82.

he Late, Late Show is on the television and most of us are sitting in the kitchen when the bells start to ring. I take a last sip of tea as I count onetwo onetwothreefourfive one onetwothreefourfive. The kitchen chairs empty as the last number comes in. Box 2515. Intervale Avenue and Kelly Street.

We can smell the smoke as the pumper turns down Intervale, and hands automatically start pulling boot-tops to thighs, clipping coat-rings closed, and putting on gloves. The pumper stops in front of a building just before we reach Kelly Street. We're about to stretch the hose when there is an anguished scream from inside the building. A boy is running out of the doorway, his shirt and hair aflame.

Ladder 31 and Chief Solwin are right behind us, and one of the ladder men goes rapidly to the boy's assistance. Willy Knipps takes the first folds of the hose and heads into the building. Carroll and I follow, dragging the rest of the hose with us. Royce and Boyle are still on the sidewalk donning masks.

Lieutenant Welch is waiting for us on the second floor, crouched low by a smoking door. There are four apartments on the floor, and three of the doors are open, their occupants fleeing. Chief Solwin arrives, stops for a moment at the top of the stairs, and then rushes into the apartment adjoining the rooms on fire. He starts kicking through the wall with all his strength. The smoke rushes through the hole, darkening the apartment and the hall. Knipps and I are coughing and have to lie on our bellies as we wait for the water to surge through the hose. Carroll has gone down for another mask. He can tell it's going to be a tough, snotty job.

Billy-o and Artie Merritt start to work on the locked door. It's hard for me to breathe with my nose to the marble floor of the hall, and I think of the beating Artie and Billy-o must be taking as they stand where the smoke is densest, swinging on the ax, hitting the door with the point of the halligan tool. The door is tight and does not give easily.

Captain Frimes arrives with Charlie McCartty behind him. "Give me a man with a halligan," Chief Solwin yells, and Captain Frimes and McCartty hustle into the adjoining apartment.

"I'm sure I heard someone in there," Chief Solwin says.

Charlie widens the hole in the wall. The Chief and Captain Frimes are on their knees as Charlie works. After furious hacking, the hole is through to the next apartment. Charlie tries to squeeze through the bay—the sixteen-inch space between the two-by-fours. He can't make it. Not with his mask on. He turns to take the mask off, but before he can get it off Captain Frimes enters through the hole.

The front door has still not been opened, and Frimes knows that only luck or the help of God will keep the whole place from lighting up. He crawls on the floor toward the front door, swinging his arms before him as if swimming the breast stroke. His hand is stopped by the bulk of a body, lying on the floor. It's a big frame, and Captain Frimes struggles to drag it toward the hole in the wall. The fire is raging in three rooms at the end of the hall, and spreading fast toward the front of the building. McCartty is just crawling through the hole as the Captain passes by with the body. "Here, Cap, here," McCartty yells.

The smoke is so thick that Captain Frimes missed the hole. McCartty grabs the body under the arms, and pulls.

Captain Frimes can hear Billy-o and Artie working on the door, and he makes a desperate effort back down the hall. He reaches the front door and feels the long steel bar of a Fox lock. Like a flying buttress, the bar reaches up from the floor and braces the door closed. Captain Frimes knows locks as well as he knows his own kids' names, and he kneels and turns the bolt of the lock. He jumps back, and the door swings open. Billy-o and Artie grab the Captain, who is overcome by smoke and can barely move now, and pull him out of the apartment.

Charlie McCartty walks past us with the body in his arms. It is a boy, about sixteen or seventeen years old. He is a strapping black youth, but McCartty is a powerful man, and carries him easily to the street. The boy is still breathing, but barely. McCartty knows that he has to get some oxygen into him if he is to live, and begins mouth-to-mouth resuscitation.

The hose comes to life with water as Billy-o and Artie pull the Captain down the stairs. Lieutenant Welch gives the "okay" to Knipps, and we start crawling down the hall. We reach the first burning room, and Knipps opens the nozzle. The room is filled with the crackling of fire, and as the water stream hits the ceiling the sound is made louder by falling plaster, steaming and hissing on the wet floor.

The fire darkens quickly, and the smoke banks to the floor. There is no escape from it, and Knipps knows that he has to push into the last room for a rest. "Give me some more line!" he yells, and his order is relayed back through the hall by Lieutenant Welch's voice: "Lighten up on the inch-and-a-half." The hose moves forward, and Knipps with it.

Boyle moves up, breathing easily in his mask. He is going to relieve Knipps on the line, but he trips in the middle of the room. He feels around the floor to see what tripped him, and his hands sink into another body. "I got a victim here!" he yells through the mouthpiece of the mask. Carroll joins him quickly, and they carry the body out.

Royce moves up to the nozzle, and Knipps says that he thinks he can make it. But Lieutenant Welch orders him to take a blow, and

Royce takes the nozzle. Knipps stands to make a quick exit to clean air, but the smoke has gotten to him. He vomits, and the stream of food and acid falls over the back of my coat and boots. He doesn't stop to apologize.

Vinny Royce moves slowly and deliberately through the second and third rooms. Lieutenant Welch is next to him all the while, saying, "You got it, Vinny. You got it," and coughing continuously. I am right behind humping the hose and leaning into it to relieve the fifty-pound-per-square-inch back pressure that is straining Vinny's arms. As the third room darkens down completely, I run to the fire-escape window and climb out of it. I lie on my back on the narrow steel strips of the fire escape, taking the air, sucking the oxygen from it, not taking the time to look at anything.

Boyle and Carroll lay the second body on the sidewalk, next to the boy McCartty carried out and is now using the mechanical resuscitator on. Carroll looks at the body before him. He is a teenager also, and his clothes are like charred bits of paper sticking to his skin. He is badly burned, and the flesh on parts of his face has opened so that it looks like there are pink patches woven into his black skin. Boyle turns away and vomits as Benny plugs the face-piece connection into the regulator of the resuscitator. He puts his finger into the face piece, testing it, making sure there is the quick, clicking sound of air being pushed and relieved—in and out, in and out. The mechanical apparatus forces pure oxygen into the lungs until they expand and build up enough pressure to push the air out again. Benny tilts the boy's head back, and fits the face piece onto the burned face. He holds the mouth-piece tightly with both hands to ensure a good seal, because the thing doesn't work if the oxygen escapes. Boyle places one hand over the other on the boy's chest. And he pumps. Like a heart. Sixty times a minute. "He's as dead as a board," Boyle says.

"Yeah," Benny says, "but we have to try."

Engine 73 stretched a line to the floor above the fire. One room was lost, but they stopped the fire there. Now they have taken up their hose, and are on their way back to their Prospect Avenue firehouse. Ladder 31 and Ladder 48 are still here, pulling the ceilings and walls. Vinny has taken his mask off, and is waiting for the men of the truck companies to finish their work. One quick bath, a final wash down, and we'll take up.

Chief Solwin is supervising the operation, and Allen Siebeck asks him, between pulls on his hook, "What happened to that guy who was on fire, Chief?"

"The police put him in the car and rushed him to the hospital, but I understand he didn't make it. The doctor pronounced him DOA."

"How the hell did he get out?" Allen asks.

"The only thing I can figure is that he got out the fire-escape window, and went downstairs and through the hall, burning all the while."

Bill Finch, Chief Solwin's aide, enters the room. "What should I do with the gas cans, Chief?" he asks.

"Just leave them here. The fire marshals will be here shortly."

While Billy-o was searching the rooms, he found two gas cans, and Artie found a third in the hall. The one in the hall was still half full.

"That's somethin', isn't it?" Vinny says, making a facial gesture of disgust and dejection. "These kids were probably torching the place, and it lit up on them. I know it sounds lousy to say, but if it happened more often people would learn, and we wouldn't have so many torch jobs."

Lieutenant Welch joins us, and we begin to talk about the fire, as we do after each job. "Did you notice that the whole place was charred?" he asks, as he leads us to the front of the apartment. We look at the walls in all of the rooms, and they are bubbled and crisp. "You can see," he says, "that there was a great amount of intense heat here, but when we got here there were only three rooms going. The kids must have spread gasoline all over, and there was a flash fire. It probably burned through the whole place for a few moments, and then burned itself out, except, of course, in the front three rooms, where there was enough oxygen to keep the fire going. It's like lighting a candle in a mayonnaise jar, and then putting the top on; the candle will burn until the flame eats all the oxygen in the jar, and then it will go out."

Two fire marshals arrive and begin to question the Chief, Captain Frimes, and Lieutenant Welch. They are dressed in wide-lapeled jackets and colorful ties. If I were in a downtown bar I would figure them for detectives, because they wear their jackets opened and have tough but handsome faces. Their job is essentially that of a police detective, but they are responsible only for crimes connected with fires. They're firefighters just like us, but they would rather wear a gun at their side than have a nozzle in their hands. I was asked once if I would like to be a marshal, but I figured that I applied to be a firefighter because I wanted to fight fires. If I had wanted to investigate crimes I would have applied to be a policeman. The marshals take down the information they think necessary, and leave for the hospital. One of the teenagers is still living, and they want to see if he can answer some questions before he dies. They take the gas cans with them.

The truckmen are finished with their overhauling work, and Vinny gives the rooms a last spray. We drain the hose, repack it, and head back to the firehouse. It is near six o'clock now, and the brightness of the day begins to invade the South Bronx.

In the kitchen again. The men haven't bothered to wash up, and they sit before their steaming cups of coffee, with smoke- and mucus-stained faces. They are talking about the ironic justice of the fire, although they don't call it ironic justice but "tough shit." None of us want to see anyone killed, but there is a sad kind of "it's either you or me" irony here. We remember all the obvious torch jobs we have been called into, all the vacant buildings, the linoleum placed over holes in the floor so the firefighters would fall to the floor below, the people killed in the rooms above a fire because the tenant below had a fight with his wife and set the place up, and the burns, cuts, and broken limbs we have suffered because of them. Any one of us could have been killed in that fire. But it was the arsonists who were killed this time.

Willy Knipps comes into the kitchen, and I remember Vinny Royce washing the vomit from my coat and boots. I had forgotten about it, but Vinny noticed it and put the nozzle on me, washing me clean. Ordinarily I would say something funny about this, something like,

"Hey, Knipps, next time you go into a fire bring a bucket with you. Huh?" But I'm too tired.

It was four days later that Benny Carroll asked me, "Did you hear about the fire we had the other night, the one where the two kids were killed?"

"I was there, Benny, don't you remember?"

"I don't mean it that way, dummo, I mean about the investigation."

"No. Tell me about it."

"Well, the marshals were here last night, and told the story. It seems that the landlord wanted that apartment vacant, and he knew that the people wouldn't be there that night. So he hired some guy to torch the place. The guy then hires the three kids to light it up, and when they were in there spreading the gasoline the guy threw a match in and locked the door on them. They're looking for the guy now for a double murder. It looks like the kid Captain Frimes got out is gonna live."

Benny was going to continue with the story, but the bells came in. Now I am on the back step of the pumper, and thinking that it wasn't ironic justice at all. It's what always happens in the South Bronx. The real devil gets away without a burn, and the children of the South Bronx are the victims.

from On Fire

by Larry Brown

Larry Brown (born 1951) fought fires in Oxford, Mississippi for 17 years before becoming a full-time writer.

I was cooking some ribs one evening and drinking a beer, taking life easy on a Saturday afternoon. The ribs were parboiling in some water, getting tender, and about dark I was going to put them over a fire on the grill, slap some barbecue sauce on them, cook my family a little feast. Maybe we were going to watch a movie, too, I don't know. That's one of our big things: cook something on the grill outside and then watch a good movie while we're eating, then kind of just fall out all over the living room to finish watching it, then sometimes even watch another one. I usually have several cold beers while I'm doing that. The ribs were going to cook for a couple of hours and I had plenty of beer.

The phone rang and my plans got changed. It was the dispatcher at Station No. 1, and he said we had a fire at the Law School at Ole Miss, and all hands were being called in. It was what we call a Code Red.

I cut off the ribs but I did take my beer. I thought if the fire wasn't too bad, a beer would be pretty good on the way back. I drove my little truck at what is an abnormal speed for me, about sixty-five. I live about ten miles from Oxford so it didn't take long to get there.

You never know what to expect except that if it's bad you can certainly expect to be dirty and exhausted and possibly coughing or throwing up or maybe even burned, your ears singed a little before it's over. I knew the building but I'd only been in the bottom of it once, and in the library once, and that was on the second floor. The fire we had that night was on the fifth, top floor.

I stopped by Station No. 1 and got my turnouts, pulling my pickup right into the truck bay where a lot of leather boots were lying, where my partners had kicked them off and left them. The turnout pants stand on low shelves, folded down with the rubber boots already inside them, so that all you have to do is step into them and pull the pants up, snap them shut, grab your coat and helmet, climb on the truck and roll out the door. Every piece of equipment in the house was gone, our big diesel pumper, the van, and the ladder truck that could reach ten stories high. The dispatcher came out for a second and said we had a working fire but they didn't know how bad it was yet. I drove fast through town, knowing where all the cops were.

The ladder truck was being set up when I pulled into the parking lot. There was a little smoke showing from the top of the building. I could see our boys in full gear down on their knees putting airpacks on. I put my turnouts on, got my gloves in one hand and my helmet in the other, and ran to report to the assistant chief in charge that I was there and ready for my assignment. Off-duty people were arriving all around me. They'd called everybody in.

The structure was a five-story building with a concrete exterior, lined with windows about seven or eight feet long and about five and a half feet tall. None of the windows were designed to open, had no hinges or handles, and the glass was tempered, somewhere between a quarter and a half inch thick. There was no outside egress to the building except through the first and top floors. It was not equipped with a sprinkler system, since it was considered to be a fireproof building, but it did have a wet standpipe system with those little piss-ant hoses.

I found out that the alarm inside the building had been going for quite a while, but people had simply ignored it. Kept walking around in there, conducting their whatever. I was told to put on an airpack and climb the stairwell with some other firefighters to the top floor and descend into the building to try and locate the fire. I donned my apparatus, found my partners, and we started up. We all had flashlights.

The rig weighs between thirty and forty pounds. It will give you about twenty minutes of air if you're lying flat on your back breathing through the respirator; that's if you're not exerting yourself. When five minutes of air is left, a little bell mounted on the tank will start ringing, loud and insistently, driven by the declining air pressure. With experience you learn to leave the mask off until you're ready to enter your dangerous atmosphere. They work just like a diver's rig, but the mask and mouthpiece are all molded together, so that the mask covers your whole face. They're called SCBA, self-contained breathing apparatus. You can enter a poisonous atmosphere, live in a superheated temperature if the rest of your body can stand it. The main purpose is to prevent the firefighter from breathing smoke.

We were already a little winded by the time we got to the top floor. As soon as we stepped into the hall, we were enveloped in heavy black smoke. It was bad enough to put the masks on. An initial search revealed nothing but more smoke and nearly zero visibility. Things were much worse than they appeared from outside, certainly. I got worried when I saw that it was impossible to see my partners' flashlight beams if they were over three or four feet away. I got everybody back together and told them to go back outside. I didn't want anybody getting separated from the group and getting lost in the smoke. We hadn't had time to bring in any safety lines or anything like that yet. It was still very early. No tactical decisions had been made. We went back down for fresh tanks and more men. I knew by then I wouldn't be getting back to those ribs any time soon.

I reported what we'd found up there: bad conditions, heavy smoke, zero visibility, no flame found yet. The ladder was operating by then and more off-duty people had arrived. Most of the people on my shift were there, including my boss, who took charge of the ladder. My two duty partners were there, getting their turnouts on, getting ready to go up. I got another tank and climbed on the ladder platform and caught a ride to the roof. There was a wide ledge, maybe twelve feet or so, outside the fifth floor. The captain of the shift on duty got off on the ledge and the rest of us went on to the roof. My boss let us off and went back down for more men and equipment. His steady, up-and-down trips, five stories high, ferrying people and supplies, would go on unceasingly for the next few hours.

The fire needed to be ventilated—that is, an opening of some sort made in the building to let the buildup of heat and smoke out, to improve visibility conditions so the fire could be located and attacked. It was a long time before that happened.

We started another search of the fifth floor. We appeared to be in a hall that was built in a large rectangle with numerous doors that opened into offices. What we didn't know was that the fire was in the very center of the building, in a lounge area that had only two doors. We wasted an enormous amount of time checking for fire in the outlying offices, working by feel and touch in a place that was solid black to the eye, a place growing uncomfortably hot. We had a bad fire, it was rapidly worsening, and we didn't have it located, although we were searching as diligently as we could. Bells started ringing on the tanks, and I realized that it might be possible for some of us to become disoriented in the smoke, run out of air, and have to pull the mask off, and maybe never make it back to safety and fresh air. We went back out to count heads and then we climbed on up to the roof.

An entry saw with a gasoline engine had been sent up in case we decided to cut a hole in the roof, but the roof was constructed of gravel over tar paper over concrete. Something else had to be done, something quick. The smoke had to be let out of the building right away, before a bad fire got any worse, before the heat intensified any more. The only thing we saw was the windows.

More people had come up, along with hoses and nozzles and ropes and more airpacks. I went over to the ladder and told my boss about the conditions, that it was evidently a bad fire and getting worse, and that we were going to have to break some windows on the fifth floor. He listened and nodded, and went down for tools.

I don't know what all happened then. Adrenaline. The next major event was the arrival via the ladder of two men with a fire ax and a heavy pry bar. I got back on the ladder platform and went with them down to the fifth-floor ledge and we walked to the corner window, a huge pane of dark glass that looked very expensive. Hundreds of people were standing below on the ground. Red and blue lights were flashing everywhere down there. The ladder was running at a high throttle, and hoses had been laid from the pumpers to the building so that we could boost the water pressure inside the standpipe system. I took a deep breath and swung the heavy pry bar as hard as I could at the window. It bounced off.

I braced my feet, tightened my helmet strap, turned the point of the tool to the glass and tried my best to shatter it. It bounced off.

I'm no ball player, never have been. But I brought the heavy bar around from behind my back with both hands gripping it like a base-ball bat and delivered all the weight of it to the center of the window and it caved in in large jagged pieces. We were immediately engulfed in a roar of dense black smoke that barreled out over us so heavily that we had to move out of it and go on to the next window. People on the ground were yelling.

We eventually broke nine windows in a row all down that side of the fifth floor, walking down the ledge, swinging the pry bar in, knocking the sharp edges of glass out of the casement. More men were delivered to the ledge and we established our entry and exit route: through a window halfway down the side, step down into a nicely upholstered Law School dean's desk chair, walk across his desk and papers, drop onto the floor, try to find the fire. I think we knocked a lot of things over. A forward command post was set up on the ledge, and the captain relayed his orders for men and equipment via walkie-talkie back to the assistant chief, who directed the ground operations from the parking lot.

That trip I went in without a mask, because the smoke was lifting a little, even though the temperature seemed to have increased. I knew that was because the fire was getting a fresh supply of oxygen, but that's something you have to deal with when you ventilate. If you can go on in and make your stop, it doesn't make a shit.

Our pumpers were feeding the standpipe system, and we got the little piss-ant hose off the rack and stretched out the line. We thought the fire was right in front of us, and we were going to crawl our way up to it and find it and fight it. But we couldn't get the valve turned on. We tried and tried and even hammered on it with spanner wrenches, but we couldn't get it to open. We sent somebody out for a pipe wrench and then got it turned on, but blew the hose completely out of the coupling from the tremendous pressure our pump operators were sending through the pipe.

It took a little while to shut it off, take off the burst hose, and put our own nozzles and hose on it. But when we had that done, we put on fresh tanks and went down the hall in a group, close to the floor. We knew where it was now, back there in that lounge.

The air was burning our ears, even down that low. All of us crawling and sliding in the water, going inside a door where the thing was feeding and getting bigger. That is a special place to be in, with men in a burning building, where you can only barely hear one another talking behind the masks, where the glow of the fire makes a light on the masks around you, where you are all panting and pulling on the hose and trying to be as small and concentrated as possible, trying to do the job. Sometimes you reach a stage of near exhaustion after only a few minutes.

All we could see was a hellish red light in front of us somewhere. But we could hear the damn thing. Everything around us was charred, the water we were crawling in was black and hot, and the only smell was that of heavy smoke. My partners had the nozzle and I had my hand on their shoulders and we were inching forward, spraying water. We slipped on the tiles until we got to the carpet and then we pushed close to the fire, to that awful heat, until it came through our turnouts and our gloves and into our knees where we knelt in the hot water. Another bell started ringing and I hollered for whoever it was to get out. Somebody left and somebody came in on the line to replace him. We kept pushing forward, yelling, urging each other on.

You have to meet the thing is what it is. You have to do something in your life that is honorable and not cowardly if you are able to live in peace with yourself, and for the firefighter it is fire. It has to be faced and defeated so that you prove to yourself that you meet the measure of the job. You cannot turn your back on it, as much as you would like to be in cooler air, as much as you would like to breathe it. You have to stay huddled with the men you are with.

We whipped that fire's ass. It fought back, leaping and dodging the water, but we kept the nozzle open and on fog and rotated it in a counterclockwise manner due to the rotation and curvature of the earth, and the water was dispersed into tiny droplets by the turbojet nozzle. The droplets were converted into steam by the heat of the fire and steam is what put the fire out.

We pulled back for a breather and more people came in to mop up small fires and start salvage and overhaul.

In the Law School dean's office I saw my partners with sootstreaked faces, exhausted beer-drinking buddies with their coats open, lying on shards of glass in the floor with cigarettes in their hands. There was an unbelievable amount of talking and confusion. I lit my own cigarette, went back across the man's nice desk and out on the ledge, and told them we'd knocked it down.

It isn't until later that the real exhaustion sets in. They sent up some cold Gatorade that was delivered while the overhaul went on, while more men, fresh men, came up, while they ferried empty air tanks back and forth to Station One for refilling at the compressor, while men worked at the station filling the tanks, while the pump operators watched the gauges and engine temperatures, while the people in charge oversaw everything from outside and talked on their walkie-talkies, while the dispatcher manned the radio, while my boss carried the platform of the ladder up and down, over and over.

I sat down on the floor and smoked a cigarette and drank some Gatorade. We all looked at each other and just shook our heads.

Later we were told that it looked like a black tornado had come out of the building when we broke the first window, and that a man from the university's physical plant department had started tearing at his hair when we started breaking the windows because they cost $1,500 apiece.

Well, yeah. But it got the smoke out. Their fireproof building didn't burn down. And we were all still alive when it was over.

The Chief

by Elizabeth Kolbert

William Feehan was the second-highest ranking official in New York City's fire department when he died on September 11, 2001. New Yorker staff writer Elizabeth Kolbert (born 1961) published this story about him in the magazine's October 8, 2001 issue.

The first and second alarms, which were transmitted together, sounded at 8:47 a.m., the third at 8:50. At 8:55, a 10-60 went out, signaling a major emergency, and four minutes later a fifth alarm sounded. The New York City Fire Department has no formal designation for a blaze that requires more than five alarms, but on September 11th there were five for the north tower and another five for the south tower, and still the alarms continued to ring, first in firehouses in Chelsea and Chinatown, and then in Brooklyn Heights and Williamsburg, and then all across the city, so that in less than thirty minutes more than a hundred companies had been called out. Ladder 24 was called from midtown, and Engine 214 from Bedford-Stuyvesant, and so was Squad 288 from Maspeth, Queens, and Ladder 105 from downtown Brooklyn. Even after the two towers collapsed and tens of thousands of people came streaming out of lower Manhattan covered with ash, the firemen kept coming.

That afternoon, Liz Feehan and her sister Tara waited for news together at Tara's house, in Belle Harbor, Queens. Three of the men in their family were firefighters, and all three were at the World Trade Center that day: Liz and Tara's father, William, the department's first deputy commissioner; their younger brother John; and Tara's husband, Brian Davan. When the phone rang, Tara picked it up and started yelling. Liz immediately concluded that the call was about one of the two younger men. Their father, the second-ranking official in the F.D.N.Y., was, she assumed, too far up the hierarchy to die in the line of duty.

William Michael Feehan had joined the F.D.N.Y. in 1959, and during the next forty-two years held every possible rank in a department that was thick with them, from "proby" to lieutenant to battalion chief to commissioner—something only two or three other people have done in the department's history. Feehan helped fight some of the worst fires in New York, including the Brooklyn Navy Yard fire, in 1960, which killed fifty people, and the Madison Square blaze, in 1966, which killed twelve. For his long, distinguished career, he was venerated by his fellow-firefighters, and also sometimes teased by them. "Billy," his friends used to say, "when you joined the department what were they feeding the horses?" At the time of his death, Feehan was seventy-one years old, six years past the mandatory retirement age for firefighters in the city, and for nearly a decade he had held what is technically a civilian post. Still, he kept handy a helmet and a rubberized suit—known as "turnout gear"—and was fit, and willing, enough to help lay hose.

Before Feehan died, few outside the department or the insular world of city government had heard of him. He did not court publicity, and he rarely attended the functions that high-ranking city officials are invited to. (A favorite excuse of his was that he had tried to stop by but couldn't find a parking space.) As first deputy commissioner, Feehan served under three different commissioners and two different mayors, a tenure that testified at once to his ability and to his equanimity. "He would quietly suggest to you to do something differently, and you always knew that it was good advice, and you always took it," the current commissioner, Thomas Von Essen, told me. Even after Feehan became deputy commissioner, his men continued to address him as "Chief," a lower but, to them, more honorable title.

Feehan began his career with Ladder 3, on East Thirteenth Street in Greenwich Village. One week after the disaster, I went down to the firehouse, a squat brick building constructed under Mayor Jimmy Walker, in 1929. The men in the company refer to it as Ladder 3 Recon, for "reconnaissance," and they like to say that when rescue units get into trouble they call Ladder 3 Recon to get them out of it. The house sits next to a photo shop and across the street from a New York University dormitory. A construction-paper sign posted in one of the dorm's windows read "NYU ♥ FDNY." Normally, the men would have been upstairs, in the firehouse kitchen, cooking dinner and watching TV, but this night they were out on the street receiving condolences, as were firemen all over the city.

On September 11th, Ladder 3 was called on the third alarm. The day shift was just arriving, and the night shift going off duty, which meant that there were two full crews in the house. The company lost twelve men out of a total force of twenty-five. It is still not known where, or how, they died. Someone had pasted pictures of the missing on a piece of poster board, and around this poster, which was propped on an easel, the sidewalk had been transformed into a makeshift shrine. There were dozens of bouquets with notes pinned to them, and candles flickering in pools of wax, and silver balloons, clearly designed for less grave occasions, printed with the message "Thank you." It was six in the evening, the time when New Yorkers start to arrive home from work. People kept coming by to drop off doughnuts and cakes and homemade cookies. An elderly man brought over a plate of apples and honey, in honor of Rosh Hashanah; a woman with red and blue tinsel stars in her hair stopped in to offer the men Shiatsu massages. A woman in her forties brought a mixed bouquet. She seemed unwilling to just add it to the general pile, so she waited for one of the firemen to notice her, and handed it to him. "You guys are the best and the bravest," she said. Then she started to cry.

The attack on the World Trade Center left thousands of people mourning fathers and mothers, colleagues, close friends, and children. It left thousands of others, in the city and beyond, who hadn't lost anyone, searching for a focus for their grief. In this context, it was natural for people to gravitate to their local firehouses. One former Manhattanite I know drove in from Westchester to visit the firehouse in his old neighborhood. He had brought a check for the relief fund—the company had lost nine members—and when the fireman he gave it to thanked him he had to turn away, he told me, because he found himself weeping uncontrollably. Not a single firehouse in the city was untouched by the disaster. Among the three hundred and forty-three firefighters who are either dead or missing are members of at least sixty companies.

The only men left in Ladder 3 are those who were not on duty on the morning of the eleventh. I asked one of them, a lieutenant, whether he felt fortunate to have been off that day. He told me the opposite was true. "I wish it was me instead of them," he said, and he felt sure, he told me, that had the situation been reversed his colleagues—his "brothers"—would have felt the same way. "The camaraderie that you have with your brothers—you'd do anything for them," he said.

William Feehan was born in Queens on September 29, 1929, and grew up in Jackson Heights. His father was a firefighter with Engine 21, and one of his uncles was a priest. In the tradition of old Irish New York, these were the career choices presented to Feehan, and although his parents tried to steer him toward the church he eventually chose the F.D.N.Y. From an early age, Feehan loved fires—he used to run down to Northern Boulevard to watch the engines go by—and in 1956, after graduating from St. John's University and serving in Korea, he joined the New York Fire Patrol, a private force financed by the insurance industry, which is still in operation.

At about the same time, a new F.D.N.Y. commissioner, Edward Cavanagh, instituted a mandatory-retirement policy, and Feehan's father, who was sixty-seven, immediately became overage. In 1992, the year he became first deputy commissioner, Feehan spoke about his father's disappointment in an interview with his oldest son, William, Jr., a human-resources executive, and a friend of his, Harvey Wang, a photographer. "My father lived till he was in his early eighties, and to the day he died I think he felt that Edward Cavanagh passed that bill just to hurt him," Feehan recalled. "I don't think a day went by when he didn't have something unkind to say about Edward Cavanagh for cutting his career short, in the prime of his life, and he carried that bitterness to the grave with him."

From the beginning, Feehan's solidity impressed those he worked with. James Manahan, a firefighter who trained with him, told me, "Billy really made his own reputation. In firefighting, it's crucial how you're perceived by the people you're working with, because when you go above a fire you've got to have trust in the guy that's beneath you. No one would think twice about going above Billy."

In 1956, Feehan married Betty Keegan, whom he had met, also in the tradition of Irish New York, in the Rockaways. Over the next decade, the couple had four children. They moved to a single-family house in Flushing, and, because it wasn't easy to support the family on a fireman's salary, Feehan moonlighted—first as a substitute teacher and later as a security guard for the Helmsley hotels. (Whenever the kids made cracks about Leona or Harry, Feehan asked them if they wanted to take out another college loan.) He also studied hard for the department exams that determine promotions. In 1964, after just five years in the department, Feehan made lieutenant. In 1972, he became a captain, and in 1979 the chief of a battalion.

A week and a half after Feehan died, I went out to the house, on Twenty-eighth Avenue in Flushing. It is, by today's standards, modest, and following Betty's death, in 1996, Feehan continued to live there alone. The day I visited, Liz Feehan, a slim, lively woman who works as a court clerk in Manhattan, was at the house, and so were her brother John and his wife, Debbie, who is a nurse. We sat in the dining room, at a table covered with a lace cloth, surrounded by the bags of Mass cards that had been left at Feehan's wake.

According to his children, Feehan was a man of great faith, and also of great optimism. When they were young, everything they presented to him was "the most special—fill in the blank—in the world," and, when they got older, every house or apartment they moved into was a "gem" or a "home run." "He was your biggest fan," Liz said. "Nothing could not be overcome. He'd say, 'We'll move on and get through this.'"

John looks a lot like the photographs of his father—the same square face and wide-set eyes. He told me that his father hadn't pushed him to become a fireman but had been relieved when he did: "He didn't know what the hell I was going to do, so he was happy that I had a job." Everyone in the department knew him as "Feehan's kid," John said. "It sounds way too pretentious, and I don't mean to be, but it was kind of like I was a prince," he told me. Often, on Saturdays, the two men would have breakfast at the North Shore Diner, in Bayside, and "talk fire." On their days off, they also liked to "buff" fires together—watch their colleagues handle a blaze and later, like a pair of critics, review it.

All of Feehan's children had felt a certain trepidation about the upcoming mayoral election and the inevitable arrival of a new administration. Their father had told them that, no matter who became mayor, he didn't think it likely that he would be asked to stay on. Liz described how their mother, long before Feehan's retirement was even on the horizon, had worried about it: "She used to say, 'I hope your father goes in a fire.' We'd say, 'Speak for yourself.' But she meant that's how he would have wanted to go."

Feehan liked to tell stories. In the interview that he did with his son and Harvey Wang, he told one about how he almost didn't make it into the Fire Department, because of his bad eyesight, and another about the time he was a captain in Harlem and the commissioner, who had come for a visit, ended up posing for photographs with a bookie. He also spoke about Charlie, a fire buff who lived for a while at Ladder 6, in Chinatown, and, having been convinced by the men that Feehan's wife was Chinese, was always plying him with fortune cookies.

Feehan was a member of Ladder 6 when, in 1970, the company was called to a fire at One New York Plaza, a fifty-story office building at the corner of Water and Broad Streets. The blaze killed two people, and helped bring about the passage of Local Law 5, which requires that all high-rises have sprinkler systems and fire alarms on each floor.

"When we were dispatched to the fire," Feehan recalled, "we left the firehouse heading down East Broadway, and an air line broke. We came to a dead halt and the chauffeur"—the driver of the fire truck—"jumped out and said we were out of service. I was a fairly young lieutenant and this was going to be my first high-rise fire, and there was no way that I was going to miss this fire. There was a hardware store right on the corner, so I sent a guy in, and I said, 'Get some tape,' and we taped this thing up. They called us, and said, 'Ladder 6, what's your location?' We lied and said that we were three blocks from them.

"I remember the chief of the department then was John O'Hagan. I remember him telling us to go to the floor above the fire, and see whether or not there was an access from one floor to the next. We went up the stairway and the floor was just so hot that we couldn't crawl in. My chauffeur, who was very senior, and a very experienced guy, said, 'It's just too hot, we've got to get out of here.' We did, and we went back down and reported to Chief O'Hagan, and told him we couldn't get in on the floor, and he said, 'If you can't make it, you can't make it.' It was like a knife in your heart.

"A short time later, there was a report that there were some people on the upper floors, and we jumped up, because we were kind of depressed from not doing the other job. A guy from the building said, 'I have an elevator that will take you directly up to the top floor.' We went down to the lobby to get this elevator, and he said, 'I'm pretty sure this elevator—' We said, 'Hold it. Pretty sure is not good enough. If we're going to get on this elevator, we have to be sure it is not going to let us off on the fire floor.' Well, to make a long story short, he couldn't guarantee that. The only way to get there was to walk. We walked from the thirty-second floor to the roof and opened the roof, and of course the people reported being trapped weren't there, and now we had to get back down.

"I remember walking down. We had to stop on every floor, because we were totally exhausted. And I remember one of the senior guys— we were sweating profusely now, we were dirty and grimy, it must have been about eleven o'clock at night—and I remember him sitting on the stairs and looking over, and he said, 'You and your frickin' tape.' "

The F.D.N.Y. has its headquarters in a building in the Metrotech complex, in downtown Brooklyn, and the deputy commissioner's office is on the eighth floor, next door to the commissioner's. A week after the attack, a new first deputy, Mike Regan, was already in place, and when I went to visit I could see that someone had dropped off a half-inch-thick departmental memo entitled "Missing as of September 17, 2001, 1400 hours." Otherwise, things in the office appeared to be pretty much as Feehan had left them. Arranged on the desk were half a dozen pictures of his grandchildren and a stack of his business cards, which he kept in a holder shaped like a fire hydrant. A collection of toy fire engines was displayed on the windowsills, and on the walls were fire-prevention posters drawn by New York City schoolchildren. Feehan's red appointment book was still lying near the phone.

In every municipal department, the commissioners are political appointees, while the people who work for them are civil servants. This distinction is keenly felt, and nowhere more so than among the members of the F.D.N.Y. At the headquarters, I picked up a copy of *Fire Works*, the department's internal newsletter. The issue, which had been published in July, included a Q & A with the commissioner. In answer to a question about mandatory training days, Von Essen had written, "When you look up hypocrisy in the dictionary, it should have UFA/UFOA written next to it." The U.F.A. is the firemen's union; the U.F.O.A. is the officers' union.

Feehan's accomplishment, almost unheard of at the Fire Department, was to be equally popular with labor and management. "Very few people are loved by City Hall and the firefighters," Vincent Dunn, a retired F.D.N.Y. senior deputy chief, told me. "Bill Feehan was to the fire commissioner what Colin Powell and Dick Cheney are to the President.

He always made the top command look stable." This was not, by all accounts, because Feehan had an accommodating nature; as one of his friends put it, "He was a tough fucking guy." Feehan didn't care for whiners, and he was especially hard on shirkers. In firefighting, it is usually left to the junior man to carry the extinguisher, or "can." One of Feehan's favorite expressions was "If you're the can man, be the can man," and it meant "Just do your job."

Once, Feehan was sitting in a restaurant when he overheard a firefighter at another table boasting that he was fit enough to return to work but planned to squeeze a few extra days out of his medical leave. The next day, the man found himself, with no explanation, assigned to a desk just outside the commissioner's office. Only after he had spent a few days wondering anxiously what had happened did Feehan call him into his office to, as another Fire Department official put it to me, "read him the riot act." More recently, Feehan was involved in a minor traffic accident while driving to the funeral of a firefighter in Staten Island. When he arrived at the office the next day, he saw his name on the list of people who were on medical leave. "More than one person got chewed out for that," John Feehan told me.

Feehan served briefly as the fire commissioner in the last days of David Dinkins's mayoralty. When Rudolph Giuliani was elected, he appointed Howard Safir to head the department, and asked Feehan to stay on as Safir's deputy. A few years later, Safir moved on to become the police commissioner. Feehan thought that he might be reappointed fire commissioner, and when Giuliani passed him over he confided his disappointment to Von Essen, the man who got the job. But, in keeping with his "be the can man" work ethic, Feehan put that disappointment aside and, Von Essen told me, "worked tirelessly to teach me and to mentor me."

During the more than four decades that Feehan served in the F.D.N.Y., the city's composition changed fundamentally, but the department's did not. The *Times* recently published two pages of pictures of the missing firefighters; there were barely a dozen African-American faces and not a single woman's. In the 1992 interview,

Feehan acknowledged that critics were right to fault the department for its lack of diversity. "We have failed in that," he said. But he went on to say that he was pained by the way the critics had broadened their attack. "When they talk about a firehouse culture, they talk about it negatively; and this disturbs me, because there is maybe not a firehouse culture but a department culture," he said. "If you destroy the culture this department has, that tradition this department has, you destroy a very basic part of this department, and we just become another city agency. I don't think that when you have a department whose men and women are expected to be ready at any moment to put their life on the line to go to the aid of a stranger, I don't think you can pay people to do that job. There has to be something beyond money that makes them do that, and I think it's the culture of the department."

"High-rise firefighting is a whole art in itself," Feehan once said. "I spent very little time in a high-rise area, and there are chiefs who know more about high-rise firefighting than I'll ever know. When you have your first high-rise fire, the thing that strikes you most is just how long it takes you to get the thing done. It is twenty or twenty-five minutes after you arrive at the scene before you are getting water out of the nozzle on the fire floor."

On the morning of September 11th, Feehan was in his office, where he typically arrived by seven-fifteen. He was at his desk when his son John called with a question about the bibliography for the upcoming lieutenant's exam. Feehan told him that it would be available soon—it was just awaiting the commissioner's approval. A few minutes later, the first plane struck.

There was no precedent for the World Trade Center fire, and no way to fight it except as if there were. Feehan rushed from his office directly to the fire's command post, which, following standard protocol for a high-rise fire, had been set up in the lobby of the burning north tower. Every fire of any significance has such a post, which is basically nothing more than a metal folding table and a set of magnetic tabs labelled with the numbers of the F.D.N.Y. companies. Whoever is in command draws a rough sketch of the site directly onto the table with a felt-tip pen and then uses the magnetic markers to keep track of where the companies have been assigned. Also following standard protocol, the first companies to arrive at the World Trade Center were ordered to get hoses up to the blaze and to try to keep the stairwells open.

When a plane hit the south tower, the command post moved to West Street. Feehan's executive officer, Henry McDonald, was at home monitoring radio traffic. "The last thing I heard over the radio was that they were moving the post 'by orders of Chief Feehan,' " he told me.

Partly shielded by the north tower, the command post on West Street survived the collapse of the south tower, at 9:59 a.m., at which point Feehan and the chief of the department, Peter Ganci, decided to move the post farther north. But before they could do so, the north tower fell. (Von Essen had been called away to brief Mayor Giuliani, and this is why he survived.) Liz Feehan told me she was sure that her father would not have regarded his death as heroic. "We don't know exactly what happened to Dad," she said. "But he would have said, 'I'm not a hero—a wall fell on me. How does that make me a hero?' That's exactly what he would have said."

Feehan's body was one of the first to be pulled from the ruins; it was found that afternoon, while his son John and his son-in-law Brian Davan were nearby, assisting with the rescue operations. The funeral was held the following Saturday at St. Mel's, in Flushing. Among the mourners were Mayor Giuliani, Commissioner Von Essen, and the Speaker of the City Council, Peter Vallone. Ganci was buried on the same day, as was the Fire Department's chaplain, Mychal Judge.

William, Jr., delivered his father's eulogy. He spoke of Feehan's love for his family, his sense of humor, his profound optimism, and, above all, his pride in his work. He told about how, on the night after the attack, he had gone down to the site of the fire to see where his father had died and had found a certain comfort there—a comfort perhaps incomprehensible to someone who is not part of a fire family. Standing amid the wreckage, which at that point was still smoldering, he realized, he said, that "there was no place on earth my father enjoyed more than a fire scene.

Bound Upon a Wheel of Fire
by Sallie Tisdale

Writer Sallie Tisdale's (born 1957) look back at her childhood recollects her experience as the daughter of a fireman.

E very winter night of my childhood, my father built a fire. Every element of the evening's fire was treated with care—with the caress of the careful man. The wood, the wood box, the grate, the coal-black poker and shovel: He touched these more often than he touched me. I would hold back, watching, and when the fire was lit plant myself before it and fall into a gentle dream. No idea was too strange or remote before the fire, no fantasy of shadow and light too bizarre.

But for all the long hours I spent before his fires, for all the honey-colored vapors that rose like smoke from that hearth, these aren't the fires of memory. They aren't my father's fires. When I remember fire, I remember houses burning, scorched and flooded with flame, and mills burning, towers of fire leaping through the night to the lumber nearby like so much kindling, and cars burning, stinking and black and waiting to blow. I loved those fires with a hot horror, always daring myself to step closer, feel their heat, touch.

My father is a fireman. My submission to fire is lamentably obvious. But there is more than love here, more than jealousy—more than Electra's unwilling need. It is a fundamental lure, a seduction of my roots and not my limbs. I am propelled toward fire, and the dual draw of fascination and fear, the urge to walk into and at the same time conquer fire, is like the twin poles of the hermaphrodite. I wanted to be a fireman before, and after, I wanted to be anything else.

Firemen are big, brawny, young, and smiling creatures. They sit in the fire hall with its high ceilings and cold concrete floors and dirty corners, waiting, ready. Firemen have a perfume of readiness. They wash their shiny trucks and hang the long white hoses from rods to dangle and dry. And when the alarm rings, firemen turn into hurrying bodies that know where to step and what to do, each with a place and duty, without excess motion. Firemen wear heavy coats and big black boots and hard helmets. They can part crowds. They are calescent and virile like the fire, proud, reticent, and most content when moving; firemen have their own rules, and they break glass, make messes, climb heights, and drive big loud trucks very fast.

Forgive me; I am trying to show the breadth of this fable. I wanted to be a fireman so much that it didn't occur to me for a long time that they might not let me. Fires marked me; I got too close. The hearth fire was my first and best therapist, the fire-dreams were happy dreams of destruction and ruin. The andiron was the ground, the logs our house, and each black space between the logs a window filled with helpless people, my father and mother and siblings. The fire was the world and I was outside and above, listening to their calls for rescue from the darting blaze, and sometimes I would allow them to escape and some-times not, never stirring from my meditative pose. If I felt unchari-table, I could watch the cinders crumble from the oak and cedar like bodies falling to the ground below and the fire turn to ashes while I, the fire fighter, sat back safe and clear and cool.

At odd times—during dinner, late at night—the alarm would sound, and my father would leap up, knocking dogs and small chil-dren aside as he ran from the house. I grew up used to surprise. He was a bulky man, and his pounding steps were heavy and important in flight; I slipped aside when he passed by.

The fire department was volunteer, and every fireman something else as well. My father was a teacher. We had a private radio set in the house, and we heard alarms before the town at large did. It was part of the privilege of fire. Before the siren blew on the station two blocks away, the radio in the hallway sang its high-pitched plea. He was up and gone in seconds, a sentence chopped off in mid-word, a bite of food dropped to the plate. Squeal, halt, go: I was used to the series; it was part of our routine.

Then my mother would stop what she was doing and turn down the squeal and listen to the dispatcher on the radio. His voice, without face or name, was one of the most familiar voices in my home, crowned with static and interruptions. My mother knew my father's truck code and could follow his progress in a jumble of terse male voices, one-word questions, first names, numbers, and sometimes hasty questions and querulous shouts. She stood in the hallway with one hand on the volume and her head cocked to listen; she shushed us with a stern tension. She would not betray herself, though I knew and didn't care; in the harsh wilderness of childhood, my father's death in a fire would have been a great and terrible thing. It would have been an honor.

The town siren was a broad foghorn call that rose and fell in a long ululation, like the call of a bird. We could hear it anywhere in town, everyone could, and if I was away from our house I would run to the station. (I had to race the cars and pickups of other volunteer firemen, other teachers, and the butcher, the undertaker, an editor from the local newspaper, grinding out of parking lots and driveways all over town in a hail of pebbles.) If I was quick enough and lucky enough, I could stand to one side and watch the flat doors fly up, the trucks pull out one after the other covered with clinging men, and see my father driving by. He drove a short, stout pumper, and I waved and called to him high above my head. He never noticed I was there, not once; it was as though he ceased to be my father when he became a fireman. The whistle of the siren was the whistle of another life, and he would disappear around a corner, face pursed with concentration, and be gone.

Oh, for a fire at night in the winter, the cold nocturnal sky, the pairing of flame and ice. It stripped life bare. I shared a room with my sister, a corner room on the second floor with two windows looking in their turn on the intersection a house away. The fire station was around that corner and two blocks east, a tall white block barely visible through the barren trees. Only the distant squeal of the alarm downstairs woke us, that and the thud of his feet and the slam of the back door; before we could open the curtains and windows for a gulp of frigid air, we'd hear the whine of his pickup and the crunch of its tires on the crust of snow. The night was clear and brittle and raw, and the tocsin called my father to come out. Come out, come out to play, it sang, before my mother turned the sound off. He rushed to join the hot and hurried race to flames. We knelt at the windows under the proximate, twinkling stars, in light pajamas, shivering, and following the spin of lights on each truck—red, blue, red, blue, red—flashing across houses, cars, faces. We could follow the colored spin and figure out where the fire must be and how bad and wonder out loud if he'd come back.

There were times when he didn't return till morning. I would come downstairs and find him still missing, my mother sleepy-eyed and making toast, and then he would trudge in. Ashen and weary, my father, beat, his old flannel pajamas dusted with the soot that crept through the big buckles of his turnout coat, and smelling of damp, sour smoke.

I should be a fire setter. I should be that peculiar kind of addict, hooked on stolen matches and the sudden conflagration in mother's underwear and father's shoes. There are plenty of them, many children, thieving flame and setting its anarchic soul free in unexpected places. But I lack that incendiary urge; my Electra is more subtle, the knotty recesses of my own desires cunning even to me.

"What we first learn about fire is that we must not touch it," Gaston

Bachelard writes in his book *The Psychoanalysis of Fire*, in the course of explaining the "Prometheus Complex" that the prohibition against fire creates. I talk about my father infrequently, always with hunger and anger; I build fires almost every winter night. But I've never built a wrong fire, and I worry over flammables like a mother hen. I'm scared of being burned and of all of fire's searing lesions. I class it with the other primitive, deadly joys: the sea deeps and flying—the runaway edge of control.

I fear one particular fire. My father was also an electrician, a tinker of small appliances. I am wary of outlets and wires of all kinds, which seem tiny and potent and unpredictable; the occult and silent river of electrical fire racing behind the walls can keep me awake nights. Electricity is just another flame, but flame refined. (In this way it is like alcohol: literally distilled.) Not long ago I put a pot of water to boil on my stove, and a little sloshed over; suddenly a roaring arc of electricity shot from beneath the pot and curved back upon itself. The kitchen air filled with the acrid smoke of burning insulation and the crackling, sputtering sound of short circuits, and I didn't have the slightest idea what to do. I wanted my father to put it out, and he was 300 miles away. It seemed the most untenable betrayal, my stove lunging out at me in such a capricious way. It seemed *mean*; that arc of blue-white current burned down my adulthood.

Prometheus stole more than fire; he stole the *knowledge* of fire, the hard data of combustion. I wanted all my father's subtle art. I wanted the mystery of firewood and the burning, animated chain saw, the tree's long fall, the puzzle of splitting hardwood with a wedge and maul placed just so in the log's curving grain. I wanted to know the differences of quality in smoke, where to lay the ax on the steaming roof, how the kindling held up the heavy logs. What makes creosote ignite? How to know the best moment to flood a fire? What were the differences between oak and cedar, between asphalt and shake? And most of all I wanted to know how to go in to the fire, what virtue was used when he set his face and pulled the rim of his helmet down and ran inside the burning house. It was arcane, obscure, and unaccountably male, this fire business. He built his fires piece by piece, lit each with a single match, and once the match was lit I was privileged to watch, hands holding chin and elbows propped on knees, in the posture Bachelard calls essential to the "physics of reverie" delivered by fire.

I build fires now. I like the satisfying scritch-scratch of the little broom clearing ash. I find it curious that I don't build very good fires; I'm hasty and I don't want to be taught. But at last, with poorly seasoned wood and too much paper, I make the fire go, and then the force it exerts is exactly the same. That's something about fire: All fire is the same, every ribbon of flame the same thing, whatever that thing may be. There is that fundamental quality, fire as an irreducible element at large; fire is fire is fire no matter what or when or where. The burning house is just the hearth freed. And the fire-trance stays the same, too. I still sit cross-legged and dreaming, watching the hovering flies of light that float before me in a cloud, as fireflies do.

How I wanted to be a fireman when I grew up. I wanted this for a long time. To become a volunteer fireman was expected of a certain type of man—the town's steady, able-bodied men, men we could depend on. As I write this I feel such a tender pity for that little, wide-eyed girl, a freeroaming tomboy wandering a little country town and friend to all the firemen. I really did expect them to save me a place.

Every spring we had a spring parade. I had friends lucky enough to ride horses, others only lucky enough to ride bikes. But I rode the pumper and my father drove slowly, running the lights and siren at every intersection and splitting our ears with the noise. We the firemen's children perched on the hoses neatly laid in pleated rows, bathed in sunlight, tossing candy to the spectators as though, at parade's end, we wouldn't have to get down and leave the truck alone again.

He would take me to the station. I saw forbidden things, firemen's lives. On the first floor was the garage with its row of trucks. Everything shivered with attention, ripe for work: the grunt of a pumper, the old truck, antique and polished new. And the Snorkel. When I was very small, a building burned because it was too high for the trucks to reach a fire on its roof; within a year the town bought the Snorkel, a basher of a truck, long, white, sleek, with a folded hydraulic ladder. The ladder opened and lifted like a praying mantis rising from a twig, higher and higher.

Above the garage was the real station, a single room with a golden floor and a wall of windows spilling light. The dispatcher lived there, the unmarried volunteers could bunk there if they liked; along one wall was a row of beds. No excess there, no redundancy, only a cooler of soda, a refrigerator full of beer, a shiny bar, a card table, a television. I guess I held my father's hand while he chatted with one of the men. In the corner I saw a hole, a hole in the floor, and in the center of the hole the pole plunging down; I peeked over the edge and followed the light along the length of the shining silver pole diving to the floor below.

I remember one singular Fourth of July. It was pitch dark on the fairgrounds, in a dirt field far from the exhibition buildings and the midway. Far from anything. It was the middle of nothing and nowhere out there on a moonless night, strands of dry grass tickling my legs, bare below my shorts. There was no light at all but a flashlight in one man's hand, no sound but the murmurs of the men talking to one another in the dark, moving heavy boxes with mumbles and grunts, laughing very quietly with easy laughs. My father was a silhouette among many, tall and black against a near-black sky. Then I saw a sparkle and heard the fuse whisper up its length and strained to see the shape of it, the distance. And I heard the whump of the shell exploding and the high whistle of its flight; and when it blew, its empyreal flower filled the sky. They flung one rocket after another, two and four at once, boom! flash! One shell blew too low and showered us with sparks, no one scared but smiling at the glowworms wiggling through the night as though the night were earth and we the sky and they were rising with the rain.

Only recently have I seen how much more occurred, hidden beneath the surface of his life. I presumed too much, the way all children do. It wasn't only lack of sleep that peeled my father's face bald in a fire's dousing. He hates fire. Hates burning mills; they last all night and the next day like balefires signaling a battle. He hated every falling beam that shot arrows of flame and the sheets of fire that curtain rooms. And bodies: I heard only snatches of stories, words drifting up the stairs in the middle of the night after a fire as he talked to my mother in the living room in the dark. Pieces of bodies stuck to bedsprings like steaks to a grill, and, once, the ruin of dynamite. When my mother died I asked about cremation, and he flung it away with a meaty hand and chose a solid, airtight coffin. He sees the stake in fire. He suffered the fear of going in.

I was visiting my father last year, at Christmastime. There are always fires at Christmastime, mostly trees turning to torches and chimneys flaring like Roman candles. And sure enough, the alarm sounded early in the evening, the same bright squeal from the same radio, for a flue fire. There have been a thousand flue fires in his life. (Each one is different, he tells me.)

As it happened, this time it was our neighbor's flue, across the street, on Christmas Eve, and I put shoes on the kids and we dashed across to watch the circus, so fortunately near. The trucks maneuvered their length in the narrow street, bouncing over curbs and closing in, and before the trucks stopped the men were off and running, each with a job, snicking open panels, slipping levers, turning valves. We crept inside the lines and knelt beside the big wheels of the pumper, unnoticed. The world was a bustle of men with terse voices, the red and blue lights spinning round, the snaking hose erect with pressure. The men were hepped up, snappy with the brisk demands. And the house—the neighbor's house I'd seen so many times before had gone strange, a bud blooming fire, a ribbon of light behind a dark window. Men went in, faces down.

My father doesn't go in anymore. He's gotten too old, and the rules have changed; young men arrive, old men watch and wait. He still drives truck. He lives for it, for the history and the books, his models, the stories, meetings, card games. But he's like a rooster plucked; I have a girlish song for Daddy, but I sing it too far away for him to hear.

I wanted to feel the hot dry cheeks of fever and roast with the rest of them. I wanted to go in, and I kept on wanting to long after my father and the others told me I couldn't be a fireman because I wasn't a man. I wanted to be the defender, to have the chance to do something inarguably good, pit myself against the blaze. I wanted it long after I grew up and became something else altogether, and I want it still.

"That which has been licked by fire has a different taste in the mouths of men," writes Bachelard. He means food, but when I read that I thought of men, firemen, and how men licked by fire have a different taste to me.

I live in a city now, and the fire fighters aren't volunteers. They're college graduates in Fire Science, and a few are women, smaller than the men but just as tough, women who took the steps I wouldn't—or couldn't—take. Still, I imagine big, brawny men sitting at too-small desks in little rooms lit with fluorescent lights, earnestly taking notes. They hear lectures on the chemistry of burning insulation, exponential curves of heat expansion, the codes of blueprint. They make good notes in small handwriting on lined, white paper, the pens little in their solid hands.

Too much muscle and nerve in these men and women both, these firemen; they need alarms, demands, heavy loads to carry up steep stairs. They need fires; the school desks are trembling, puny things, where they listen to men like my father, weary with the work of it, describing the secrets of going in.

from Young Men and Fire
by Norman Maclean

Norman Maclean (1902–1990) spent the last 14 years of his life studying the Mann Gulch Fire of 1949. This excerpt from his book describes what happened to 15 Smokejumpers who participated in the Forest Service's greatest tragedy.

E ven on the first run over the fire, all pertinent pieces of the plane and its universe began to fall into place and become one, preparatory to the jump—the crew, the overhead, the pilot, the airplane, the gulch, the fire in it, and the sky between, all readying themselves for the act. Jumping is one of the few jobs in the world that leads to just one moment when you must be just highly selected pieces of yourself that fit exactly the pieces of your training, your pieces of equipment having been made with those pieces of yourself and your training in mind. Each of the crew is sitting between the other's legs, and all this is leading to a single act performed between heaven and earth by you alone, all your pieces having to be for this one moment just one piece. If you are alive at the end of the act, it has taken about a minute—less, if you are not alive. The jump is that kind of beauty when everything has to be in perfect unison in order for men to commit themselves to what once done cannot be recalled and at best can be only slightly modified. It becomes the

perfectly coordinated effort when a *woof* is heard on earth as the parachute explodes open within five seconds after the jumper steps into the
sky. If it's more than five seconds, a handle has to be pulled to release
the emergency chute.

The pilot now was circling to see how close he could get the plane and
the jumpers to the fire. The circles became closer by becoming smaller
and nearer to the ground. Sometimes a Smokejumper pilot gets so near
to the ground after the crew jumps but before he can pull his plane out
of the face of a mountain that he returns to the base in Missoula with
evergreen boughs in his landing gear. That is also beautiful, but mathematically can't happen often.

It was the time now for the drawing together of the overhead and
the pilot. The spotter and the foreman lay on the floor with only the
open door between them; the spotter and the pilot were joined
together by earphones. The pilot was Kenneth Huber, a good one. He
had been flying for the famous Johnson Flying Service for four years
and during the war had transported paratroopers.

The Johnson Flying Service did all the flying for the Smokejumpers
in Missoula on contract and was as much a western legend as the
jumpers themselves. In the Northwest, Bob Johnson, the owner, was
a kind of Paul Bunyan of the air. Huber told Cooley over the earphones that his altimeter showed the plane had dropped a thousand
feet in a few minutes and that because of the suction of air in the
gulch he was going to jump the men above the ridge—at two thousand feet instead of the customary twelve hundred. Cooley knew as a
result that the crew and cargo on landing would be scattered more
than usual, and this information affected Cooley's and Dodge's
choice of a landing area.

If Bob Johnson had been piloting his own plane, he probably would
have taken it into the gulch and arrived back in Missoula physically
exhausted from lifting his plane out of the cliffs, and the plane would
have been ornamented with Christmas boughs.

On their first pass over the fire, the pilot, the spotter, and the
foreman were already looking for a possible jump site, but the job of

picking one was primarily the spotter's. The pilot's job, since he generally uses instruments when jumping his men, is to report what he can see on his instruments, and he had already reported considerable wind turbulence in the gulch. Both Cooley and Dodge, looking through the open door, immediately noticed a possible jump area, right on top of the ridge and right in front of the fire on its upgulch side. But almost immediately they said "no" and shook their heads in case "no" could not be heard across the open door. Naturally, they were trying to drop their men close to the fire—but without endangering them or their equipment, and a change in the wind, which was blowing upgulch from the river, so close to a fire front might have been the end of both. They were starting with the knowledge from the instruments that the wind had dropped the plane a thousand feet in minutes, and to this they could add their own stored-up knowledge that the top of a mountain is a world particularly devoid of equilibrium. As Cooley, the most experienced of the overhead, said later in explaining his rejection of this landing site, if you have wind turbulence to start with, you should know ahead of time that there will be even more of it at the top of a mountain and that, at the top, one side will have an upwind and the other side a downwind. Those who died later died near the top of a mountain in the upwind.

On the next pass Cooley selected a jump area near the head of the gulch on its north side where "the slope gradually goes off into the bottom and your jumper more or less hits equilibrium." Cooley later told the Forest Service's Board of Review that he estimated the jump area to be "a strong half mile from the closest point of the fire" and five hundred feet below it in elevation—not only below it but on its flank and, important also, with few trees and rocks. Dodge finally accepted the site, although first objecting because a helicopter couldn't land there in case injured men had to be brought out.

So they all tried to think of everything, but the pilot thought primarily of his instruments, and the foreman thought primarily of his crew, and the spotter thought primarily of everything and made the decision.

Then the crew began to stir. They were sitting straddle-legged on the floor, their backs to the cockpit, each man fitting snugly between the legs of the man behind him so that all sixteen jumpers and their equipment could be packed into the plane. They were almost literally one body—the equipment of each man next to him where the seat had been and each man between the legs of the man behind. Since the beginning of the flight, the assistant spotter, Jack Nash, had been checking their equipment. Now the men stirred to check themselves, figuring they had better do their own checking since they were going to have to do their own jumping.

On the next pass over the fire the assistant spotter stood by the side of the open door and dropped the hunter orange drift chutes, and on the next circle the spotter estimated the distance and direction the wind had blown the chutes so he could tell how far ahead of their target he should drop the jumpers.

The first "stick" stood up, a stick being the number of men, usually three or four, who are jumped on each run over the landing area. They stand in front of the open door, one behind the other, the front man with his left foot forward. They are closer together than ever. The man behind the first man stands with his right foot forward so that after the first man jumps the second man can make one step forward with his left foot and be where the first man was.

It is the assistant spotter's job to snap the jumper's static line to a rod in the roof of the plane. The other end of the static line is snapped to his parachute. It is twelve feet long and, if all else goes well, will automatically open the jumper's parachute after he has fallen twelve feet. So as the moment for the jump approaches, the men and the plane get closer and closer together. Some jumpers won't allow the assistant spotter to snap their static line to the plane—they do it themselves. They also have to be careful when they jump not to hang themselves in their own lines. One has. On the next pass they started jumping. The foreman jumped first.

Nearly every jumper fears this moment. If he continues to miss sleep because of it, he doesn't tell anybody but he quits the Smokejumpers and joins up with something like the crew that makes trails. Whatever he tries, it is something close to the ground, and he never tries jumping again because it makes him vomit.

Fear could be part of the reason they were jumping only fifteen men on this day—one had become sick on the flight over. Although he was an experienced jumper, his repressions had caught up with him and he had become ill on each of his flights this season and had not been able to jump. This was a rough trip, and after he had vomited and crawled out of it and his jump suit, he must have made his decision. When he landed back in Missoula, he resigned from the Smokejumpers.

It was a record temperature outside and the air was turbulent, so much so that Sallee once told me that they were all half sick and trying to be in the first stick to jump and get on the ground. But, weather aside, it was hard to know on what day this or that good man had built up more anxiety than he could handle, and at the last minute on this day this crew of fifteen was jumping four sticks of 4-4-4-3. On the ground, however, the crew was to pick up another firefighter who had been fighting the fire alone, so when the showdown came the crew was again sixteen.

The fear of the jumpers is a complicated matter, because in some ways a part of each of them is not afraid. Most of them, for instance, believe that God is out there, or a spirit or a something in the sky that holds them up. "You wouldn't dare jump," they say, "if it was empty out there." Also they say, "Why be afraid? You are jumping in a parachute, and the government made the parachute, didn't it?" This is connected with their thinking that guys who hang glide from the tops of the big mountains surrounding Missoula are crazy. "They're crazy," the Smokejumpers say. "They don't have a government parachute." So in some strange way they think they are jumping on the wings of God and the government. This does not keep them from worrying some nights—maybe every night—before they jump, and it does not keep some of them from vomiting as they are about to jump.

Understandably, Smokejumpers have an obsession about their

equipment. Although they change from one fixation to another, equipment is nearly always somewhere on their mind, and, as they get close to the jump, equipment is about all that is on their mind. They know they are about to live or die on a man-made substitute for wings furnished by the government. They start saying to themselves, as if it had never occurred to them before, "What the hell does the government know about making a parachute that will open five seconds after it starts to fall? Not a damn thing. They just farm it out to some fly-by-night outfit that makes the lowest bid." As the jump nears their general fears focus on what seems the least substantial and the most critical piece of their equipment—the static line that is supposed to jerk the parachute open with a *woof* twelve feet after it drops from the plane.

The attention the jumper has to pay to the elaborate and studied ritual of jumping helps to keep his fears manageable. He stands by the spotter lying on the left of the door, who holds the jumper by the left foot. The next signs are by touch and not by word—the whole flight is made with the door open, unless it is going to be a very long one, so words can't be trusted in the roar of the wind. Using the sill of the open door as a gunsight, the spotter waits for the landing area to appear in it and next allows for the wind drift. The spotter then says "Go," or something like that, but the jumper doesn't step into the sky until he feels the tap on the calf of his left leg, and in his dreams he remembers the tap. With the tap he steps into the sky left foot first so that the wind drift will not throw him face-first into the plane's tail just to his left. He leaves for earth in the "tuck position," a position somewhat like the one he was in before he was born. This whole business of appearing on earth from the sky has several likenesses to nativity.

The jumpers are forced into this crouched, prenatal moment almost by the frame of things. The jumper, unlike the hang glider, is not up there for scenic purposes. He comes closer to plummeting than to gliding. He is to land as close as possible to the target the spotter has picked, and all the jumpers are supposed to do the same so no time will be lost in collecting and piling their stuff in the same pile and being off to the fire. In order to drop as straight as possible, the jumpers originally would stand straight up in front of the door of the plane and the spotter would say, "Do you see the jump spot down there?" But if the jumper was a new man, the spotter wouldn't look to see if the jumper was seeing. He knew the jumper would be standing rigid with his eyes squeezed shut, looking as if he were looking at the distant horizon. But the spotter, needing to be sure that at least he was heard, would ask again, "Do you see the jump spot down there?" And the new jumper, frozen on the horizon, would say, "Yes, sir." Then he would get the tap on the left leg, but before he could jump he had to crouch in the tuck position because the favorite plane of the early Smokejumpers was the Ford TriMotor that had just a small opening for a door. So it was more or less the frame of things that forced a Smoke-jumper to be born again as he jumped.

His whole flight to the ground takes an average of only a minute. This minute is about the only moment a Smokejumper is ever alone, and it is one of the most lonely moments in his life. A Smokejumper never is sent alone to a fire; the minimum number is two; at their base Smokejumpers live in their dormitory with roommates or, if they live in Missoula, with their families; at night they are with their girls and often with other Smokejumpers who are with their girls, and if they get into a fight at a bar they are immediately supported by these other Smokejumpers. For the eternity of this one minute Smokejumpers are alone. It is not that they lose faith in God for that moment. It is just that He is not there anymore or anywhere else. Nothing is there except the jumper and his equipment made by the lowest bidder, and he him-self has thinned out to the vanishing point of being only decisions once made that he can't do anything about ever after.

The moment the jumper starts falling is umbilical; he starts by counting, putting "one thousand" in front of each number to slow each count to a second. If he gets to "one thousand five," he knows he is in trouble and pulls the handle that releases the emergency chute on his chest. If, however, his umbilical relation to the plane is properly severed by his twelve-foot static line, his regular parachute explodes, the *woof* vibrates in the rocks below, and his feet are thrown over his head. So it is to be born in the sky—with a loud noise and your feet where your head ought to be. So it is to be born in the sky with a loud noise—the moment you cease to be umbilical you become seed, blown by the wind. It is very lonely for a young man to be seed in the wind. Although you are seed, the sky still seems like the womb and you as seed are blown around the sky's interior parts until you light on the top of a tree or hard rocks or grass, the grass often being only a cover for hard rocks. If you land on the top of a tree, you are probably lucky, especially if you have a long rope in your pocket by which you can let yourself down to the rocks—but only a small percentage when they touch earth land on the tops of trees. Try as they may to avoid landing on rocks, many do. Landing smoothly from the sky does not come naturally to man.

As in life generally, it is most common to land in grass that thinly covers very hard rocks. If a jumper lands on flat ground at all, it is something like jumping off the roof of an automobile going twenty-five miles an hour, and in 1949 he finished his jump by taking the "Allen roll," landing sideways, with the right side from the hip down taking the shock, the upper part of the body continuing to pivot to the right until the body falls on its back and then rolls over on its knees. As a jumping instructor once said, the roll is to spread the pain all over the body.

So it is to appear on the earth from the sky. It is not surprising, considering the punishment the jumper takes at both ends of the jump, that no big man can be a Smokejumper, and we have to remind ourselves from time to time that, although we keep saying "men," most of them are still close to boys and that they are not very big boys. Most of the seventeen or eighteen thousand visitors a year at the Smokejumper base in Missoula, having heard, possibly from the Smokejumpers themselves, that the Smokejumpers are the Forest Service's best, expect to see the Minnesota Vikings professional football team practicing outside their dormitory, but instead they see teams of fairly ordinary-looking boys playing volleyball, their sizes ranging from five feet four to six feet two, with a maximum weight in 1949 of 190 pounds. The name of the game is not important to Smokejumpers. The competition is. In the Smokejumpers they don't recruit losers or big men, who don't seem to be made to drop out of the sky.

This was a fairly rough landing. Sallee lit in a lodgepole, his feet just off the ground, but none of the rest of them were lucky enough to break their fall. They rolled through rocks, although only Dodge was injured. Hellman and Rumsey came to help him and found him with an elbow cut to white bone, the cut somehow self-sealed so that it did not bleed. They bandaged the elbow, and Dodge said only that it was stiff, and the next day he said only that it was stiffer.

They crawled out of their jump suits that made them look part spacemen and part football players. In 1949 they even wore regular leather football helmets; then there was wire mesh over their faces, the padded canvas suit (with damn little padding), and logger boots. They tagged their jump suits and stacked them in one pile. Their work clothes, unlike their jump suits, were their own, and they were mostly just ordinary work clothes—Levis and blue shirts, but hard hats. None in this crew appeared in white shirts and oxfords, although Smoke-jumpers have appeared on fires in their drinking clothes when there has been an emergency call and they have been picked up in a bar, and a jumper is quite a sight in a white shirt and oxfords after he has been on a fire for three or four days and had a hangover to start with.

Then the plane began to circle, dropping cargo. It was being dropped high and was scattering all over the head of the gulch. Because the cargo had been dropped at two thousand feet instead of the customary twelve hundred so the pilot would not have to take his plane close to the ridgetops in the heavy winds, the men had to collect the cargo over at least a three-hundred-square-yard area. In those days the bedrolls were dropped without benefit of parachutes and popped all over the landscape, some of them bouncing half as high as the trees. The parachutes were made of nylon because grasshoppers like the taste of silk. In a modern tragedy you have to watch out for little details rather than big flaws. By the end, every minute would count, but it took the crew some extra minutes to collect the cargo because it was so scattered. Suddenly there was a terrific crash about a quarter of a mile down the canyon from the landing area. It turned out to be the radio, whose parachute hadn't opened because its static line had broken where it was attached to the plane. Another detail. The pulverized radio, which had fallen straight, told the crew about how far downgulch from the landing area they had been jumped, so the spotter must have been allowing for about a quarter of a mile of wind drift. It also told them something else—that the outside world had disappeared. The only world had become Mann Gulch and a fire, and the two were soon to become one and the same and never to be separated, at least in story.

They finished collecting and piling up their cargo. Dodge estimated that the crew and cargo were dropped by 4:10 p.m. but that it was nearly 5:00 before all the cargo had been retrieved.

Dodge made the double L signal on the landing area with orange sleeves, signaling to the plane, all present and accounted for. The plane circled twice to be sure and then headed for the outside world. It headed straight down Mann Gulch and across the glare of the Missouri. It seemed to be leaving frighteningly fast, and it was. It had started out a freight train, loaded with cargo. Now it was light and fast and was gone. Its departure left the world much smaller.

There was nothing in the universe now but the terminal glare of the Missouri, an amphitheater of stone erected by geology, and a sixty-acre fire with a future. Whatever the future, it was all to take place here, and soon. Of the Smokejumpers' three elements, sky had already changed to earth. In about an hour the earth and even the sky would all be fire.

They could see the fire from their cargo area, at least they could see its flank on the Mann Gulch slope, and even at five o'clock they were not greatly impressed. Rumsey didn't think any of them regarded it as dangerous, although he did think it would be hard to mop up because it was burning on steep and rocky ground.

Then they heard a shout from the fire, but it was impossible to distinguish the words. The crew had been led to believe before they left Missoula that there would be a ground crew on the fire (hence, their having no maps), so Dodge told the squad leader, Bill Heilman, to take charge of the men and see that they ate something and filled their canteens while he himself took off for the fire to find out who was on it.

They spent only about ten minutes at the cargo area before they started tooling up. Sallee and Navon carried the saws; the rest were double-tooled. They thought they were going to work. Actually they were leaving an early station of the cross, where minutes anywhere along the way would have saved them.

Since their tools had better fit our hands if we are going to a fire, we should try them on here and see how they would have been used if the fire had been reached while it was at its present size of about sixty acres. At that size it is doubtful that the crew would have tried to hit it on its nose—it is dangerous business to attack a good-sized fire straight on.

Instead, they would have started flanking it close to its front and tried to steer it into some open ground, some stretch of shale or light grass where the fire would burn itself out or burn so feebly that it would be safe to take on directly. It's a ground fire of this size that, as suggested earlier, is brought under control by digging a fire-line around it, a shallow trench two to three feet wide scraped deep enough to expose mineral soil. All dead leaves, needles, even roots are removed so that nothing can burn across it. If any dead trees lie across it, they also must be removed and likewise any standing trees with low branches that the fire might use to jump the line. To put a fire "under control" is to establish and then hold such a line around it, especially around the part of it that is most likely to advance. What follows is called "mopping up," working back from the fire-line into the interior of the fire, digging shallow graves and dropping still-burning trees into them, and of course burying everything on the ground that smokes.

The tools that perform these two operations are, with one exception, those that have done most of the hard work of the world—axes, saws, and shovels.

Sallee says he was single-tooled and was carrying a saw, and Navon started with the other saw, which he soon traded off to Rumsey, who was carrying the heavy water can. Power saws, of course, were already invented, but those early ones were mechanical monsters; it took a whole crew just to crank one, so they were of no use to the Smoke-jumpers until well into the 1950s. The crew's two saws would have been two-man handsaws, and in making a fire-line would have been used to cut trees lying across the line or standing too close to it. In mopping up, they would have been used to drop the burning snags.

The not-always-clear references to tools by the two surviving crew members indicate that besides these two handsaws the crew had two or three shovels and eleven or twelve Pulaskis. Laird Robinson, who when I first met him was information officer at the Smokejumper base in Missoula, says that number sounds about right for a crew of sixteen at that time.

Even the numbers show that the Smokejumpers' tool of tools was the Pulaski. It was the forest firefighters' one invention, primitive but effective, invented strictly for firefighting. It was even named after the Forest Service's most famous firefighting ranger, Edward Pulaski, who in 1910, when many thought the world was ending in flames, put a gunnysack around his head and led forty-two half-paralyzed men through smoke to a deserted mining tunnel that he remembered. The cold air rushed out of the tunnel and was replaced by heat so intense it set fire to the mining timbers. Pulaski kept the fire in the tunnel under control by dipping water with his hat from a little stream that went by the mouth of the shaft, and he had enough control over his men to make them lie flat with their mouths on the ground. He was badly burned and finally passed out, and from time to time they all fell unconscious. But all recovered except five men and two horses.

The Pulaski is a kind of hybrid creation, half ax and half hoe. I remember the first one I ever used, an early, handmade one, nothing more than a double-bitted ax with one bit left on and a little hoe welded to where the other ax-bit had been. Even after all these years the Pulaski is still the tool for digging fire-lines. A little hoe goes deep enough because its job is to scrape the stuff that would burn off the surface of the ground. So the hoe makes the line; the ax-bit chops little trees or shrubs along the line that might let the fire jump across, and it has other uses, such as chopping roots. When the foreman ends his first lesson to his trainees on how to use a Pulaski, he says, "For the next couple of hours, all I want to see are your asses and your elbows."

Behind the crew with the fast Pulaskis come a couple of men with shovels, who clean out and widen the fire-line, and, of course, in the mopping-up operations, shovels are all-important in making shallow graves and burying whatever is still smoking.

The crew strung out on the trail. Those with the unsheathed saws were behind because the long teeth and rakers of the saws make them hard to carry and dangerous to follow too closely; most of the double-tooled men were carrying Pulaskis and for the second tool either a shovel or a water canteen or a first-aid kit or a rattlesnake kit. The flank of the fire was in plain view only half a mile across the gulch. Although from the cargo area its most advanced front on top of the ridge was not visible, they had seen it from the sky and remembered that on top of the ridge it was burning slowly downhill into a saddle. They had no trouble guessing what they would be doing ten or fifteen minutes from now when they caught up to their foreman and the fire. He would line them out on both the Mann Gulch and Meriwether flanks to make fire-lines that would keep the fire from spreading farther down either canyon and so limit its advance to the top of the ridge where, forced into the saddle and light grass, it would be easy to handle. Dodge would space the men with Pulaskis about ten to fifteen feet apart, depending upon the ground cover, and they wouldn't raise their heads until they had caught up to the man in front of them. Then they would tap him on the leg with a Pulaski and say "Bump." If the two men right behind had also finished their stretch, they would say "Bump Three." To a Smokejumper, "Bump" is a musical word if he is the one who sings it out.

When Smokejumpers work next to a regular crew of Forest Service firefighters, they take pleasure in leaving them bruised with "bumps."

As the crew started for the south side of the gulch, they had it figured out before they even had an order. They would work all night establishing a line around the fire. From then on, it would depend. The Smokejumpers couldn't be touched when it came to getting a line around a fire, but they usually didn't win medals in mopping it up. They were all in the business for money—the forestry school students, the fancy M.A., M.D., and Ph.D. students, and especially the jump-happy boys who hoped to make enough money in the summer to shack up all winter in Honolulu. So there was no use putting a little fire out of its misery too soon when you would be paid overtime.

The crew started up the side of the gulch toward the fire. It was about five o'clock. The next day a wristwatch of one of the boys was found near his body. Its hands were permanently melted at about four minutes to six. This must come close to marking the time when it was also over for most of the others. So there were about fifty-six minutes ahead of them, time to do only a little thinking, and undoubtedly only a little is all they did.

It is not hard to imagine what was in their heads. They knew they were the best and they were probably thinking at least indirectly about being the best, sizing up the fire ahead as a kind of pushover. They thought of what they were in as a game and they were the champs and the fire didn't look like much competition. They already had developed one of the best ways of facing danger in the woods, the habit of imagining you are being watched. You picture the mountainsides as sides of an amphitheater crowded with admirers, among whom always is your father, who fought fires in his time, and your girl, but even more clearly you can see yourself as champion crawling through the ropes. You would give this small-time amateur fire the one-two, and go home and drink beer. It was more than one hundred degrees on that open hillside, and all of them were certainly thinking of beer. If anything troubled them, it was the thought of some guy they had tangled with in a Missoula bar who they were hoping would show up again tomorrow night. And each boy from a small town such as Darby, Montana, or Sandpoint, Idaho, was undoubtedly thinking of his small-town girl, who was just finishing high school a year behind him. She had big legs and rather small breasts that did not get in the way. She was strong like him, and a great walker like him, and she could pack forty pounds all day. He thought of her as walking with him now and shyly showing her love by offering to pack one of his double-tools. He was thinking he was returning her love by shyly refusing to let her.

The answer, then, to what was in their heads when they started for the fire has to be "Not much."

Like the frontier cavalry, the Smokejumpers didn't kill themselves off at the start of a march. They loosened up for about a quarter of a mile downgulch and then began to climb toward the fire, but they hadn't climbed more than a hundred yards before they heard Dodge call to them from above to stay where they were. Shortly he showed up with Jim Harrison, the recreation and fire prevention guard stationed at the campground at the mouth of Meriwether Canyon. Harrison had spotted the fire late in the morning while on patrol duty, returned to Meriwether Station, and tried unsuccessfully to radio both Missoula and Canyon Ferry Ranger Station outside Helena at 12:15, ten minutes before the fire was first officially reported by the lookout on Colorado Mountain, thirty miles away. After he had tacked a sign on the station door, "Gone to the fire. Jim," he again had climbed the fifteen-hundred-foot precipice between Meriwether Canyon and Mann Gulch, and had been on the front of the fire alone until Dodge found him around five o'clock. He had tried to do what he was supposed to do— stop the fire from burning down into scenic Meriwether Canyon. Meriwether Canyon is a chimney of fifteen-hundred-foot precipices and pinnacles. In minutes it could draw flames through the length of its funnel and be heat-cracked rocks forever after. It is one of America's tourist treasures, and Harrison had fought to save it. Later, two sections of fire-line that he had scraped with his Pulaski were found burned over at the top of the ridge between Meriwether and Mann. His tracks were there too, burned over.

Harrison was known to many of this crew because he had been a

Smokejumper himself the summer before in Missoula, and ironically had switched to patrol duty and cleaning up picnic grounds to please his mother, who was afraid smokejumping was dangerous. Now here he was with Dodge and this crew of Smokejumpers on its mission of August 5, 1949, and he might as well have run into General Custer and the Seventh Cavalry on June 25, 1876, on their way to the Little Big Horn.

In addition, as recreation and patrol guard he could not have been in as good physical shape as the jumpers—the forest supervisor's description of his job makes clear that primarily he was a "recreation guard," keeping the public grounds and facilities at Meriwether Landing tidy for the tourists, and only upon special assignment was he to get into patrol and fire prevention work. As the supervisor told the Board of Review, Harrison had made only one patrol before August 5. Realizing he was in need of exercise, Harrison would hike up to his patrol point on his days off, but he couldn't have been in shape to keep up with the jumpers if the going got tough. And yet, that day he had twice climbed the perpendicular trail to the top of the ridge between Meriwether and Mann and fought fire alone for four hours while the Smokejumpers had done nothing but jump and walk a quarter of a mile plus a hundred yards.

Both Sallee and Rumsey record briefly the crew's meeting with Dodge and Harrison after those two had left the front of the fire. Sallee reports Dodge as saying that all of them "had better get out of that thick reproduction" because "it was a death trap" and then instructing Hellman to return the crew to the north side of the gulch and head them down the canyon to the river. Rumsey and Sallee agree Dodge didn't look particularly worried: "Dodge has a characteristic in him," Rumsey told the Board. "It is hard to tell what he is thinking." And Dodge probably wasn't yet alarmed, since he told Hellman that, while the crew was proceeding toward the river, he and Harrison would return to the cargo area at the head of the gulch and, as the others had already done, eat something before starting on the trail.

Still, it is clear Dodge hadn't cared for what he saw when he took a look at the front of the fire. He said it was not possible to get closer to the flames than one hundred feet and the "thick reproduction" he was worried about was a thicket of second-growth Ponderosa pine and Douglas fir that had sprung up after an earlier fire and was tightly interlaced and highly explosive, especially with the wind blowing upgulch. Primarily, the retreat to the river was for the safety of the crew, but if the wind continued to blow upgulch, the crew could attack the lower end of the fire from its rear or flanks to keep it from spreading, especially into Meriwether Canyon, which, like a good chimney, drew a strong updraft. If worse came to worst and the wind changed and blew downgulch, the crew could always escape into the river.

Dodge gave Hellman still another order—not to take the crew down the bottom of the gulch but to "follow contour" on the other slope, by which he meant that the crew should stay on the sidehill and keep on an elevation from which they could always see how the main fire on the opposite side was developing.

Hellman led the crew across the gulch and started angling for the river, and, sure enough, it happened as it nearly always does when the second-in-command takes charge. The crew got separated and confused—considering the short time Dodge was gone, highly confused and separated by quite a distance. Sallee says they ended up in two groups, five hundred feet apart, far enough apart that they couldn't see each other, and so confused that Sallee's group thought they were in the rear only to have to stop and wait for the rear group to catch up. Rumsey says that part of the time Navon, the former paratrooper from Bastogne, was in the lead. He was the one really professional jumper—and professional adventurer—among them and evidently was always something of his own boss and boss of the whole outfit if it looked to him as if it needed one.

This is all that happened in the twenty minutes Dodge was gone. But instead of being just a lunch break for the boss, it also was something of a prelude to the end. At least it can make us ask ahead of time what the structure of a small outfit should be when its business is to meet sudden danger and prevent disaster.

In the Smokejumpers the foreman is nearly always in the lead and the second-in-command is in the rear. On the march, the foreman sizes up the situation, makes the decision, yells back the orders, picks the trail, and sets the pace. The second-in-command repeats the orders, sees that they're understood, and sees that the crew is always acting as a crew, which means seeing that the crew is carrying out the boss's orders. When they hit a fire, the foreman again is out in front deciding where the fire-line should go and the second-in-command is again in the rear. He repeats the foreman's orders, he pats his men on the back or yells at them, and only if he can't himself get them to do what they should does he yell to the foreman, "They're making lousy line."

Although the foreman has little direct contact with his men, even on a friendly basis, his first job is to see that his men are safe. He is always asking himself, Where is a good escape route?

It is easy to forget about the second-in-command, who has a real tough job. He is the one who has to get the yardage out of the men, so he has to know how to pat them or yell at them and when. He has to know his men and up to a point be one of them, but he has to know where that point is. Being second in command, he will have a hard time, especially when he first takes command. A little friendship goes a long way when it comes to command, and they say Hellman was a wonderful fellow, but that may be part of the reason why, when he first took command, the outfit became separated and confused.

It could also have been partly the crew's fault. Now that they weren't going to hit the fire head on, some of the excitement was gone. Fighting a fire from its rear is not unusual, but it doesn't show how much horsepower you have. The crew, though, was still happy. They were not in that high state of bliss they had been in when they expected to have the fire out by tomorrow morning and possibly be home that same night to observe tall dames top-heavy with beer topple off bar stools. On the other hand, attacking the fire from the rear would make the job last longer and mean more money, and, in a Smokejumper's descending states of happiness, after women comes overtime. Actually, the priority could be the other way around. To the crew the fire was nothing to worry about.

Dodge felt otherwise as he and Harrison sat eating at the cargo area near the head of the canyon, from where he could see almost to the river. He told the Board of Review, "The fire had started to boil up, and I figured it was necessary to rejoin my crew and try to get out of the canyon as soon as possible."

He picked up a can of Irish white potatoes and caught up to his crew roughly twenty minutes after he had left them. It was "about 5:40," according to his testimony. Dodge had Hellman collect the crew, then station himself at the end of the line to keep it together this time while he himself took the lead and headed for the river. Things went fast from then on but never fast enough for the crew to catch up and keep ahead of disaster.

Rod Norum, who is one of the leading specialists on fire behavior in the Forest Service and still a fine athlete, as an experiment started out where Dodge rejoined his crew and, moving as fast as possible all the way, did not get to the grave markers as fast as the bodies did. Of course, there was nothing roaring behind him.

When the crew crossed back from the south to the north side of Mann Gulch where they had landed, they crossed from one geography into another and from one fire hazard into one they had never dealt with before. Mann Gulch is a composition in miniature of the spectacular change in topography that is pressed together by the Gates of the Mountains. Suddenly the Great Plains disappear; suddenly the vast Rocky Mountains begin. Between them, there is only a gulch or two like Mann Gulch for a transition from one world to another. Before the fire the two sides of Mann Gulch almost evenly divided the two topographical and fuel worlds between them—a side of the gulch for each world. The south side, where the fire had started, was heavily timbered. In the formal description of the *Report of Board of Review:* "At the point of origin of the fire the fuel type consisted of a dense stand of six- to eight-inch-diameter Douglas fir and some ponderosa pine on the lateral ridges."

But it was a different type of fuel on the north side, where the crew was now on its way to the river. "At the point of disaster the tree cover consisted of stringers of scattered young ponderosa pine trees with occasional overmature ponderosa pine trees. The ground cover or understory which predominated was bunch grass with some cheat grass." Essentially the north side of Mann Gulch was rocky and steep with a lot of grass and brush and only a scattering of trees. The south side was densely timbered.

The difference between the two sides of the gulch is after all these years still clearly visible. On the south side the charred trees stood until their roots rotted. Then winds blowing upgulch from the Missouri left them on the ground, unburied but paralleling each other, as if they belonged to some nature cult ultimately joined together by the belief that death lay in the same direction. At times they look as if they had been placed there—black-draped coffins from some vast battle awaiting burial in a national cemetery on a hillside near a great river, if not the Potomac then the Missouri.

On the north side, where the crew was angling toward the river, there are white crosses with bronze plates and a few black odds and ends. Not much else. The men died in dead grass on the north slope.

Several generalizations will help with what lies ahead if we remember that they are only generalizations. A fire in dense timber builds up terrific heat but not great speed. As Harry Gisborne has said, a big run for a crown fire is from half a mile to a mile an hour. A grass fire, by comparison, is usually a thin fire; it builds up no great wall of heat—it comes and is gone, sometimes so fast that the top of the grass is scarcely burned. Sometimes so fast it doesn't even stop to burn a homesteader's log cabin. It just burns over and around it, and doesn't take time to wait for the roof to catch on fire. Even so, since the great fire catastrophe of 1910, far more men had been killed by 1949 on fast, thin-fueled grass fires east of the Continental Divide in Montana than on the slow, powerful fires in the dense forests of western Montana.

Arthur D. Moir, Jr., supervisor of the Helena National Forest, generalizing in his 1949 testimony about the Mann Gulch fire, said fires east of the Continental Divide in Montana "are smaller, and because of less fuel, are more quickly controlled." But he went on to add that to his knowledge "only two men have been burned in forest fires in Idaho and western Montana since 1910," whereas he counted thirty-five who had burned to death east of the Divide in fast grass.

The grass and brush of Mann Gulch could not be faster than it was now. The year before the fire, the Gates of the Mountains had been designated a wilderness area, so no livestock grazed in Mann Gulch, with the result that the grass in places was waist high. Since it was early August with blistering heat, the worst of both fire-worlds could occur— if a fire started in the deep timber of the southern side, where most fires start, and then jumped to the explosive grass and shrubs of the northern side, as this one might, and did, it could burn with the speed of one of those catastrophic fires in the dry gulches of suburban Los Angeles but carry with it the heat of the 1910 timber fires of Montana and Idaho. It could run so fast you couldn't escape it and it could be so hot it could burn out your lungs before it caught you.

Things got faster and shorter. Dodge says they continued down-gulch about five minutes, Sallee says between an eighth and a quarter of a mile, which is saying about the same thing. Dodge was worried— evidently no one else was. The fire was just across the gulch to be looked at, and that's evidently what they were doing. They were high enough up the slope now that they could almost peer into its insides. When the smoke would lift, they could see flames flapping fiercely back and forth, a damn bad sign but they found it interesting.

Navon was in his element as a freewheeler, alternating between being benevolent and being boss. He had lightened Rumsey's load by trading him his saw for Rumsey's heavier water can, so Rumsey especially was watching the scenery as it went by. He observed that the fire was burning "more fiercely" than before. "A very interesting spectacle," he told the Board of Review. "That was about all we thought about it."

Of the stations of the cross they were to pass, this was the aesthetic one. On forest fires there are moments almost solely for beauty. Such moments are of short duration.

• • •

Then Dodge saw it. Rumsey and Sallee didn't, and probably none of the rest of the crew did either. Dodge was thirty-three and foreman and was supposed to see; he was in front where he could see. Besides, he hadn't liked what he had seen when he looked down the canyon after he and Harrison had returned to the landing area to get something to eat, so his seeing powers were doubly on the alert. Rumsey and Sallee were young and they were crew and were carrying tools and rubbernecking at the fire across the gulch. Dodge takes only a few words to say what the "it" was he saw next: "We continued down the canyon for approximately five minutes before I could see that the fire had crossed Mann Gulch and was coming up the ridge toward us."

Neither Rumsey nor Sallee could see the fire that was now on their side of the gulch, but both could see smoke coming toward them over a hogback directly in front. As for the main fire across the gulch, it still looked about the same to them, "confined to the upper third of the slope."

At the Review, Dodge estimated they had a 150- to 200-yard head start on the fire coming at them on the north side of the gulch. He immediately reversed direction and started back up the canyon, angling toward the top of the ridge on a steep grade. When asked why he didn't go straight for the top there and then, he answered that the ground was too rocky and steep and the fire was coming too fast to dare to go at right angles to it.

You may ask yourself how it was that of the crew only Rumsey and Sallee survived. If you had known ahead of time that only two would survive, you probably never would have picked these two—they were first-year jumpers, this was the first fire they had ever jumped on, Sallee was one year younger than the minimum age, and around the base they were known as roommates who had a pretty good time for themselves. They both became big operators in the world of the woods and prairies, and part of this story will be to find them and ask them why they think they alone survived, but even if ultimately your answer or theirs seems incomplete, this seems a good place to start asking the question. In their statements soon after the fire, both say that the moment Dodge reversed the route of the crew they became alarmed, for, even if they couldn't see the fire, Dodge's order was to run from one. They reacted in seconds or less. They had been traveling at the end of the line because they were carrying unsheathed saws. When the head of the line started its switchback, Rumsey and Sallee left their positions at the end of the line, put on extra speed, and headed straight uphill, connecting with the front of the line to drop into it right behind Dodge.

They were all traveling at top speed, all except Navon. He was stopping to take snapshots.

The world was getting faster, smaller, and louder, so much faster that for the first time there are random differences among the survivors about how far apart things were. Dodge says it wasn't until one thousand to fifteen hundred feet after the crew had changed directions that he gave the order for the heavy tools to be dropped. Sallee says it was only two hundred yards, and Rumsey can't remember. Whether they had traveled five hundred yards or two hundred yards, the new fire coming up the gulch toward them was coming faster than they had been going. Sallee says, "By the time we dropped our packs and tools the fire was probably not much over a hundred yards behind us, and it seemed to me that it was getting ahead of us both above and below." If the fire was only a hundred yards behind now, it had gained a lot of ground on them since they had reversed directions, and Rumsey says he could never remember going faster in his life than he had for the last five hundred yards.

Dodge testifies that this was the first time he had tried to communicate with his men since rejoining them at the head of the gulch, and he is reported as saying—for the second time—something about "getting out of this death trap." When asked by the Board of Review if he had explained to the men the danger they were in, he looked at the Board in amazement, as if the Board had never been outside the city limits and wouldn't know sawdust if they saw it in a pile. It was getting late for talk anyway. What could anybody hear? It roared from behind, below, and across, and the crew, inside it, was shut out from all but a small piece of the outside world.

They had come to the station of the cross where something you want to see and can't shuts out the sight of everything that otherwise could be seen. Rumsey says again and again what the something was he couldn't see. "The top of the ridge, the top of the ridge.

"I had noticed that a fire will wear out when it reaches the top of a ridge. I started putting on steam thinking if I could get to the top of the ridge I would be safe.

"I kept thinking the ridge—if I can make it. On the ridge I will be safe. . . . I forgot to mention I could not definitely see the ridge from where we were. We kept running up since it had to be there somewhere. Might be a mile and a half or a hundred feet—I had no idea."

The survivors say they weren't panicked, and something like that is probably true. Smokejumpers are selected for being tough, but Dodge's men were very young and, as he testified, none of them had been on a blowup before and they were getting exhausted and confused. The world roared at them—there was no safe place inside and there was almost no outside. By now they were short of breath from the exertion of their climbing and their lungs were being seared by the heat. A world was coming where no organ of the body had consciousness but the lungs.

Dodge's order was to throw away just their packs and heavy tools, but to his surprise some of them had already thrown away all their equipment. On the other hand, some of them wouldn't abandon their heavy tools, even after Dodge's order. Diettert, one of the most intelligent of the crew, continued carrying both his tools until Rumsey caught up with him, took his shovel, and leaned it against a pine tree. Just a little farther on, Rumsey and Sallee passed the recreation guard, Jim Harrison, who, having been on the fire all afternoon, was now exhausted. He was sitting with his heavy pack on and was making no effort to take it off, and Rumsey and Sallee wondered numbly why he didn't but no one stopped to suggest he get on his feet or gave him a hand to help him up. It was even too late to pray for him. Afterwards, his ranger wrote his mother and, struggling for something to say that would comfort her, told her that her son always attended mass when he could.

It was way over one hundred degrees. Except for some scattered timber, the slope was mostly hot rock slides and grass dried to hay.

It was becoming a world where thought that could be described as such was done largely by fixations. Thought consisted in repeating over and over something that had been said in a training course or at least by somebody older than you.

Critical distances shortened. It had been a quarter of a mile from where Dodge had rejoined his crew to where he had the crew reverse direction. From there they had gone only five hundred yards at the most before he realized the fire was gaining on them so rapidly that the men should discard whatever was heavy.

The next station of the cross was only seventy-five yards ahead. There they came to the edge of scattered timber with a grassy slope ahead. There they could see what is really not possible to see: the center of a blowup. It is really not possible to see the center of a blowup because the smoke only occasionally lifts, and when it does all that can be seen are pieces, pieces of death flying around looking for you—burning cones, branches circling on wings, a log in flight without a propeller. Below in the bottom of the gulch was a great roar without visible flames but blown with winds on fire. Now, for the first time, they could have seen to the head of the gulch if they had been looking that way. And now, for the first time, to their left the top of the ridge was visible, looking when the smoke parted to be not more than two hundred yards away.

Navon had already left the line and on his own was angling for the top. Having been at Bastogne, he thought he had come to know the deepest of secrets—how death can be avoided—and, as if he did, he had put away his camera. But if he really knew at that moment how death could be avoided, he would have had to know the answers to two questions: How could fires be burning in all directions and be burning right at you? And how could those invisible and present only by a roar all be roaring at you?

• • •

On the open slope ahead of the timber Dodge was lighting a fire in the bunch grass with a "gofer" match. He was to say later at the Review that he did not think he or his crew could make the two hundred yards to the top of the ridge. He was also to estimate that the men had about thirty seconds before the fire would roar over them.

Dodge's fire did not disturb Rumsey's fixation. Speaking of Dodge lighting his own fire, Rumsey said, "I remember thinking that that was a very good idea, but I don't remember what I thought it was good for. . . . I kept thinking the ridge—if I can make it. On the ridge I will be safe."

Sallee was with Rumsey. Diettert, who before being called to the fire had been working on a project with Rumsey, was the third in the bunch that reached Dodge. On a summer day in 1978, twenty-nine years later, Sallee and I stood on what we thought was the same spot. Sallee said, "I saw him bend over and light a fire with a match. I thought, With the fire almost on our back, what the hell is the boss doing lighting another fire in front of us?"

It shouldn't be hard to imagine just what most of the crew must have thought when they first looked across the open hillside and saw their boss seemingly playing with a matchbook in dry grass. Although the Mann Gulch fire occurred early in the history of the Smoke-jumpers, it is still their special tragedy, the one in which their crew suffered almost a total loss and the only one in which their loss came from the fire itself. It is also the only fire any member of the Forest Service had ever seen or heard of in which the foreman got out ahead of his crew only to light a fire in advance of the fire he and his crew were trying to escape. In case I hadn't understood him the first time, Sallee repeated, "We thought he must have gone nuts." A few minutes later his fire became more spectacular still, when Sallee, having reached the top of the ridge, looked back and saw the foreman enter his own fire and lie down in its hot ashes to let the main fire pass over him.

In this story of the outside world and the inside world with a fire between, the outside world of little screwups recedes now for a few hours to be taken over by the inside world of blowups, this time by a colossal blowup but shaped by little screwups that fitted together tighter and tighter until all became one and the same thing—the fateful blowup. Such is much of tragedy in modern times and probably always has been except that past tragedy refrained from speaking of its association with screwups and blowups.

This story some time ago left the inside world at its very center—Dodge had come out of the timber ahead of his crew, with the fire just behind. He saw that in front was high dry grass that would burn very fast, saw for the first time the top of the ridge at what he judged to be about two hundred yards above, put two and two together and decided that he and his crew couldn't make the two hundred yards, and almost instantly invented what was to become known as the "escape fire" by lighting a patch of bunch grass with a gofer match. In so doing, he started an argument that would remain hot long after the fire.

At the time it probably made no sense to anyone but Dodge to light a fire right in front of the main fire. It couldn't act as a backfire; there wasn't any time to run a fire-line along its upgulch edge to prevent it from being just an advance arm of the main fire. Uncontrolled, instead of being a backfire it might act as a spot fire on its way upgulch and bring fire from behind that much closer and sooner to the crew.

Dodge was starting to light a second fire with a second match when he looked up and saw that his first fire had already burned one hundred square feet of grass up the slope. "This way," he kept calling to his crew behind. "This way." Many of the crew, as they came in sight of him, must have asked themselves, What's this dumb bastard doing? The smoke lifted twice so that everyone had a good chance to ask the question.

The crew must have been stretched nearly all the way from the edge of the timber to the center of the grassy clearing ahead, where Dodge was lighting his fire. Rumsey and Sallee say that the men did not panic, but by now all began to fear death and were in a race with it. The line had already assumed that erratic spread customary in a race where everything is at stake. When it comes to racing with death, all men are not created equal.

At the edge of the timber the crew for the first time could have seen to the head of the gulch where the fire, having moved up the south side of the gulch, was now circling. From the open clearing they also could see partway toward the bottom of the gulch, where it was presumably rocks that were exploding in smoke. They didn't have to look behind— they could feel the heat going to their lungs straight through their backs. From the edge of the clearing they could also see the top of the ridge for the first time. It wasn't one and a half miles away; to them it seemed only two hundred yards or so away. Why was this son of a bitch stopping to light another fire?

For the first time they could also see a reef twelve to twenty feet high running parallel to the top of the ridge and thirty yards or so below it. This piece of ancient ocean bottom keeps the top of the ridge from eroding, as the rock lid on the top of a butte on the plains keeps the butte from eroding into plains. But no one was thinking of geology or probably even of whether it would be hard to climb over, through, or around. At this moment, its only significance was that it seemed about two hundred yards away.

When the line reached its greatest extension, Rumsey and Sallee were at the head of it—they were the first to reach Dodge and his fire. Diettert was just behind them, and perhaps Hellman, although these two stand there separately forever and ask the same question, What did Rumsey and Sallee do right that we did wrong? For one thing, they stuck together; Diettert and Hellman went their separate ways.

The smoke will never roll away and leave a clear picture of the head of the line reaching Dodge and his burned bunch grass. Dodge later pictured the crew as strung out about 150 feet with at least eight men close enough together and close enough to him so that he could try to explain to them—but without stopping them—that they could not survive unless they got into his grass fire. At the Review, he made very clear that he believed there was not enough time left for them to make it to the top of the hill, and events came close to supporting his belief. In the roar and smoke he kept "hollering" at them—he was sure that at least those closest to him heard him and that those behind understood him from his actions. In smoke that swirled and made sounds, there was a pause, then somebody said, "To hell with that, I'm getting out of here," and a line of them followed the voice.

The line all headed in the same direction, but in the smoke Dodge could not see whether any of them looked back at him. He estimated that the main fire would hit them in thirty seconds.

In the smoke and roar Rumsey and Sallee saw a considerably different arrangement of characters and events from Dodge's. Indeed, even the roommates differ from each other. Both agree with Dodge, however, that the line was stretched out, with a group at the head close to Dodge, then a gap, and then the rest scattered over a distance that neither could estimate exactly but guessed to be nearly a hundred yards. In fact, when in the summer of 1978 Rumsey, Sallee, Laird Robinson, and I spent a day together in Mann Gulch, the two survivors told Laird and me they were now sure some of the crew had fallen so far behind that they were never close enough to Dodge to hear whatever he was saying. The implication of Dodge's account is that they all passed him by, but Rumsey and Sallee believed that some of them hadn't. As to the head of the column, Sallee limits it to three—himself and Rumsey plus Diettert, who was also a pal and had been working on the same project with Rumsey before the two of them were called to the fire. To these three, Rumsey adds Hellman, the second-in-command, and indeed suggests, with Dodge agreeing, that it was Hellman who said, "To hell with that, I'm getting out of here," and so furnishes the basis for the charge that Hellman was doubly guilty of insubordination by being near the head of the line after Dodge had ordered him to the rear and by encouraging the crew to ignore Dodge's order to remain with him and enter his fire. Rumsey's testimony, however, will never settle Hellman's place in the line and hence his role in the tragedy, for Sallee was positive and still is that Hellman was at the head of the line when Dodge ordered the men to drop their tools but that he then returned to the tail of it, repeating Dodge's order and remaining there to enforce it. So direct testimony leaves us with opposite opinions of Hellman's closing acts as second-in-command of Smokejumpers on their most tragic mission. Either he countermanded his superior and contributed to the tragedy or, according to Sallee, being the ideal second-in-command, he returned to the rear to see that all the crew carried out the foreman's orders and to keep their line intact.

An outline of the events that were immediately to come probably would not agree exactly with the testimony of any one of the survivors or make a composite of their testimony, as might be expected, but would be more like what follows, and even what follows will leave some of the most tragic events in mystery and litigation.

Rumsey, Sallee, and Diettert left Dodge as one group and took the same route to the reef; two of them survived. Some of the crew never got as high up the slope as Dodge's fire. Hellman reached the top of the ridge by another route and did not survive. The rest scattered over the hillside upgulch from the route taken by the first three, and none of those who scattered reached the top. As Sallee said the summer we were together in Mann Gulch, "No one could live who left Dodge even seconds after we did."

In fact, the testimony makes clear that Diettert, Rumsey, and Sallee scarcely stopped to listen to Dodge. As Rumsey says, "I was thinking only of my hide." He and Diettert turned and made for the top of the ridge. Sallee paused for only a moment, because he soon caught up with Diettert and Rumsey, and actually was the first to work his way through the opening in the reef above. When asked at the Review whether others of the crew were piling up behind while he stood watching Dodge light his fire, Sallee said, "I didn't notice, but I don't believe there were. Rumsey and Diettert went ahead—went on—I just hesitated for a minute and went on too."

In the roar of the main fire that was now only thirty seconds behind them they may not even have heard Dodge, and, if they did hear words, they couldn't have made out their meaning. Rumsey says, "I did not hear him say anything. There was a terrible roar from the main fire. Couldn't hear much."

It probably wasn't just the roar from without that precluded hearing. It was also the voice from inside Mount Sinai: "I kept thinking the ridge—if I can make it. On the ridge I will be safe. I went up the right-hand side of Dodge's fire."

Although Sallee stopped a moment for clarification, he also misunderstood Dodge's actions. "I understood that he wanted us to follow his fire up alongside and maybe that his fire would slow the other fire down." Like Rumsey, Sallee interpreted Dodge's fire as a buffer fire, set to burn straight up for the top and be a barrier between them and the main fire. And like Rumsey, Sallee followed the right edge of Dodge's fire to keep it between them and the fire that was coming up the gulch.

The question of how Hellman reached the top of the ridge after leaving Dodge at his fire cannot be answered with certainty. What is known is that he made his way from where Dodge lit his fire to the top of the ridge alone, that he was badly burned, that he joined up with Rumsey and Sallee after the main fire had passed, that he told Rumsey he had been burned at the top of the ridge, and that he died the next day in a hospital in Helena. The most convincing guess about how he reached the top of the ridge is Sallee's. When he and I stood on the ridge in the summer of 1978, I asked him about Hellman's route to the top and he said that naturally he had thought about it many times and was convinced there was only one explanation: while he, Rumsey, and Diettert followed the upgulch (right) side of Dodge's fire and so for important seconds at least used it as a buffer protecting them from the main fire coming upgulch, Hellman must have followed the opposite, or downgulch, side of Dodge's fire and so had no protection from the main fire, which caught him just before he could get over the ridge.

Sallee talks so often about everything happening in a matter of seconds after he and Rumsey left Dodge's fire that at first it seems just a manner of speaking. But if you combine the known facts with your imagination and are a mountain climber and try to accompany Rumsey and Sallee to the top, you will know that to have lived you had to be young and tough and lucky.

And young and tough they were. In all weather Sallee had walked four country miles each way to school, and a lot of those eight miles he ran. He and Rumsey had been on tough projects all summer. They gave it everything they had, and everything was more, they said, than ever before or after.

As they approached the reef, its significance changed for the worse. They saw that the top of the ridge was beyond the reef, and unless they could find an opening in it, it would be the barrier keeping them from reaching the top. They might die in its detritus. The smoke lifted only twice, but they saw a crevice and steered by it even after it disappeared again. "There was an opening between large rocks, and I had my eye on that and I did not look either way," Sallee says.

Halfway up, the heat on Rumsey's back was so intense he forgot about Dodge's buffer fire, if that is what it was, and, having spotted the opening, headed straight for it. It was not only upslope but slightly upgulch and to the right. In the smoke nothing was important but this opening, which was like magnetic north—they could steer toward it when they couldn't see it. Rumsey was in the center. Sallee was even with him on his left; Diettert was just a few steps behind on his right.

The world compressed to a slit in the rocks. Rumsey and Sallee saw neither right nor left. When asked at the Review whether they saw pincers of fire closing in on them from the sides, they said no; they saw only straight ahead. Ahead they saw; behind they felt; they shut out the sides.

To them the reef was another one of those things—perhaps the final one—that kept coming out of smoke to leave no place to run from death. They can remember feeling sorry for themselves because they were so young. They also tried not to think of anything they had done wrong for fear it might appear in the flames. They thought God might have made the opening and might take it away again. Besides, the opening might be a trap for the sins of youth to venture into.

Beyond the opening and between it and the top of the ridge they could see no flames but there was dense smoke. Beyond the opening in the smoke there could be fire—beyond, there could be more reefs,

reefs without openings. It could be that beyond the opening was the end of God and the end of youth. Maybe that's what Diettert thought.

Rumsey and Sallee felt they were about to jump through a door in a plane and so had to steady themselves and believe something was out there that would hold them up. It was as if there were a tap on the leg. Sallee was in the lead and was first through the crevice. It was cooler, and he believed his faith had been confirmed. He stopped to lower the temperature in his back and lungs. Rumsey was through next. As a Methodist, he believed most deeply in what he had been first taught. Early he had been taught that in a time of crisis the top of a hill is safest. It was still some distance to the top, and he never stopped till he got there.

Diettert stopped just short of the opening. On his birthday, not long after his birthday dinner and just short of the top of the hill, he silently rejected the opening in the reef, turned, and went upgulch parallel to the base of the reef, where for some distance there is no other opening. No one with him, neither Rumsey nor Sallee, saw him do this—it is known by where his body was found. Diettert, the studious one, had seen something in the opening he did not like, had rejected it, and had gone looking for something he did not find. It is sometimes hard to understand fine students. Be sure, though, he had a theory, as fine students nearly always have.

While Sallee was cooling his lungs, he looked down and back at Dodge and the crew and for the first time realized why Dodge had lit his fire.

> I saw Dodge jump over the burning edge of the fire he had set and saw him waving his arms and motioning for the other boys to follow him. At that instant I could see what I believe was all the balance of the crew. They were within twenty to fifty feet of Dodge and just outside the burning edge of the fire Dodge had set. The last I recall seeing the group of boys, they were angling up the slope in the unburned grass and fairly close to the burning edge of the fire Dodge had set. . . .

When Dodge first set the fire I did not understand that he wanted us boys to wait a few seconds and then get inside the burned-out grass area for protection from the main fire.

Dodge's description of his fire is mostly from inside it.

> After walking around to the north side of the fire I started as an avenue of escape, I heard someone comment with these words, "To hell with that, I'm getting out of here!" and for all my hollering, I could not direct anyone into the burned area. I then walked through the flames toward the head of the fire into the inside and continued to holler at everyone who went by, but all failed to heed my instructions; and within seconds after the last man had passed, the main fire hit the area I was in.

When asked at the Review if any of the crew had looked his way as they went by, he said no, "They didn't seem to pay any attention. That is the part I didn't understand. They seemed to have something on their minds—all headed in one direction."

He wet his handkerchief from his canteen, put it over his mouth, and lay face down on the ground. Whether he knew it or not, there is usually some oxygen within fifteen inches of the ground, but even if he knew it, he needed a lot of luck besides oxygen to have lived, although Rumsey and Sallee were to say later that the whole crew would probably have survived if they had understood and followed Dodge's instructions.

It is doubtful, though, that the crew had the training and composure to interpret Dodge's instructions even if some of his words reached them over the roar. The close questioning Rumsey and Sallee received later at the Review revealed that their training in how to meet fire emergencies consisted of a small handful of instructions, four to be exact and only one of which had any bearing on their present emergency. The first was to backfire if they had time and the right situation, but they had neither. The second was to get to the top of the ridge where the fuel is usually thinner, where there are usually stretches of rock and shale, and where the winds usually meet and fluctuate. This is the one they tried, and it worked with only seconds to spare. The third instruction was designed to govern an emergency in which neither time nor situation permits backfiring or reaching a bare ridgetop. When it's that tough, the best you can do is turn into the fire and try to work through it, hoping to piece together burned-out stretches. The fourth and final warning was to remember that, whatever you do, you must not allow the fire to pick the spot where it hits you. The chances are it will hit you where it is burning fiercest and fastest. According to Dodge's later testimony, the fire about to hit them had a solid front 250 to 300 feet deep—no one works through that deep a front and lives.

Even if the crew's training had included a section on Dodge's escape fire, it is not certain that the crew would have listened to Dodge, would have entered the fire and buried their faces in the ashes. When asked at the Review if he would have gone into Dodge's fire had he received previous instruction about it, Rumsey replied, "I think that if I had seen it on a blackboard and seen it done and had it explained so that I understood it I think I surely would have gone in—but of course you never can tell for sure."

Dodge survived, and Rumsey and Sallee survived. Their means of survival differed. Rumsey and Sallee went for the top and relied on the soul and a fixation from basic training. The soul in a situation like this is mostly being young, in tune with time, and having good legs, an inflexible destination, and no paralyzing questions about what lies beyond the opening. When asked whether he had "ever been instructed in setting an escape fire," Dodge replied, "Not that I know of. It just seemed the logical thing to do." Being logical meant building one fire in front of another, lying down in its ashes, and breathing close to the ground on a slight elevation. He relied on logic of a kind and the others on time reduced to seconds. But no matter where you put your trust, at a time like this you have to be lucky.

The accounts that come down to us of the flight of the crew up the hillside nearly all conclude at this point, creating with detail only the happenings of those who survived, if only for a day, as Hellman did, or, like Diettert, at least reached the reef. Counting these two, only five are usually present in the story that goes on up the ridge. Only a sentence or two is given to those who, when last seen by Dodge, were all going in one direction and when seen finally by Sallee were angling through openings in the smoke below him as he looked down from the top of the ridge. Although they are the missing persons in this story, they are also its tragic victims. There is a simple aspect of historiography, of course, to explain why, after last seen by the living, they pass silently out of the story and their own tragedy until their tragedy is over and they are found as bodies: no one who lived saw their sufferings. The historian, for a variety of reasons, can limit his account to firsthand witnesses, although a shortage of firsthand witnesses probably does not explain completely why contemporary accounts of the Mann Gulch fire avert their eyes from the tragedy. If a storyteller thinks enough of storytelling to regard it as a calling, unlike a historian he cannot turn from the sufferings of his characters. A storyteller, unlike a historian, must follow compassion wherever it leads him. He must be able to accompany his characters, even into smoke and fire, and bear witness to what they thought and felt even when they themselves no longer knew. This story of the Mann Gulch fire will not end until it feels able to walk the final distance to the crosses with those who for the time being are blotted out by smoke. They were young and did not leave much behind them and need someone to remember them.

from Fire on the Rim
by Stephen J. Pyne

Stephen J. Pyne (born 1949) spent 15 sum-

mers on the fire crew at the North Rim of the

Grand Canyon.

B y September the changes cannot be denied. We notice it first in the sky: the days shorten, and sunlight slanting through the trees is bright but cool. Autumn cold fronts, driven and hard, replace the serendipitous storms of summer. Clouds no longer build up in lazy white blossoms but race across the sky in dark streaks. Blustering westerlies replace the tidal flow of winds between Plateau and Canyon. Local circumstances are overwhelmed by larger events.

It is the beginning of the end of fire season. The very large fuels are as dry as they will get, and the canopies reach a moisture minimum as they prepare for dormancy. Grasses and herbaceous species cure. The aspen gradually change to oranges and yellows, the ponderosa lighten as they prepare for needle cast, and mixed conifer are dappled with color. Except in the wettest of years, the fuels can still burn; but the burning periods become briefer, and the sources of ignition more remote. The fire crew, too, breaks up. The onset of school sends some collegians back for fall semester and, by reducing Park visitation, reduces the overall pool of seasonal reserves. The first departures, in August, are absorbed with little shock; but by September the losses mount, and the more crewmen who leave, the more who want to leave. Like a waterdog in the sun, hope begins to dissipate. Possibilities have become, to varying degrees, realities.

Yet the aspen display, the subsidence of a delicate Indian summer, the daily emergencies that keep a reduced work force comfortably busy—all make for a rewarding tour. And it has not yet ended. These are not preparations for winter, since no one stays, but a prolongation of summer for as long as it can endure, which means for as long as there are fires. We find new projects and close out old ones, haul firewood by the truckload, hustle about the cache, and prepare for a round of prescribed burns. There are still fires to come. There can always be more fires.

The storm starts on Friday afternoon and continues for two days.

There is nothing to do but busy ourselves in the fire cache and drink coffee in the Fire Pit. This is no afternoon shower, but a full-blown storm system; thunder, hail, lightning, rain crowd us day and night. Cold and damp, everyone bundles in jackets. This late in the year we doubt that the forest can dry out completely again. Yet there is reason to hope that a smoke or two will survive.

We move the coffeepot from the Pit to the cache. Somewhat on a whim a few weeks earlier I had ordered a set of fire training films from the regional office. All day Saturday we watch films in the cache. We eat popcorn and lie on paper sleeping bags and think what a miserable way this is to end fire season. The rumble of wet thunder, an empty promise, punctuates the film's sound tracks.

Late Sunday afternoon there is a smoke report.

Point Sublime: Sunrise

Thumper and I take the pumper quickly through the slats of shadow and cool sunlight, down the unnamed valley in which the Sublime Road, dry and clear of debris, makes its final run. We left the cache early in order to rendezvous with some South Rim brass who wanted to land at a little-used helispot near the prescribed fire plot, but they radioed to say they would be delayed for at least another hour. So we drive on, our windows up and the heater on. Suddenly the narrowing valley opens. The Canyon is thrust upon us. The Canyon is everywhere. The road to the overlook, another mile away, veers upward to a spiny desert peninsula that will take us to Point Sublime.

Everyone has a favorite viewpoint, but Sublime, by consensus, is special. I park the pumper. There is no one else around and no evidence that anyone has been here for weeks. Thump leads as we walk down to the point and sit on a rock shelf that dangles over the brink. The cliff below our feet drops instantly to the Redwall, where another peninsula extends a further mile or so toward the River. The lower peninsula echoes the upper, and it creates one of the miracles of Sublime: you have the feeling that you are watching the viewpoint that you are watching from. At Point Sublime—midway in the Canyon—you can see everything.

Every other viewpoint is inevitably compared with the perspective at Point Sublime, and every other viewpoint is found wanting. Each has its special signature, and many are better than Sublime for this effect or that. But Sublime has everything, and it has it all the time. It is the universal Canyon overlook. So effective is it at orchestrating Canyon scenery that it almost loses its own identity, and that may be its unique attribute. At Sublime the Kaibab becomes vanishingly small. The Rim is reduced to an infinitesimal presence, like a mathematical point. You see the Canyon as though suspended over the brink. The sweep of the Canyon matches the sweep of the sky. At sunrise it appears as a great lake of shadows that breaks up into shafts of sunlight and glowing rock. At noon it is clear and still and sunburned with Canyon colors. At sunset it presents two panoramas from a common vantage point, one with the sunset and the other against it, as shadows sweep like ether around butte and gorge, and the sun and moon move in a minuet of light and space. At Point Sublime, there is only the Canyon, and a Beyond—an enormous tableland that stretches to mountains that appear blue and purple along empty horizons beneath an endless sky.

The supreme Canyon vantage point, Sublime is best viewed alone. Bring too many people here at one time, and they become distracted, restless. Send a crew to Sublime for lunch and they will start tossing pebbles over the brink, then larger stones, and end up rolling off boulders. The Point is barren of any but very small and very large rocks.

As a geographic presence Point Sublime encompasses a vast sphere of influence. To say of something that it is "near Sublime" can mean anywhere from Tiyo to Swamp Point. The power of Sublime is such that the Park will not deny access to it by visitors. It means that the Sublime Road will not be considered a mere fireroad, that it will not be abandoned (even if it cannot be maintained), and this demands that the whole Sublime region must be denied wilderness status. Sublime has equally influenced Canyon history, for Clarence Dutton set the climax to his *Tertiary History* at the Point and communicated a view from the Kaibab that no one since has ever approached. If you want to experience the Canyon, go to Point Sublime.

Thump and I watch the sun bring the buttes to life, like breath on glowing coals. We barely know our own presence, hushed by the supreme stillness of a Canyon sunrise. Then our reverie snaps. The Park radio crackles, "Seven-two-six, this is 210. I'm lifting off the South Rim for Site S-1, near Point Sublime. ETA fifteen minutes." The watch is over. We have just enough time to rendezvous at the helispot.

The smoke—faint and camouflaged among packs of waterdogs—is reported by Scenic Airlines as somewhere north of Swamp Point. Tom and I start the blue pumper toward the Shinumo Gate as the storm reluctantly begins to clear. The sky swirls with great white and black chunks of cloud pierced here and there by patches of blue.

The smoke is north of Castle Canyon, just inside the Park boundary. We can see streamers of smoke on the ridge. Grass Canyon is heavy with cold fog; waterdogs move like squirrels among the trees; the grass is coated with dampness, and wet pine needles glisten in reds and oranges. By the time we reach the boundary we are soaked. Brushing against tree branches shakes down cascades of suspended rainwater. I have a poncho, Tom does not. Our boots are saturated.

The fire is small, wholly contained within the lightning scar of a green ponderosa. We need only drop the tree so that the part of the twisting scar which actually contains the fire faces the sky. Hidden, the fire will build up heat and gradually worm through the log and enter the surrounding, drying landscape, but exposed, the fire will go out. The work goes quickly.

Tom is at the end of his rookie year. He arrived with tie-dyed bell-bottom pants, floppy hair, sandals, and a belief that firefighting was a team sport, but without cheerleaders, like soccer. But he has learned quickly, the SWFFs like him, and he is a natural athlete. He will return next season. Before we hike back to the pumper I cut holes in a plastic garbage bag for arms and head and have Tom wear the bag as a raincoat.

The sky clears, and the night, frosted with stars, turns cold as quartz. The main haul road takes us near the Conoco station in V. T. Park, and we stop for a snack. Tom chews a candy bar and grips a coffee cup while the Milky Way arches over us like a plume.

Smokechasing with Bone

Bone spots a faint drift of smoke.

He stops the pumper, gets out to check the wind direction—light from the southwest—and points the pumper in that direction. The pine forest is open, if rocky, and the old fireroad to Cape Final is irrelevant. Bone steers through and around some outcrops, bypasses a large downed ponderosa, and, with supreme indifference, passes over the trace of the old road. His net draws closer. Cape Final is the conclusion to a blunt peninsula, and there is no escape. "Get out and swamp," he tells the fern feeler with him. He is met with bewilderment and orders the fern feeler to take the wheel—"Drive like you're walking on eggs," he says with disgust—and seizes a pulaski. What I wouldn't give for a Longshot, he thinks, but everyone else is on a fire, or on his way to a fire. He pauses and scans the forested horizon, then treads,

light as a long hunter, through the wood. He will track the smoke to
Chuar Butte if necessary.

The fire, of course, is the easy part. Hot-spotting is just common
sense, and even line construction is obvious—drudgery disguised by
adrenaline. The early fire is the fun part of being a Longshot. Spot the
flames and smoke through tall timber. Scout pine and fir reproduction
as they flare like blowtorches. Watch the snags belch smoke and
embers and bellow with hollow growls. Call for help. Spray dirt with
shovels; crash through half-rotted logs with pulaskis; scrape against
rock and soil with McLeods and shovels. Slap down a flame here.
Scratch a line there. Burn out over here. Listen to the rumble of an
unseen air tanker just above the trees, and watch as the slurry descends
in a pink cloud or a spray or a clump to coat, wash, or smash through
the scene. Chain-saw through thickets, over logs, into snags. Cry out
alarms and insults, cough through clouds of smoke, and gasp for
breath in the foul air and against the tug of pack straps. Move; move
on; and move again, while the air is frantic with shouts and the noise
of flames, aircraft, chain saws, pumps, clanging tools, and dull slaps of
dirt. Anyone can like that. Almost everyone can suppress a fire with a
little training; even tourists put out campfires daily. And after smokechasing and hot-spotting are done, fires belong to hotshots and big
shots, not Longshots.

What takes instinct, and what shows character, are smokechasing
and mop-up. What makes a Longshot is knowing how to get to fires
and how to leave them. That can't be taught. It is learned by example.
It is learned by doing and by perseverance. Nothing can happen until
there are fires and the fires are found; that is the most important lesson
a Longshot can learn. Finding your fire may take hours, maybe days.
Sometimes it seems to take years.

Bone turns down the volume of his radio and smiles. The bust is
insane. Leo and John-Boy are cautiously feeling their way through the
Asbestos Forest, stumbling over downed timber, with rolls of flagging
in their teeth and another mile, at least, to go. Pferd and Dean from
Mars have rushed their attack, missed their fire altogether, and hauled

themselves up a distant empty ridge; now Pferd is climbing a tree to see where they are. Rich and Kenny are executing a bizarre mating dance with Recon 1, neither able to see, only to hear, the other, and now recon has apparently lost not only the two smokechasers but their smoke as well, and vapidly flaps its wings over Walhalla. Charlie and Dash are incommunicado—or just plain lost, their radio 10-7 somewhere in the Forest. But he, Bone, and this miserable fern feeler have spotted smoke.

His senses alert—eyes darting for a patch of grey, nose sensitized to the acrid odor of woodsmoke, ears poised for a telltale crack or hiss—Bone waves to the fern feeler to shut off the engine and wait. Gripping his pulaski like a rifle, he stalks on.

The forest dries, and lost smokes clamor for attention.

Early Tuesday morning a smoke is reported along E-1, atop the high ridge that segregates E-1 from Fuller Canyon. Mac and B. Gray park the blue pumper along the entrance road and begin the brutal hike in, first along the open meadows, then up the tangled forest floors, still wet and slippery, that mantle the monstrous ridges. The smoke column spirals up like incense, above the ridges, and they can see it from the road. Mac is convinced that they should be able to hike directly to it by sight. But once into the woods, they can see nothing. They return to the pumper, take a bearing on the smoke, and compass blindly into the burn. B. Gray mutters under his breath and trudges mindlessly on—a fire drone, soon to depart the Rim forever.

The fire consists of a flaming, gigantic ponderosa. Fire entered it, however, from an adjacent, lightning-shattered aspen, and not until the fire smoldered away from the aspen and entered the pine was there anything to see. With the ground wet, the fire will not spread easily, so Mac prepares to drop the snag along its lean. An ember, however, floats into B. Gray's eye, and Mac requests help. It takes a small corps to transport B. Gray, temporarily sightless, back to the Area, and Wil remains with Mac on the fire. Already the smoke is fast disappearing in the damp air.

Shortly after lunch another smoke is reported in the vicinity of Uncle Jim Point. Duane and Uncle Jimmy set out on the trail. Meanwhile, I take a compass bearing from TT-1; then E.B. and I drive to the Lodge parking lot, where there is a small nature shelter. There I take another bearing. The parking lot is full of people, who happily ignore us and the smoke. The Lodge and ranger station are far enough apart, and Uncle Jim Point is close enough, that the two sightings can be crossed with some accuracy. The fire, we estimate, is about a quarter mile north from the point. I radio that information to Duane and Uncle Jimmy, who quickly locate the Avuncular fire. The source tree, it seems, long ago tumbled over and burned to ash—patches of white powder with bony chunks of charcoal scattered in a feeble outline like a rudely barbecued skeleton.

The days are warm and dry, and the Rim, shaking off the massive storm, edges into Indian summer. We spend Wednesday checking the two fires and reconditioning our gear. The rangers, too, are roused to life. Two hikers have failed to close out their hiking permit to Thunder River. The rangers tentatively organize for a search and want to know if they can use Recon 1. The hikers' vehicle, Recon 1 reports, is at the trailhead. The hikers are still in the Thunder River area.

In midafternoon, Recon 1 sights two smokes, both within the Park, in the vicinity of the Saddle Mountain Burn. The two fires are within an air mile of each other, and we send two crews. One fire is possibly accessible by pumper; the other, only by foot. But Recon 1, impatient with our progress and eager to search the Rim for yet more smokes, confuses the two crews and the two fires. Uncle Jimmy and E.B.—their fire maps spread over the hood of the pumper—are given directions for a hike into the Iron Triangle, while Wil and I are told to drive the Three-quarter Ton a hundred yards into a fire that is in fact a mile and a half away. By the time the confusion is recognized, by the time we each return to our vehicles and start over, hours have passed. Uncle Jimmy and E.B. drop the source snag, hose down the ground fire, clear away some brush, and depart in good conscience. Wil and I, however, discover a large, long-smoldering burn in mixed conifer in which fire has crept extensively around the moist forest floor. There are active flames only on the large logs, and small branch wood carries the fire down into the deeper layers of duff; but mop-up will take hours. It may take all night. Sometime around midnight, unrequested but welcome, Uncle Jimmy and E.B. follow our trail of flags into the fire to help mop up.

Shortly after dawn Thursday, Scenic Airlines reports a smoke on Swamp Ridge. The Kid and Duane hike south from the Swamp Point road on a casual compass bearing suggested by Recon 1 before they arrived. When they reach the Rim and find nothing, they invite Recon 1 to try again. Contact is difficult. They try to locate each other by sound, then with a smoke grenade, then with the compass as a signal mirror. Finally they move to an outcrop projecting onto the Rim itself. This time they are marched back another half mile to a knoll of mature ponderosa flooded with a messy understory of white fir. There a few logs burn, while a huge smoking snag reaches to the sky like a colossal, supplicating hand sculpted out of black granite.

There are more smokes on the Rim; we know it in our bones.

The Thunder River search gears up incrementally. The rangers have designated some ground parties to hike the trail and request 210 for aerial observation. There is not much more we can do to help. The similarities between a search and a fire are superficial, all in the area of logistics. There is a rhythm to firefighting, a sequence of steps from first report to extinction, that is not true of a search. It is hard to say when a search starts and when it concludes. Even as it begins, a "missing" hiker may have already reappeared home, or taken a detour and forgotten to close out a permit, or be dead. A search can end instantly— or never. The missing person may never be found. A fire does not know it is being searched for.

On the Rim, fire is endemic, persistent, natural; the smokes from the Labor Day storm are pursued—make themselves available for pursuit—because they are evolutionary and ecological survivors. We come and go, we are found and lost; but the fires are eternal, and each fire creates the circumstances for more fires. Lost persons are, almost by definition, not native to the area. They are visitors and transients, usually lost in the Canyon, who must relate to the River, not the Rim. They look for water, not fire. Steadily the rangers gear up. We lend them canteens, batteries, assorted supplies. No one in the hikers' families has heard from them.

At midmorning on Friday another smoke is sighted, in the great wasteland north of The Basin and west of Lindbergh Hill. There is no obvious access, not even a helispot. Eric and Dana pause for a minute by the W-1 junction. If they drive to Lindbergh Hill, they will have an easy route in— all downhill. But they will have an equally difficult hike out, and they will have to depend on sophisticated compassing and flagging. There is no shortcut. They decide to take the long walk across The Basin to Robber's Roost Spring; from there they can call upon Recon I for a compass bearing, and they can use the spring to fill up fedcos. Still, they will require several hours just to reach the fire, another hour to drop the snag, many more hours to mop up even if the duff is wet. They place frozen rib steaks in their firepacks. Deep in the Plateau they will rely on the surface drainages, however deranged, to position themselves. When they get hungry, they will build a fire and roast their steaks —the Ribsteak fire. They can follow the drainages back, even at night.

The search moves into high gear. The Park brings in dogs and trackers, flies the Esplanade with two helos, and fields half a dozen ground teams. One party discovers a track; another, an empty canteen. The searchers locate a pack, with a note pinned to it that reads "Keep looking. Please." The signs, the presumed track across the red rock, appear to be heading for the springs. The field parties use channel 2, avoiding the Park repeater, so we hear nothing of what transpires. The lead party located a second pack. The helos and ground teams and dogs converge south of Monument Point. Then a smoke is reported "near Point Sublime."

The fire is pinpointed by Recon 1 in the northeast quarter of Section 29. It is not only adjacent to the Sublime Road, within sight of the Rim, but inside an old burn. Wil and I take the blue pumper and locate the fire—an archetypal snag fire—without difficulty. Everything around is burned out. The scene is surreal, as though from some ancient, fire-swept world. The source tree is a green ponderosa with a huge catface at the base, probably a result of the previous burn. There are no surface fuels to spread the fire, which sizzles within the lightning scar like a suppressed scream. If the smoke were anywhere else, we might have taken days to find it. The Dream fire.

Wil cranks up the slip-on and hoses down the burning cavities as I prepare to fell the snag. McLaren, acting as an aerial observer in 210, flies over our position. Do we need any assistance? he asks kindly. No, we reply, we have located the fire. "We found those two hikers," he continues, impassive and calm. "They were both dead."

As the crews return, we gather at the cache. There is much to do. Our firepacks and the pumpers are half empty; old tools and disassembled saws cry out for repair; and the crew, fatigued from long nights, is starting to show wear. The spare ration bin is cleaned out. Every sleeping bag is dirty. Ranger King stops by to return some borrowed quart canteens and headlamps. Compulsively, helplessly, he talks about the search.

The hikers, it seems, tried everything. They even ignited some signal fires—clumps of bunch grass, a pinyon. But they were outside the fire regimes of the Rim, and it would have required an incredible coincidence for the pulse of smoke to have been sighted. No one saw anything, and the two hikers knew it. They apparently died from falls sustained during a desperate attempt to scramble down the Redwall to the water they saw but could not reach. They were probably dead before the search began.

When I close my eyes that night, I see the Dream fire. I see a bright small flame along the Rim. On one side is Canyon, dark and bottomless, and on the other, a fire-gutted forest.

Point Sublime: Noon
Sublime is empty.

The atmosphere is ideal—clear and dry, too warm for a jacket and too cool to strip off a fireshirt. A few stray cumuli drift across the Canyon, but otherwise the scene is an aching, royal blue. Jack and I

take our sack lunches from the pumper, grab a canteen, and proceed to
a pinyon, on the west side of the Point, which has shaded generations
of Longshots. We hang the canteen from a broken limb. In the noon
sunlight, even at this time of year, everything is bleached and distinct
in the cloudless sky. We munch on some cans of ration crackers salvaged from the recent fires. After a while it becomes a trifle cool under
the shaded pinyon, and we want to see the rest of Sublime, so we
shuffle over to the very tip of the Point. Heat radiates from the limestone rocks. We lean against some large boulders. When I look down,
I have the sensation that I am soaring.

The mind drifts.

The revelation of the Canyon began when Captain Cardenas of the
Coronado Expedition visited the South Rim, probably near Desert
View, in 1540 and tried to reach the River. He was followed by the
Franciscan missionary Father Garcés, who inspected the Havasupai
Indians in the 1770s while en route to the Hopi mesas. But nothing
permanent came of either visit.

Stories were propagated by American trappers, however, about a
"Big Canyon" on the Colorado River of the West, and during the Utah
War of 1857–58 the Army Corps of Topographical Engineers spon-
sored an expedition up the Colorado River that crashed a steamboat at
Black Canyon, traveled down Diamond Creek into the gorge of the
western Grand Canyon, then visited the Havasupais and exited along
the South Rim. The Ives Expedition, whose report was published in
1861, communicated the first images of the Canyon—mostly those of
the inner gorge—to Western civilization. Further exploration was
thwarted by the Civil War.

Then came John Wesley Powell. A former major under Grant, Powell
piloted a handful of wooden dories down the Colorado from Green
River, Wyoming, to Pierces Ferry, Nevada, in 1869. His was the first
authenticated descent through what Powell called the "Grand
Canyon," and his account of the adventure, *Exploration of the Colorado
River of the West*, made Powell's reputation, catapulted him into
national prominence as a scientific administrator, and established a

genre of river writing that has never been surpassed. On the basis of his
exploits, Powell organized the Geographical and Geological Survey of
the Rocky Mountain Region. Not to be outdone, the peacetime Army
tried to recapture its glory days by sponsoring the Geographical and
Geological Survey West of the Hundredth Meridian under Lieutenant
George Wheeler. Wheeler confronted Powell head-on in 1871 by trying
to take small boats up the gorges of the Colorado, much in the manner
of Ives, and succeeded in getting some of his party to Diamond Creek.
There Wheeler's explorers exited, carrying away visions of Army glory
along with their baggage train.

The future lay with Powell. Within a year he organized a second trip
down the River. This time, buffeted by high spring floods, the party
departed the western Canyon at Kanab Creek. Powell subsequently
established a base camp at Kanab and inaugurated the scientific inventory of the region. Most of the creators of the Grand Canyon as a cultural phenomenon—as an exemplar of geology, as romantic earth
biography, as an icon of American nationalism—were associated with
Powell or his survey or its institutional successor, the U.S. Geological
Survey. Through them the Canyon was introduced to, and preserved by,
American intellectual culture. Photographers like Timothy O'Sullivan,
E. O. Beaman, William Henry Jackson, and Jack Hillers; artists like
Thomas Moran, fresh from his glorious canvasses of the Yellowstone,
and William Henry Holmes, a genius in the metamorphosis of topo-
graphic illustration into art; cartographers, like Amon Thompson; geol-
ogists, like Clarence Dutton, on loan from the Army, and G. K. Gilbert,
willingly shanghaied from the Wheeler Survey; artist-historians, like
Frederick Dellenbaugh—all contributed; and their collective masterpiece, *Tertiary History of the Grand Canyon District*, did for the genre of
Rim writing what Powell's *Exploration* did for the genre of river writing.

The climax of the book was set at Point Sublime. There Dutton
summarized the geologic evolution of the Canyon and traced the
evolution of a scenic day. When intellectuals traveled to the Grand
Canyon, however, they generally went to the North Rim. The North
Rim brought the Grand Canyon into high culture. Later visitors, like

the quietly influential Charles Walcott, also followed Powell's direc-
tions to the North Rim—in Walcott's case, to the Nankoweap Basin.
Collectively they established the parameters of our understanding of
Rim, River, and Canyon.

What has changed since then is the relative importance of high culture and popular culture and the significance of North Rim and South.
Originally the Rim (and Canyon) were more accessible through the
Mormon settlements of Utah than through an Arizona populated
largely by hostile Indians. The Colorado River did not join the two
rims but segregated them, and until the 1890s, the North Rim was the
more prominent. Then came the transcontinental railroads. With the
construction of the Atchison, Topeka & Santa Fe Railroad through
Flagstaff, the tourist connection to the Canyon rapidly shifted from the
North Rim to the South; Baedeker advised tourists to take the railroad
to Flagstaff, then a stage to the South Rim; even Powell and Gilbert
directed the 1894 International Geological Congress, on tour of the
United States, to the South Rim, along rail lines. When Moran returned
to make the Canyon a central icon of his landscape art, he did so under
commission from the Santa Fe Railroad and he painted from the South
Rim. When President Teddy Roosevelt in 1903 proclaimed the Canyon
a national treasure, "the one great sight every American should see," he
did so on the steps of the luxury hotel the El Tovar, positioned between
the Rim and a new railroad terminus at Grand Canyon Village. Paved
highways followed the railroad routes. Not until the late 1920s, after
the construction of Rainbow Bridge, was it possible to drive from South
Rim to North without crossing the Colorado River by ferry. During the
1920s, too, under the See America First campaign, the National Park
Service actively promoted automobile traffic to the parks. Automobile
tourism massed at the South Rim, and Park politics, then as now, followed the visitor. The process of intellectual assimilation began on the
River and on the North Rim, but popular culture clustered on the
macadamized roads and overlooks of the South. There the Park established its headquarters.

The geomorphic differences between the two rims are pronounced.

The bulk of the Kaibab Plateau lies to the north of the River, and most of the Canyon's expansion comes from its erosion. The South Rim is folded into gentle waves; the North Rim is gouged into retreating peninsulas that leave in their wake strings of decaying buttes and mesas. The difference in elevation between Bright Angel Point on the North Rim and Grand Canyon Village on the South is over twelve hundred feet. But here geography fails as a guide to bureaucracy. Politically, it is the South Rim that looks down upon the North. The superintendent of Grand Canyon is, in reality, the CEO of the South Rim.

On the north side, there is simply too much Rim and too few tourists. It is too removed from major thoroughfares, its entrance a dead-end road, not a side street on the way to Los Angeles or Las Vegas. With the exception of Cape Royal, the North Rim's grand overlooks are too remote for heavy tourist visitation. There is too little Canyon, too little River, and too few people. While Point Sublime is open to the public, its perspective is, as Dutton made clear, to an intellectual Canyon.

The advent of the wilderness movement altered the balance of power within the Park, but not to the advantage of the North Rim. Joseph Wood Krutch's book *Grand Canyon: Today and All Its Yesterdays* (1958) reestablished the liaison between Canyon and a vigorous intellectual culture for the first time since Dutton and Powell. By appealing to the concept of wilderness, Krutch redefined the place of the Canyon in the moral geography of American civilization. The new associations were needed to make up for the old ones that had been lost. The Canyon's status as an exemplar of earth science had eroded badly as new conceptions of geologic time evolved, as new theories like plate tectonics directed scientific attention to other phenomena, and as a new era of exploration returned images of Antarctica, the deep oceans, the outer planets and their moons. Symbolically, the publication of Krutch's book coincided with the International Geophysical Year, which effectively announced that new era of exploration and planetary science.

When high culture and popular culture converged again on the Canyon, as they did during the dam controversies of the 1960s, the

River, not the Rim, became the object of attention, and the Canyon became synonymous with the River. By then the Park bureaucracy was firmly ensconced on the South Rim, and what made the River important was not its idea—its wilderness penumbra—but the phenomenal explosion of tourists attracted to it, the advent of mass tourism by raft, and the promulgation of popular literature, movies, and television images. The dialogue between North and South became a trilogue among North Rim, South Rim, and River. South Rim and River grew at the expense of the North Rim.

We as Longshots know the intellectual Canyon poorly, but we are encouraged by the example of Dutton—Dutton of the North Rim. He knew that the Canyon did not have to be transcribed into words but only interpreted. He knew that to be understood, it had to be absorbed into American civilization and that intellectuals would have to do that job because the folk—the usual frontier pioneers—were not present. He knew that appreciation would have to be cultivated by linkages with the literary, scientific, artistic, and esthetic canons of the day. This was done. The Canyon became an icon of American civilization, and its discovery a major event in cultural history. When in the mid-twentieth century linkages to the universe of Herbert Spencer, Alexander von Humboldt, and Captain Clarence Dutton became irrelevant, new linkages had to be forged, and with often dramatic effect they were.

Yet all this was, finally, an agenda for tourists and intellectual transients. It was a means by which to communicate understanding to those who did not live there—by which a civilization with its origins elsewhere in very different times and places could relate to the Canyon. Idea had to substitute for experience. As it became vulgarized, image— mass-produced and industrially uniform—substituted for idea. But we live on the Rim. We see the Canyon daily, not as an exotic spectacle but as a reference point, an informing presence. We know it by its sensory impressions.

We know it through fire, and we understand fire in such elemental terms as dirt, water, winds, needles, trees, rocks, sod, duff, punk, sun, clouds. We talk about fires in terms of very mundane natural phenomena and unencumbered human relationships. We know the lunar cycle because it governs the caliber of evening light. We know storm patterns because they bring lightning and rain. We know tree types and biotas and soils, all of which control what kind of fire burns and what kind of mop-up is demanded. We know that the forest cover shields fires from the wind, because we hear the wind in the canopy and don't feel it on the ground. We know that the ponderosa pine enjoys a peculiar symbiosis with fire, because we find most of our fires among the pines. We know about the strange hydrology of the Kaibab because we have to carry water to drink and to put out fires. We understand the differential between Rim and River because River trips, not Strip trips, are used as rewards. We appreciate the distinction between Rims, because we live on one and are governed by the other. We know the Canyon through its fires and its influence on Rim fires, and we know from painful experience that Plateau and Canyon don't mix. Smokey's Third Rule (Canyon corollary): Keep your fire on the Rim. It is good firefighting but bad politics.

You don't have to know very much to be a Longshot. Most of the crew have some college education, and a few possess advanced degrees; but they leave their academic learning at the entrance station. The chief mental requirement for a good firefighter is resourcefulness; the chief physical attribute, stamina. Two or three seasons are enough to master the basic lore of firefighting. Good fires have ample dirt, easily scraped duff, clean-burning needles, simple access, working saws and radios, unrotted snags. Bad fires do not. In their detail and particularities, fires are infinite, and as a scientific problem, tremendously complex and abstruse. But there is a difference between knowing and doing. While fire in the abstract is not easily knowable, firefighting on the North Rim is. While the North Rim may not be easily assimilated by intellectual systems, it is completely livable. While the Canyon cannot perhaps be described, it can be experienced. We understand the idea of wilderness because it affects the way we fight fire. We experience the particulars and know the generalities through them. Like the Canyon, those ideas are not always seen but are always there.

We know why artists and scientists were drawn to Point Sublime, because we are, too. Point Sublime is to the Canyon what The Basin is to the Plateau. Ironically, it is hostile to the most important contemporary idea about the Canyon—wilderness. Sublime's road denies the western Rim legal status as wilderness, and there is no direct connection from the Point to the all-defining River. You can see Boucher Rapids from Point Sublime, but there are no trails to the River from the Point. Point Sublime is not on the way to anywhere else. You have to go to Sublime for itself.

Point Sublime is the ultimate overlook, the ideal and most challenging vantage point for a Canyon tourist. But for someone who lives on the Rim, it offers an incomplete experience. The Canyon needs sense as well as ideation. The scene needs shadows and clouds and smoke as well as sunlight. Sublime is a place to visit, and we come often; it is not a place to live. We want instead that restless, tidal tension. Sublime can be too idealized. Sublime in the noonday sun blinds and bleaches. We want a place with fire. We want the Rim.

Jack and I startle awake.

Perhaps there has been chatter on the radio, or some biological clock has sounded an alarm that lunch is over, or we unconsciously hear the whine of a distant tourist flight through Muav Saddle. We blink in the sunlight. Jack points skyward. Overhead three turkey vultures circle lazily in the thermals. We gather our trash and, stiff-legged, walk back to the pumper.

The smoke is sighted early Saturday morning—a big smoke, near Tiyo. Barbara Red Butte gives a 15 degree azimuth. Recon 1 will be delayed, so we quickly sharpen some spare saw chains, fill some extra canteens with oil, toss a few extra handtools onto the pumpers, and replenish the slip-on tanks. As Recon 1 lifts off, we head for Tiyo.

Everyone goes. Recon 1 reports that the fire is near the junction of W-1D and the old W-1D-B. It is about three acres in size and spreading steadily. I take Uncle Jimmy, and outfitted with packs and handtools we start out on a loose compass bearing for the fire. Dana will follow and flag a proper route. The fire is only a couple of hundred yards distant, and with a little saw work we should be able to bring in the pumpers. For now we hot-spot and scout the fire. We'll need help.

I request some reserves and the water truck. McLaren informs us that there is an air tanker at Prescott, and we take the hint. "Send it." Dana arrives with the rest of the regulars. We organize into two small squads and begin putting in scratch lines around the fastest-spreading heads. In places the needles and duff are too thick to scrape with a McLeod, so we trench with shovels. When the air tanker arrives, I have it split its load into two parts, one along each of the two most active fronts. Good drops; between the retardant and the scratch line we contain the fire. The cost of control, however—deferred for the moment—is that mop-up will be crummy, an unsavory mix of dense duff and slurry. We complete the scratch lines; then I send one squad back for the pumpers while the other improves the fireline, bucks up some heavy logs, and drops two burning snags. When controlled, the fire is about five acres in size, the biggest of the bust.

The reserves arrive later that morning, and I start them on line patrol and mop-up along the perimeter while we break for lunch. Most of us have not eaten today. There are signs of fatigue as the afternoon grades into an endless round of bottomless mop-up. For some it is time to end not only the bust but the season. The fire smolders uncontrollably just beneath the surface crust of retardant; its spread is marked by tiny vents of smoke, like fumaroles in the Valley of Ten Thousand Smokes, as though hundreds of cigarettes were buried within the needles. I release the reserves before dinner, and we continue to mop up until we exhaust the water in both our slip-ons and the water truck, then pack it in for the night. We reach the fire cache about 2100 hours and fill up the slip-ons and water truck before heading off to Skid Row. One slip-on is decommissioned with a broken drive belt.

When we depart the cache early the next day, maintenance insists that one of its operators drive the water truck—easy overtime for a Sunday—and we agree. Ross has some fire experience. No amount of OT, however, will tempt the Park mechanic to search through his supply of fan belts for the other slip-on. No matter, only one pumper crew will go early. The others we leave behind to recondition equipment and make a quick inventory of the fire cache; they can join us at the Tiyo fire in a couple of hours. The fire itself is a landscape of small smokes—loose, disorganized, smoldering. Wil scrapes together enough embers and branches for a small campfire and heats some water for coffee.

Mop-up continues with what might be termed professional resignation. It has to be done, and even as the morning sun heats the ground, the smokes diminish. It is with some surprise, then, that we hear from Barbara Red Butte around noon that she has a smoke in sight at approximately 14 degrees azimuth. McLaren interrupts to observe that this is probably the Tiyo fire. An hour later, as the smoke grows, Red Butte wants to know how much smoke our fire is putting up. We can't see a flame anywhere and are only a couple of hours away from complete extinguishment. Not much, we tell Red Butte. "Then you have another fire," she announces.

McLaren sees it as soon as he lifts off the helipad at the South Rim. The fire is burning on the long peninsula, flanked by Rim on both sides, that ultimately converges at Point Sublime. We leave Ross on the Tiyo fire, request that someone be sent to help him baby-sit the final embers, and take off with a roar. Phlegmatic, imperturbable McLaren has found an edge to his voice. He calls for an air tanker, but the nearest available ship is in Boise and cannot arrive for several hours. I mention the busted fan belt on the slip-on. "Tell me what size you want, and I'll get it from the South Rim," he says. Lookouts from Kendricks Peak to Dry Park call in the smoke. We request Forest Service assistance, and the North Kaibab mobilizes two engine crews. We request all the North Rim reserves that can be rounded up. McLaren drops a fan belt to us from the helicopter as we pause near a clearing on the Sublime Road. This, I think in a glow of adrenaline, this is what it is all about. And it is about all we are good for.

The fire is about fifteen acres, burning parallel with a ridgetop, and it has already started a one-acre spot fire perhaps one hundred fifty feet ahead of the flaming front. The ridge—steep and rocky on its southern exposure—trends southwest to northeast. By the time we make a quick reconnaissance the Forest Service has arrived. Red Butte must have reported the smoke on the Forest radio net to its dispatcher, and the crews probably started toward the Park before we officially requested them. We divide the fire into two sectors. Park crews will work the south; Forest crews, the north. There is not much to do but cut line where it can be most easily done, then burn out. More reserves will arrive within an hour. The air tanker should arrive within two.

I flag a proposed line, then double back past the Perk crew and begin burning out with a fusee. McLaren hovers overhead in 210, injecting a note of calmness and curiosity. The burnout along the flanks proceeds well. The Park crews pull back from the Sublime fire; our line is relatively straight, short, and rapid through pockets of light fuel. The Forest crews work much closer. They crowd the fire's flank, putting in a line on the steep shoulder of the ridge. There will be problems with rolling firebrands later, I think; better if they sacrificed some acres and put the fireline on the other side of a shallow draw to the north; the draw would act as a ditch to catch even rolling logs. But it is too late now. Burning out along the head of the fire is touchy. Trees torch, and we finesse the burnout by backing the fire against strong, dry winds. Several spot fires flare up, but at last we tie our lines together. We let our backfire and the wildfire burn into each other and watch for new spots. When the two fires meet, there is a rush of wind. The Kid finds one spot, and Uncle Jimmy another. Yet we are winning. Then we hear the roar.

The air tanker, a B-17—not expected for another hour: it appears that BIFC dispatchers have forgotten again that Arizona stays on mountain standard time—is sighted through the trees. We have no communications with it whatsoever. We expect that it will make a dry run, establish contact, then return for a precision drop. Instead, the slurry spills out of the fuselage, and we hit the ground. The retardant atomizes and settles over the fire in a pink fog. It knocks out our backfire. Then, as suddenly as it appeared, the plane vanishes. It is too late for another drop today, and the plane heads for Cedar City.

We improve our lines, complete some burnout, and note danger spots. There are a couple of snags on the northeast corner that are too broken to fell safely. The BI arrives, and we send him to where he can watch the burning snags. Finally we break for dinner. The fire is contained. We estimate its size at sixty to seventy acres; the perimeter fireline is more than a mile long.

Most of the reserves want to return to the Area. Stay for a couple more hours, I plead, then we will release you. Reluctantly they agree. The Forest Service wants to remain as long as possible. Someone remembers the BI, and we find him asleep by the snags and send him home with the reserves. As regulars, of course, we will remain all night—some on patrol, the rest to sleep. Around midnight we release the Forest Service.

For the next three days we mop up the Sublime fire. For a while we think we have discovered a way to get pumpers to the fireline, but we dent one vehicle and abandon the scheme. Instead, we lay hose up the ridge from the Sublime Road. We request reserves to assist with mop-up—so vast is the fire—and we get some. There is even a hot meal from the Lodge. Each night after the first we leave a couple of Longshots on the fire, while the rest of us return to the Area. Our exhilaration fades. We are exhausted; our equipment is a mess; the cache is almost unusable; one slip-on is dented, and the other disabled; we are down to two cases of C rations. But we need only one more day to finish the Sublime fire and wrap up the season. The fire and accident reports should keep us busy for the rest of the month. Uncle Jimmy reminds us that we have yet to recheck the old fires. But we are thinking about big paychecks and big replacement orders. The fire will allow us to restock the cache over the winter.

It is time to think beyond this season.

Mopping Up; or, Tell Me Again When It Is *Really* Over

Uncle Jimmy has a fedco, and Eric a shovel. Eric digs up a chunk of duff, and Uncle Jimmy sprays it, while Eric flips the duff over, chops it into pieces, and mixes it with dirt. Then he digs up another chunk, and Uncle Jimmy sprays that. Wil has only a shovel. He pushes it into the ground with his boot—good, well-drained soil here—bends over to lift up the shovel head, turns it over, and chops with it as though he were churning butter. A small smoke spirals upward from the pile. He repeats his actions, then he digs the shovel into the ground exactly adjacent to it and begins all over again. Tim attempts, with negligible success, to do the same thing with a pulaski, using the grub end to lift and the ax and grub ends alternately to chop and stir. With shovels Duane and I scrape smoldering leaders of fire from unburned duff—in effect, installing scores of small, internal firelines within the general perimeter of the fire. The smoldering sections are piled, then spaded into holes. "Dirt," Wil yells, "is better than water." Uncle Jimmy answers back that "water is better than dirt." But Dana can stand no more of either. With a shout he masses a hundred square feet of smoking duff into a great mound and ignites the pile with a fusee. The pile refuses to flame. Instead, it billows in great puffs of acrid smoke that spread over the fire like smog.

The hardest part of controlling a snag fire is finding it, but the hardest part of suppressing a fire is mopping it up. It is one thing to know how to get to a fire, and something else to know how and when to leave it. Only a small fraction of a fire burns within the flaming front; most of a forest's fuels are consumed by a disorganized medley of flaming and smoldering combustion after the front has passed. A fire is not out until the fire in the duff is out. It is not a lesson anyone wants to hear, and one only a small minority learn.

There are some places where the surface fuels are light and burnout is more or less complete; grass and brush are like this. Almost universally, however, the North Rim has a heavy mat of semidecomposed humus, fresh needles, and windfallen branches, even whole trees that can burn for days. There are places, too, where standards for mop-up are lax, where the dull, meticulous labors of mopping up acres of smokes are superseded by a loosely conducted "patrol." The South Rim favors this approach and flaunts it before

North Rimmers. But the consequences of leaving unburned fuels and pockets of combustion untouched are generally unpleasant. It may mean continual observation or incessant, casual mop-up for a crew; it may mean that those who return to inspect the fire must mop up for those who first abandoned it; or it may mean that the fire flares up or even escapes. On the North Rim our standards are simple: we mop up to the last smoke, and we return twenty-four hours after the last smoke to check the burn before officially calling the fire out.

As a result, we know the duff better than any other part of the Rim forest. The humid understory of the spruce-fir forest has the worst duff. Short needles refuse to fluff into deep, porous fuelbeds so that sustained flaming combustion is replaced by a malingering, creeping process of glowing combustion. Recently cast needles are covered with a cobweb of fine branches. Underneath they do not rest upon mineral soil but intercalate with rocks and the stringy lignin residue of largely decomposed trees; organic soil replaces mineral soil. Fires tend to be large in area and low in intensity—a hundred square feet of flame and four acres of mop-up. The real fuelbed in spruce-fir is the tree canopy, and high-intensity fires are invariably crown fires. Without copious quantities of water, mop-up in spruce-fir, or in most mixed conifer, is interminable.

By contrast, ponderosa pine has deeper, more sharply defined fuelbeds of long needles that support flaming combustion. The deep duff, moreover, is layered. The boundary between duff and mineral soil is sometimes sharply drawn, but above the soil there is a shallow layer of finely ground needles, an organic powder that can, improbably, carry glowing combustion. Then come several layers of needles, progressively decomposing and compacting like the transformation of snow into firn. Near the surface, small branches interweave with the duff, and on the surface are windfall and fresh needle cast. Each of these layers has a different fuel moisture, and each may burn out of sync with the others. The ways in which wet and dry fuels may combine to burn are endless. Only during intense droughts is the entire duff equally dry.

There are many techniques for extinguishing all smokes, but a good strategy is to begin with the large fuels and work down. Drop any burning snags and protect dead, as-yet-unburned snags by scraping a fireline around them. Break up the big burning logs into small pieces, chop out fire and embers, cool each piece with dirt or water, and toss it into a cleared zone, a boneyard. That sweeps the fire of everything but duff. Isolate the burned from the unburned duff. Then mix the burned duff with equal parts of dirt, water, and sweat. Spade it over, spray it, dump, chop, and mix; then begin again; and again. Divide the fire into sectors, and force crewmen to stay in their sector until every smoke is extinguished. For prolonged mop-up, bring in extra crewmen. Wait twenty minutes from the last smoke until you abandon the fire. Typically, some canteens or a fedco and a few handtools are left behind. Then return twenty-four hours later to inspect the burn, remove the remaining tools, and pull the flagging. When you return, write up the fire report: draw a map, code the fire behavior data, narrate the events. The fire is not over until its report has been filed. The pen is mightier than the pulaski.

In practice, everyone has his own favorite technique. The simplest and most direct approach is usually, in the long run, the surest. But one way or another, mop-up has to be done. That may take a long time. It takes patience to outwait fire. Duff is deep and complex, like memory. You just can't abandon a fire after hot-spotting or lining it. Worst of all is to bury it. Better to let a fire flame on and watch it in casual patrol, or indifferently tinker with this smoking duff pile or that, than to bury it and leave. A fire can smolder under dirt or retardant or wet needles for days. It can smolder for years.

Dana, Eric, Duane, Tim, Wil, Uncle Jimmy, and I have been mopping up for three days now, and each day has been slower than the last. Rather than fall back on basics, we are inspired by the tedium into innovations in the theory and practice of mop-up. We are becoming smoke-happy. When we close our eyes, we see tiny spirals of smoke. There are smokes everywhere; they emanate from tree trunks; they appear in our firepacks, sleeping bags, pumpers; they spiral insidiously out of every tiny mound of needles. We are haunted by infinitesimal smokes for which there is no escape and no limit.

Dana pounds his smoking mound with a shovel, and Eric joins him, while both scream incoherently. Uncle Jimmy's fedco leaks so badly his pants are soaked and become caked with ash, but when he looks down at his boots, he thinks he can see small smokes emerging from the eyelets. Wil sits down at the boneyard and stares toward the sun. If there are smokes in his sector, they will catch the light and be quickly apparent. One rises from the rotted log; another appears in a small hole where he had stirred dirt and duff. He sighs and drags himself to his feet. That night, as we bed down, the stars appear like white embers in a cosmic duff.

Dana is sure he sees a smoke emerging from Cassiopeia.

This should be our last day on the Sublime fire. Some pockets of duff remain on the far side, but with extra hose we hope to get close enough at least to fill up fedcos from the pumper without the half hour walk that has crippled us so far. Then the Park dispatcher reports that Scenic Airlines has sighted a smoke near Swamp Point. It seems impossible.

Its location is uncannily close to the site of the Back fire. Before we abandon the Sublime fire completely, we request that two reserves be sent out to watch; then we take the pumpers up the Sublime Road to W-4 and onto the Swamp Point road; we request Forest Service assistance; we order an air tanker; and we suggest to the BI—then, as always, back in the Area—that he order a hot meal from the Lodge. When we stop, our vehicles are next to the flagging of the Back fire, and the bearing that Recon 1 gives us to the Swamp fire is so close to the old route that we decide to follow the flags in. The Swamp fire is, in fact, exactly adjacent to the Back fire. A reburn or an independent start—we can't say. There is too much fire on the scene to worry at present about causes. Dispatch informs us that a C-119J will arrive within thirty minutes.

With saws we clear away a swath ahead of the active north flank— a volatile medley of snags, heavy fir reproduction, thick needles, and downed logs—then wait for the tanker. I tell the pilot to split his load four ways, one drop to each side of the fire. Then we back well off. After each load I rush in, assess the accuracy of the drop, inform the pilot where I want the next, and retreat. Each drop is exactly on target. The fire is contained. The slurry and heavy fuels will make for messy mop-up, but we are too fatigued—too high on adrenaline and momentum—to care much about the next day or even the coming night. It is enough that the fire is stopped. Two Forest Service engine crews arrive, and we cut line together. Before darkness deepens further, we drop a few snags and buck up some burning logs near the line. Tom locates some large pockets of soil along the fireline, and we excavate them for dirt and recycle them as boneyards. Several of the holes are knee-deep.

Then we retire to our packs—what passes for a fire camp—and to some food. There isn't much. We have a few spare cans of crackers and miscellaneous fruitcakes and nut rolls. The Forest Service crews share their rations, and we promise them a hot meal later. It has been a crazy, extraordinary bust, and we have gone far beyond our supplies, beyond what any of us has experienced before, beyond what any of us could have believed possible. In our exhaustion we begin to believe that we can go on—that we can extemporize—forever.

The Forest crews want to know more about the bust. Nothing so extensive has occurred in the Forest. Uncle Jimmy assumes patrol duties around the fireline. The conversation soon deteriorates into BI stories. We forget, for an instant, about the smoke in our headlamps, the cold wind and our aching, lifeless legs. The Forest crews cannot get enough, and they contribute some new stories. Neither side will concede the last word, so the pace of outrageous stories accelerates. In the distance we hear the scrape of tools as Uncle Jimmy methodically digs in one of the boneyards and throws dirt on a burning limb. The Forest crews want to know how Big Bob could have become an FMO, how the Park plans to build a future fire program. Fossey tells them the future can take care of itself and proceeds with another BI story. The laughter is infectious. Then we hear footsteps and see headlamps, and out of the smoke step the BI and a maintenance man with trays of hot food. Embarrassment hangs over the scene like smoke trapped under a morning inversion. "Thanks," Duane says meekly. The BI has already eaten, of course, so we suggest to him that he patrol the fireline. "Sure," he nods, his lower lip curled. "Right away." The food slacks our hunger, but not our sense of guilt. A few minutes later, some twenty yards away, we see the BI's headlamp disappear, accompanied by a shout, into one of the boneyard holes in the fireline. He never returns to camp.

There is nothing left but tedious mop-up, brutalizing in its simplicity, and it is pointless to keep a full crew all night. Without water, mop-up will be difficult, and this time we will have to stay with the fire to the last smoke. Yet we also need to rework the cache and recheck the other fires. All we require tonight is for someone to stay with the Swamp fire. Uncle Jimmy reappears and promptly volunteers.

He is the oldest of the Longshots and the least known beyond his life on the Rim. Wiry, indefatigable, compulsively enthusiastic, Uncle Jimmy seems to be in a state of suspended animation, growing older without aging. He is excitable and meticulous, ruthless in exercise, a good Longshot. He despises Big Bob. If he has plans for the winter, he has kept them to himself. He has told The Kid something about traveling around and maybe working part-time on the Forest and maybe learning a trade like carpentry. He once confided to Duane that he might have been better off to stay with the Army (he was a paratrooper), that his sergeant had told him he would never make it in civilian life. He was the first recruit this season, arriving in April, he will probably hang on as long as the fire account holds out this fall, and he has indicated that he can report next spring as soon as we can pay. Now he appears before us like some kind of fire gnome—haloed by a week's growth of beard grimy with ash and dirt, thick stringers of black hair tied with a bandanna around his forehead, bright eyes in a gaunt face. He has a sad, fanatical look. Like most of us, Uncle Jimmy does not want the bust to end. Unlike many, he cannot afford to have it end.

It is decided that the rest of us will retire to the Area, put the slipons and our gear in shape, and return to the Swamp fire in the morning.

Even if we rise early, however, so many things need to be reconditioned and so much time must be expended in the drive that we probably won't reappear until midmorning or later. That bothers Uncle Jimmy not in the slightest. He is poor with reports but good in the field. He obliterates a fire with meticulous attention, until nothing is left, because he knows there will always be—there have to be—more fires, another season. Besides, I remember, tomorrow is his lieu day. Overtime. The longer our delay, the larger his paycheck. When we leave we see Uncle Jimmy scrounging through the campsite, bustling like a shrew, hoarding unused ration cans.

We reach the fire cache shortly before midnight. For the next two days we recheck old fires and continue to dry-mop at Swamp. The days shorten and the nights turn cold with frost.

The bust is over.

Point Sublime: Sunset

The Tiyo fire, the Dream fire, the Sublime fire—we check them all, and there are no lingering smokes. Not enough of the workday remains to return to the cache before 1700 hours, but there is enough daylight left to drive to Sublime and watch the sunset. "Oh, hell," says Donnie. "Let's do it. Our time."

The afternoon clouds are breaking up, and a twilight wedge, still large and diffuse, begins to take shape. The wedge is more distinct in the autumn than in the summer because the air is cooler and more stable, and the refracted light is broken into strata. Our eyes rove restlessly over the panorama. Too often our view of sunsets away from the Area is compromised by our need to exploit every minute of sunlight to locate a fire or fell a snag—everything is refracted through the prism of fire. But now the fires are extinguished. Now we have the time to watch.

It is a complex and dynamic scene. The sunset is doubled: there is one to the east, with the sun, and one to the west, against it. Their effects are utterly different. One accents Canyon and light; the other, shadow and sky. The drama repeats daily, with the timeless play of dusty pale light on butte and mesa and gorge, with shadows washing through the Canyon like a tide. The rocks dull in intensity and brighten in color. The sky condenses from diffuse pastels into a brilliant wedge, compressed by an encroaching spectrum of blues—light blue at the horizon, and above that an immensely soothing royal blue, and finally a navy blue salted with early stars. Distant mountains are silhouetted in lavender, then blue.

We study both views, looking equally to past and to future. It is easier, however, to look back on a season, when everything that must happen has happened, than to stare at the sunlight with only hope to shield the eyes, and increasingly we look back. The Canyon fades before a murky, indistinct grey—the first in a sequence of shadow land-scapes. Shadows sweep over the Canyon in wave upon wave, each layer darker than the last, until the gorge is swallowed in blackness, and the final drama transfers to the sky. The darkness grows; the wedge shrinks. Orange fades to lemon along the sharpened horizon, and as the sun meets horizon, it flares defiantly into orange and blood red, like a muted fire, before vanishing.

Yet there is more. There is not one process at work but two—not only the tidal sunset but the breakup of a storm. Light plays not just, as with the sunset, against rock sculptures—immobile, the dynamism of the scene set by the sinking, refracting lights; it plays also against the clouds. Here they tower into pinks and magentas, there they furrow into purples, blues, yellows, and greys, and everywhere virga shimmers downward like colored veils. Sunset and storm combine into a fugue of colors and shapes and motions. The storm breaks apart, the clouds shred and darken into black ink spots that interrupt and silhouette the enveloping twilight wedge before they shrivel away with the dying sun.

It is the supreme Canyon spectacle. Neither sunset nor storm alone but their interplay makes the scene Sublime; the Grand Ensemble, as Dutton called it, is put into complex motion. It could only be improved with a little smoke. It is an attribute of woodsmoke that the bulk of its particulates have diameters roughly comparable with the wavelengths of white light. In daylight smoke can obscure and lessen Canyon scenery.

But at sunset, when the particulates magnify and scatter the refraction of sunlight, the scene is dramatically enhanced. Smoke intensifies the color and highlights the texture of sky and earth. Add a little fire, and the scene could be not merely viewed but lived.

Yet the power of the view resides equally in the viewer. The Point captures two analogous motions in the lives of its observers—one seasonal and one secular. The experience is not just of a place or a time or an event but of the whole lot in a crazy, incongruous mix. It is the North Rim and youth and fire. It is falling trees and hot-spotting and growing up and SWFFs and walking through blue night winds and flaming trees and C rations and moonlight on Canyon clouds. It is Saddle Mountain and Powell and The Dragon and Walhalla. It is the endlessly recycled summers and the irreversible storm of youth in dynamic counterpoint. It is fire on the Rim.

A few flakes of ink-black cloud drift by. The darkness arcs downward; stars and moon create a new sky; moonlight reverses the pattern of light and shadow. Warm winds from the Canyon mix with cool air from the Plateau. The future has become past.

Suddenly we feel the cold. The Point is wholly exposed. From everywhere there is the sound of distant, rushing winds.

from USFS 1919: The Ranger, the Cook
and a Hole in the Sky
by Norman Maclean

Norman Maclean (1902–1990) wrote this fictional story based on his own experiences working for the U.S. Forest Service, which he did as a teenager and again in his mid-twenties.

And then he thinks he knows
The hills where his life rose . . .
—Matthew Arnold, "The Buried Life"

I was young and I thought I was tough and I knew it was beautiful and I was a little bit crazy but hadn't noticed it yet. Outside the ranger station there were more mountains in all directions than I was ever to see again—oceans of mountains—and inside the station at this particular moment I was ahead in a game of cribbage with the ranger of the Elk Summit District of the Selway Forest of the United States Forest Service (USFS), which was even younger than I was and enjoyed many of the same characteristics.

It was mid-August of 1919, so I was seventeen and the Forest Service was only fourteen, since, of several possible birthdays for the Forest Service, I pick 1905, when the Forest Division of the Department of the Interior was transferred to the Department of Agriculture and named the United States Forest Service.

In 1919 it was twenty-eight miles from the Elk Summit Ranger Station of the Selway Forest to the nearest road, fourteen miles to the top of the Bitterroot Divide and fourteen straight down Blodgett Canyon to the Bitterroot Valley only a few miles from Hamilton, Montana. The fourteen miles going down were as cruel as the fourteen going up, and far more dangerous, since Blodgett Canyon was medically famous for the tick that gave Rocky Mountain Fever, with one chance out of five for recovery. The twenty-eight-mile trail from Elk Summit to the mouth of Blodgett Canyon was a Forest Service trail and therefore marked by a blaze with a notch on top; only a few other trails in the vast Elk Summit district were so marked. Otherwise, there were only game trails and old trappers' trails that gave out on open ridges and meadows with no signs of where the game or trappers had vanished. It was a world of strings of pack horses or men who walked alone—a world of hoof and foot and the rest done by hand. Nineteen nineteen across the Bitterroot Divide in northern Idaho was just before the end of most of history that had had no four-wheel drives, no bulldozers, no power saws and nothing pneumatic to take the place of jackhammers and nothing chemical or airborne to put out forest fires.

Nowadays you can scarcely be a lookout without a uniform and a college degree, but in 1919 not a man in our outfit, least of all the ranger himself, had been to college. They still picked rangers for the Forest Service by picking the toughest guy in town. Ours, Bill Bell, was the toughest in the Bitterroot Valley, and we thought he was the best ranger in the Forest Service. We were strengthened in this belief by the rumor that Bill had killed a sheepherder. We were a little disappointed that he had been acquitted of the charges, but nobody held it against him, for we all knew that being acquitted of killing a sheepherder in Montana isn't the same as being innocent.

As for a uniform, our ranger always wore his .45 and most of our regular crew also packed revolvers, including me. The two old men in the outfit told the rest of us that "USFS" stood for "Use 'er Slow and Fuck 'er Fast." Being young and literal, I put up an argument at first, pointing out that the beginning letters in their motto didn't exactly fit

USFS—that their last word "Fast" didn't begin with S as "Service" did. In fact, being thickheaded, I stuck with this argument quite a while, and could hear my voice rise. Each time, they spit through the parting in their moustaches and looked at me as if I were too young to say anything that would have any bearing on such a subject. As far as they were concerned, their motto fitted the United States Forest Service exactly, and by the end of the summer I came to share their opinion.

Although our ranger, Bill Bell, was the best, he did not shine at cribbage. He put down his cards and said, "Fifteen-two, fifteen-four, fifteen-six, and a pair are eight." As usual, I spread out his hand and counted after him. All he had was an eight and a pair of sevens, a hand he always counted as eight. Maybe the eight card gave him the idea. "Bill," I told him, "that's a six hand. Fifteen-two, fifteen-four, and a pair are six." Being wrong always made Bill Bell feel somebody was insulting him. "Damn it," he said, "can't you see that eight card? Well, eight plus seven. . . ." The cook, still wiping dishes, looked over Bill's shoulder and said, "That's a six hand." Bill folded up his cards and tossed them into the pile—whatever the cook said was always right with Bill, which didn't make me like the cook any better. It is always hard to like a spoiled cook, and I disliked this one particularly.

Even so, I had no idea how much I was going to dislike him before the summer was over, or, for that matter, how big a thing another card game was going to be. By the middle of that summer when I was seventeen I had yet to see myself become part of a story. I had as yet no notion that life every now and then becomes literature—not for long, of course, but long enough to be what we best remember, and often enough so that what we eventually come to mean by life are those moments when life, instead of going sideways, backwards, forward, or nowhere at all, lines out straight, tense and inevitable, with a complication, climax, and, given some luck, a purgation, as if life had been made and not happened. Right then, though, I wasn't thinking of Bill as being the hero of any story—I was just getting tired of waiting for him to make the next deal. Before he did, he licked his fingers so he wouldn't deal two or three cards at a time.

It was hard to figure out how Bill could be so different when he had a rope in his hands—with a rope he was an artist, and he usually was doing something with one. Even when he was sitting in the ranger station he would whirl little loops and "dab" them over a chair; either that or tie knots, beautiful knots. While the crew talked, he threw loops or tied knots. He was a sort of "Yeah" or "No" guy to human beings—now and then he talked part of a sentence or a sentence or two—but to his horses and mules he talked all the time, and they understood him. He never talked loud to them, especially not to mules, which he knew are like elephants and never forget. If a mule got balky when he was shoeing him, he never reached for anything—he just led him out in the sun and tied up one front foot and let him stand there for a couple of hours. You can't imagine what a Christianizing effect it has, even on a mule, to stand for a couple of hours in the hot sun minus a foot.

Bill was built to fit his hands. He was big all over. Primarily he was a horseman, and he needed an extra large horse. He was not the slender cowboy of the movies and the plains. He was a horseman of the mountains. He could swing an ax or pull a saw, run a transit and build trail, walk all day if he had to, put on climbing spurs and string number nine telephone wire, and he wasn't a bad cook. In the mountains you work to live, and in the mountains you don't care much whether your horse can run fast. Where's he going to run? Bill's horse was big and long-striding, and could walk all day over mountain trails at five miles an hour. He was a mountain horse carrying a mountain man. Bill called him Big Moose. He was brown and walked with his head thrown back as if he wore horns.

Every profession has a pinnacle to its art. In the hospital it is the brain or heart surgeon, and in the sawmill it is the sawyer who with squinting eyes makes the first major cut that turns a log into boards. In the early Forest Service, our major artist was the packer, as it usually has been in worlds where there are no roads. Packing is an art as old as the first time man moved and had an animal to help him carry his belongings. As such, it came ultimately from Asia and from there across Northern Africa and Spain and then up from Mexico and to us probably from Indian squaws. You can't even talk to a packer unless you know what a cinch (*cincha*) is, a latigo, and a manty (*manta*). With the coming of roads, this ancient art has become almost a lost art, but in the early part of this century there were still few roads across the mountains and none across the "Bitterroot Wall." From the mouth of Blodgett Canyon, near Hamilton, Montana, to our ranger station at Elk Summit in Idaho nothing moved except on foot. When there was a big fire crew to be supplied, there could be as many as half a hundred mules and short-backed horses heaving and grunting up the narrow switchbacks and dropping extra large amounts of manure at the sharp turns. The ropes tying the animals together would jerk taut and stretch their connected necks into a straight line until they looked like dark gigantic swans circling and finally disappearing into a higher medium.

Bill was our head packer, and the Forest Service never had a better one. But right now he was having a hard time figuring out which of his three remaining cards he should play. He would like to have taken off his black Stetson and scratched his head, but the first thing he did when he dressed in the morning was to put on his black hat, and it was the last thing he took off when he went to bed. In between he did not like to remove it. Before he got around to pushing it back on his head and playing a card, I found myself thinking of some of the trips I had taken with him across the Bitterroot Divide.

As head packer, Bill rode in front of the string, a study in angles. With black Stetson hat at a slant, he rode with his head turned almost backward from his body so he could watch to see if any of the packs were working loose. Later in life I was to see Egyptian bas-reliefs where the heads of men are looking one way and their bodies are going another, and so it is with good packers. After all, packing is the art of balancing packs and then seeing that they ride evenly—otherwise the animals will have saddle sores in a day or two and be out of business for all or most of the summer.

Up there in front with Bill, you could see just about anything happen. A horse might slip or get kicked out of the string and roll frightened downhill until he got tangled around a tree trunk. You might even have to shoot him, collect the saddle, and forget the rest of what was scattered over the landscape. But mostly what you were watching for took Bill's trained eye to see—a saddle that had slipped back so far the animal couldn't breathe, or a saddle that had slipped sideways. In an outfit that large, there are always a few "shad bellies" that no cinch can hang on to and quite a few "bloaters" that blow up in the morning when the cinch touches them and then slowly deflate. Who knows what? The trouble may have started back in the warehouse where the load cargoer couldn't tell weight or didn't give a damn and now an animal was trying to keep steady across the Bitterroot Divide with lopsided packs. Or maybe the packs balanced, but some assistant packer had tied one higher than the other. Or had tied a sloppy diamond hitch and everything slipped. The Bitterroot Divide, with its many switchbacks, granite boulders, and bog holes, brought out every weakness in a packer, his equipment, and his animals. To take a pack string of nearly half a hundred across the Bitterroot Divide was to perform a masterpiece in that now almost lost art, and in 1919 I rode with Bill Bell and saw it done.

The divide was just as beautiful as the way up. In August it was blue with June lupine. Froth dropped off the jaws of the horses and mules, and, snorting through enlarged red nostrils, the animals shook their saddles, trying without hands to rearrange their loads. Not far to the south was El Capitan, always in snow and always living up to its name. Ahead and to the west was our ranger station—and the mountains of Idaho, poems of geology stretching beyond any boundaries and seemingly even beyond the world.

Six miles or so west of the divide is a lake, roughly two-thirds of the way between Hamilton and Elk Summit, that is the only place where there is water and enough grass to hold a big bunch of horses overnight. K. D. Swan, the fine photographer of the early Forest Service, should have been there to record the design of the divide—ascending in triangles to the sky and descending in ovals and circles to an oval meadow and an oval lake with a moose knee-deep beside lily pads. It was triangles going up and ovals coming down, and on the divide it was springtime in August.

The unpacking was just as beautiful—one wet satin back after another without saddle or saddle sore, and not a spot of white wet flesh where hair and hide had rubbed off. Perhaps one has to know something about keeping packs balanced on the backs of animals to think this beautiful, or to notice it at all, but to all those who work come moments of beauty unseen by the rest of the world.

So, to a horseman who has to start looking for horses before daybreak, nothing is so beautiful in darkness as the sound of a bell mare.

While I was sitting there thinking of how Bill was a major artist and how even the knots he tied were artistic, he had somehow got ahead of me in the cribbage game, at which he was a chump. At least, I was a lot better than he was at cribbage, once the favorite indoor pastime of the woods. We even played it outdoors, and often on the trail one of us would carry a deck of cards and a cribbage board in his pack sack, and in the middle of the morning and afternoon we would straddle a log and have a game.

Bill really wasn't ahead, but I was going to lose unless he played like a Chinaman. We both were in striking distance of 121, which is the end of the game in cribbage, and I had the advantage of counting first. I needed only eight points, which normally I should have been able to make with a decent hand plus the "pegging." But I had a lousy hand, just a pair of fours, and a pair is worth only two points, so I would have to peg six to make 121, and that's a lot. In case you don't know cribbage, about all Bill had to do to stop me from pegging six was not to pair anything I put down. I started the pegging by playing one of my fours, and, so help me, he had a four in his hand and he snapped it down. "I'll take two for a pair of fours," he said. As I told you, all I had in my hand was a pair of fours. I put down the third four, and in cribbage three of a kind counts six, so I had 121 and the ball game, and a start toward discovering that somehow artists aren't sharp at cards.

Actually, I had heard rumors in Hamilton, which was Bill's headquarters in the Bitterroot Valley, that the local small-town gamblers could hardly wait for Bill to get his monthly check. Among the local housemen and shills he was supposedly noted for playing poker as if he breathed through gills. Knowing how Bill hated to lose, I was some-what surprised that he hadn't also been acquitted of shooting a shill.

Knowing Bill, I also knew that he was sore at me, at least for the moment, so I thought, "Let's see if a change of games won't change the luck." Of course, three can play a lot more card games than two. As the cook was finishing dishes, I asked him, "Why don't you cut in on a nickel-and-dime game? Poker? Pinochle? You and Bill name it."

I'll never forget that cook; in fact, he was to become one of my longest memories. Even out in the woods, he wore low canvas shoes. He turned his shoes toward me and said, "I never play cards against the men I work with." This wasn't the first time the cook had made this stately speech to me, so I started disliking him all over again. His name may have been Hawkins, but I really think it was Hawks and in memory I made it into Hawkins because in some book there was a character I didn't like by the name of Hawkins.

Bill and I played one more game of cribbage trying to get over being sore, but we weren't successful. I picked up the cards and put them in their case and the case on the only shelf in the cabin. Before I reached the door the cook had picked them up and was sitting at the table shuf-fling. He dealt out four hands. Then he went around the first three hands again, quickly giving each hand one or two cards as if each hand had asked to draw. He paused, however, before giving himself cards. Then with one motion he picked them all up. After shuffling, he dealt out five hands, sometimes four, never three, lest I get the idea that he would play with Bill and me. I stood there watching him shuffling and dealing. It was worth watching. After about five minutes, he picked up all the cards with one swoop, stuck them in the case and the case on the shelf and started for bed. I closed the door and started for the tent where the crew slept. I liked him less than ever.

There were only four of us in the "regular crew," plus the lookouts who were stationed on the high peaks, plus the ranger and the cook. The regular crew was hired by the month (sixty dollars per) for the summer—the ranger was the only one in the district who was hired all year. Earlier in the season, there had been a big fire in the district and an emergency crew of over a hundred men had been hired on the streets of Butte and Spokane, but the fire had been put out and the emergency crew sent back to town. Our small regular crew now was building trail about three miles from the station—grade A trail, too, with about a twenty-foot right-of-way and no more than a six-percent grade. A twenty-foot swath through the wilderness with no trees or brush left standing and, instead of going over an outcropping of rocks with a short steep pitch in the trail, we blasted through the rocks to keep the trail from gaining more than six feet of altitude every hundred feet. Tons of dynamite and we could have taken a hay wagon down our mountain boulevard. Of course, all we needed were trails wide enough to get pack horses through without the packs getting caught between trees, and in a few years the Forest Service revised the specifications and gave orders for the back country to be opened with as many trails as possible. Still, it is proper when young to strive for gigantic perfection that doesn't make sense, and today somewhere in the jungles of Idaho is a mile or two of overgrown boulevard leading nowhere, not even to a deserted Mayan temple.

Of the regular crew of four, two were old men and two were young punks. There was Mr. McBride and his redheaded son. Mr. McBride was a jack-of-all-trades who had worked at different ranches in the Bitterroot Valley and his son was trying to be like his father. Mr. Smith was the old man of the crew and was always worried about his bowels. He was addressed as "Mr. Smith." He was dignified and took small, aged steps on large legs that made his feet look tiny. He had been a miner and he naturally was our powder man, and a good one. Since there were four of us and Mr. McBride had a son, Mr. Smith looked upon me as his. That's how I was elected to the dynamite, which made me sick. Before I had started the job I had heard stories that if you touch dynamite and then your face you will get a headache. Maybe I was carried away by the story, because as long as I worked on the powder I always had headaches. Maybe, though, at seventeen I wasn't quite big enough to swing a double jackhammer all day.

When you are blasting, naturally you first make a hole in the rock for your powder. Nowadays it is done with a pneumatic drill; then it was done by hand and jackhammer. If you worked in a team of two it was called "double jacking." One man held the drill, and every time the other man hit the head of it with the jackhammer the man holding the drill would turn it slightly until the bit completed a circle. This was the outline for the hole, and the same thing went on until the hole was dug, stopping only when the man holding the drill said, "Mud." Then the hammer man gratefully rested while the man holding the drill took a very small dipper and cleaned out the hole. Otherwise, the man with the hammer kept swinging, and, if by chance just once he missed the small head of the drill and the hammer glanced off he would mutilate the hand or arm of the man holding the drill. Sometimes it seemed that Mr. Smith had forgotten how to say "Mud," and I would look down and see the heads of two or three drills, on each of which Mr. Smith had the same hand, the skin of which was already freckled by age. I no longer think that rubbing my face gave me the headaches.

This morning the headache started earlier than usual. I can't give you any very clear reason why I disliked the cook so much. I was honest enough with myself to say that I might be jealous of him. Although I was only seventeen, this was my third summer in the Forest Service, two of them working for Bill, and he had started to show me how to pack, and in return I would do him favors like coming back to camp in the morning to pack out lunch to the crew. I couldn't figure how this cook had moved into first place. Everything he said or did was just perfect, as far as Bill was concerned. Besides, I didn't like his looks—he looked like a bluejay, cocky, with his head on a slant and a tuft of hair on top of it. A bluejay with low canvas shoes. Mostly, though, I didn't need reasons to dislike him. When you get older, you become rational more or less, but when you are young you know. I knew this cook was a forty-cent piece.

It wasn't helping my headache either to think of the ranger being sore at me. I said to myself, "Take it easy, and keep your big mouth shut. It's nothing and it will blow over." Then I repeated to myself, "Keep your big mouth shut," but I knew I wouldn't. I had formed principles to compensate for having started work when I was fifteen. I had missed a lot, I knew—the swimming hole, summer girls, and a game called tennis which was played in white flannels with cuffs. I would say to myself, "You decided to go into the woods, so the least you can do is be tough." I hadn't felt this way at fifteen when I first worked for Bill, but that was the way I felt now at seventeen. Even though Bill was my model and an artist—maybe because he was—at seventeen something in me was half-looking for trouble with him.

Before noon who should come along but the cook packing our lunch. He said to me, "The ranger wants you to come back to camp after you eat."

When I got back to camp, Bill was in the cabin we used as a warehouse, building the packs for the string that was going to Hamilton soon. I didn't ask him why he had sent for me and he didn't say. I just started helping him build and balance the packs, and tried to keep my mind on what I was doing, partly because building packs is never a mechanical job. Not even when you're packing the simplest stuff like tin cans, which go into boxes called "panyards," made of rawhide, wood, or canvas, that are hung on the prongs of the saddle. You can't forget to wrap each can in toilet paper, or the labels on the cans will rub off and you won't be able to tell peaches from peas. And the heaviest cans have to go to the bottom, or the pack will shift. Then each of the two side packs has to weigh the same and together (with the top pack) they shouldn't weigh more than 175 pounds for a horse or 225 for a mule—at least, those were the Forest Service regulations then, but they were twenty-five pounds too heavy if the animals weren't to be bone heaps by the middle of the summer. I don't care who you are, I'll bet you that without a scale you can't build two packs weighing the same and together weighing 150 or 200 pounds when a top pack has been added.

After we had packed for a while, I forgot to wonder why the ranger had sent for me. Maybe it was just to help him box things up. Then, while we were working with our heads bent, I heard the cook come by jingling the knives and forks the crew had used for lunch.

Still working on a pack, I heard myself say, "I don't like that son of a bitch."

Bill lifted a pack and put it down. Inside I heard myself say, "Keep your big mouth shut." Outside, I heard myself add, "Some day I am going to punch the piss out of him." Bill stood up and said, "Not in this district you won't." He looked at me for a long time, and I looked back still crouched over my pack. I figured that at this moment crouching was a good position. Finally, we both went back to work.

Bending and lifting, he began to tell me about how the morning had gone. "The lookout on Grave Peak quit this morning." "Yeah?" I said. "Yeah," he said. "He came off that mountain in about three jumps." It was nearly twelve miles to the top of the peak. "Do you know what he said to me?" he asked. "No," I said. I wasn't happy about how this was going to end. "The lookout said, 'Give me my time. This is too tough a job for me, fighting fire in the day and sleeping with rattlesnakes at night.' " After lifting the pack again for weight, he went on, "Seems that he put his hand on the bed to pull back the blanket and he felt something shaped like a fire hose. Do you believe it?"

At Bear Creek, where I first worked for Bill, there had been a lot of rattlers on those bare mountainsides. On a steep sidehill trail, the up side can be as high as your hand, so you could almost brush those rattlesnakes as you swung along. And, being cold-blooded, they could be attracted to the warmth of a bed at night. But I hadn't seen a rattlesnake this summer in Elk Summit, although it was the adjoining district.

"No, I don't believe it," I said. "Why not?" he asked. "It's too high up there for rattlesnakes," I said. "Are you sure?" he asked, and I told him I wasn't sure but I thought so. Still working with the packs he said, "Why don't you go up on the lookout for a couple of weeks and find out?"

I didn't ask him when; I knew he meant now. I lifted the two packs until I thought they were balanced, and then started for the door. He added, "If you spot any fires, call them in. And, if there's a big rain or snow, close up camp and come back to the station."

I knew it would be dark before I got to Grave Peak, so I asked the cook to make me a sandwich. I had a big blue bandanna handkerchief, and I put the sandwich in the handkerchief and tied the handkerchief to my belt in the middle of my back. I picked up my razor, toothbrush, and comb, and my favorite ax and Carborundum stone. Then I strapped on my .32-20 and started up the high trail. I knew I had been sent into exile.

It was twelve miles and all up, but I never stopped to rest or eat the sandwich. Bill seemed to be watching all the time. By walking hard I kept even with daylight until near the end. Then darkness passed over me from below—just the dazzling peak above told me where I was going.

For the first few days, I was too tired to think about my troubles. I was still half-sick from the dynamite and I still dragged from that big fire we had fought in late July, so I spent most of my time just looking the place over and getting things squared away.

Modern lookouts live on top of their peaks in what are called "birdcages"—glass houses on towers with lightning rods twisted around them so that the lookouts are not afraid of lightning striking them, and for twenty-four hours a day can remain on the towers to watch for lightning to strike and smoke to appear. This, of course, is the way it should be, but in 1919 birdcages, as far as we knew, were only for birds. We watched from the open peak and lived in a tent in a basin close to the peak where usually there was a spring of water. From my camp to the lookout was a good half-hour climb, and I spent about twelve hours a day watching mountains.

Near the top there were few trees and nearly all of them had been struck by lightning. It had gone around them, like a snake of fire. But I was to discover that, on a high mountain, lightning does not seem to strike from the sky. On a high mountain, lightning seems to start somewhat below you and very close by, seemingly striking upward and outward. Once it was to knock me down, toss branches over me and leave me sick.

The basin where my tent was pitched was covered with chunks of cliff that had toppled from above. I did not see a rattlesnake, but I shared the basin with a grizzly bear who occasionally came along flipping over fallen pieces of disintegrated cliff as he looked for disproportionately small grubs. When I saw him coming, I climbed the highest rock and tried to figure out how many hundreds of grubs he had to eat for a square meal. When he saw me, he made noises in his mouth as if he were shifting his false teeth. In a thicket on top of a jack pine, I found the skeleton of a deer. Your guess is as good as mine. Mine is that the snow in the high basin was deep enough to cover the trees, and the deer was crossing the crust and broke through or was killed and eventually the snow melted. There was a tear in my tent so when it rained I could keep either my food or my bed dry, but not both.

Since this was not my first hitch as a lookout, I knew what to watch for—a little cloud coming up a big mountain, usually in the late afternoon when the dews had long dried and the winds were at their height. And usually it detached itself from the mountain and went on up into the sky and became just a little cloud. Once in a while it would disappear on the mountain, and then you didn't know what you had seen— probably a cloud but maybe a puff of smoke and the wind had changed and you couldn't see it now, so you marked it on your map to watch for several days. In a lightning storm you marked every strike to watch, and sometimes it was a week later before one of them became a little cloud again and then got bigger and began to boil. When a cloud began to boil, then it wasn't a cloud, especially if it reflected red on the bottom. It could mean fire even when the cloud was two or three miles down the canyon from where it was first seen, because, if there were no wind, smoke could drift a long way behind a ridge before rising again where it would show. So that's the way a fire first looks to a lookout: something—you don't know what—usually in late afternoon, that may go away and not come again and, if it comes back and is smoke, it may be quite a long way from the fire.

A possible late-afternoon cloud has no resemblance to what a fire looks like if it gets out of control, and it was often impossible in those early years to get men quickly on a fire when it was in the back country where there were no roads and sometimes not even trails, and of course long before there were planes stationed in Missoula ready to drop chemicals and smoke jumpers.

Instead, when a fire got out of control the Forest Service hired a hundred or so bindle stiffs off the streets of Butte or Spokane at thirty cents an hour (forty-five cents for straw bosses), shipped them to some rail station near the end of a branch line, and walked them the final thirty-five or forty miles over "the wall." By the time they reached the fire, it had spread all over the map, and had jumped into the crowns of trees, and for a lot of years a prospective ranger taking his exam had said the last word on crown fires. Even by my time he was a legend. When asked on his examination, "What do you do when a fire crowns?" he had answered, "Get out of the way and pray like hell for rain."

Our big fire that summer had been big enough so that I was still tired and my eyes still ached from smoke and no sleep, and big enough so that for years it crowned in my dreams, but it wasn't in the class of those fires of 1910 that burned out the Coeur d'Alene and great pieces of the Bitterroot. The smoke from those fires drifted seven hundred miles to Denver, and in my home town of Missoula the street lights had to be turned on in the middle of the afternoon, and curled ashes brushed softly against the lamps as if snow were falling heavily in the heat of August. Of course, no other fires on record were as big as those of 1910, but the one of 1919 was the biggest I was ever on.

It came in a rage and a crown to the top of the ridge. You may know, when a fire gets big enough it generates its own wind. The heat from the fire lightens the air, which rises in the sky, and the cooler air from above swoops down to replace it, and soon a great circular storm enrages the fire and the sky is a volcanic eruption of burning cones and branches descending in streamers of flames. The fire stands on the ridge, roaring for hell to arrive as reinforcement. While you are trying to peer through it to see the inferno on its way, suddenly somebody yells, "God, look behind. The son of a bitch has jumped the gulch." One hundred and eighty degrees from where you have been looking for the inferno and half-way up the opposite ravine a small smoke is growing big where one of those burning cones or branches dropped out of the sky and trapped you with a fire in your rear. Then what do you do?

Of course, the men who had been brought in from Butte or Spokane were dead tired and barefoot long before they reached the fire. At the hiring hall in Butte and Spokane each had to have a good pair of boots and a jacket to be employed, so they took turns in the alley changing the one good pair they had. Now all but one of them had marched across the Bitterroot wall in poor street shoes, and, not being able to keep ahead of the pack train, they ate twenty-eight miles of dust. They were bums off the street, miners out of the holes for the summer with the hope of avoiding tuberculosis, winos, and Industrial Workers of the World, who had been thick in Butte and Spokane during World War I. Since it was only the summer after the war, we ordinary working stiffs were still pretty suspicious of IWWs. Those of us who belonged to the regular crew (that is, who were paid sixty dollars a month instead of thirty cents an hour) said that IWW meant "I Won't Work," and we were also sure that they were happy to see our country burn. For whatever reason, we had to spend as much time patrolling them as we did the fire. First we had to get them to the top of the opposite ridge before the new fire arrived there, and a lot of them only wanted to lie down and go to sleep with the great fire coming from behind. It was the first time I ever saw that sometimes death has no meaning to men if they can lie down and sleep. We kicked them up the hill, while they begged to be left lying where they were, and we beat the new fire to the top. Then we made a "fire trench," just a scraping two or three feet wide to remove anything that would burn, like dry needles or duff. In front of the fire trench we built piles of dry twigs and then we waited for the wind to turn and blow back toward the new fire coming up the side of the ravine. We waited until the foreman gave us the signal before we lit the piles of twigs and sent fires burning back into the main one. This is known as "backfiring" and for once it worked, although if the wind had shifted again to its original direction, all we would have done was give the fire a head start on us. We did not sleep for three days. Some of us had to carry drinking water in warm canvas sacks up a thousand-foot ridge. The rest of us slowly extended the fire trench down the sides of the fire. The bottom of it we let go for a while—a fire doesn't go very far or fast downhill.

We had done a good job in heading off the fire. What you do in the first couple of hours after you hit a fire is what counts, and if it isn't right you had better take that young ranger's advice and give yourself over to prayer. Bill and the man he had made fire foreman had both experience and gift, and it takes gift as well as having been there before to know where to hit a fire hard enough to turn it in its tracks. When it's less than 110 degrees and nothing is about to burn you to death or roar at you and your lungs will still breathe the heat and your eyes aren't closed with smoke, it's easy to state the simple principles of a science, if that's what it is. All you're trying to do is to force the fire into some opening at the top of the ridge that's covered with shale and rocks or, if such openings don't abound in your vicinity, to force it into a thin stand of alpine pine or something that doesn't burn very fast. But with the inferno having arrived and the smoke so thick you can see only two or three men ahead of you, it's gift and guts, not science, that tells you where the head of the fire is, and where an open ridge is that can't be seen, and where and when the wind will turn and whether your men have what it takes to stand and wait. Don't forget this last point when you place your men—it isn't just horses that panic when the barn burns. But we were placed right and either we had guts or we were too sick to care. Anyway, we stood and the wind stayed with us and we crowded the big fire with our backfires and turned it into the timberline.

But every time we got the fire under control, something strange would happen—the fire would jump our fire trench, usually at some fairly ordinary place, so we became sure that IWWs were rolling burning logs over the trench and starting the fire off again. If they were, it was probably just to keep their jobs going, but that wasn't what we thought, and anyway it didn't matter much what we thought—the fire kept jumping the line everywhere until I and the red-headed kid were picked to patrol the fire. The fire foreman told us to carry revolvers. That's all we were told. I still ask myself why the two youngest in the outfit were given this assignment. Did they think we were so young that we would make a big show of ourselves but would freeze in the clutch and wouldn't shoot? Or did they think we were so young we were crazy enough to shoot almost sight unseen? Or did they think that nobody, especially the IWWs, could answer these questions? Anyway we patrolled miles and miles through burning branches and feathered ashes so light they rose ahead of us as we approached. We didn't look for trouble and we didn't find any. Also, we didn't pray, but finally the rains came. The other kid being red-headed, I think he would have shot. That wouldn't have left me much choice.

I don't suppose Bill would have sent me up to the lookout if he knew how much I needed a couple of days of rest, a thought that gave me a good deal of pleasure. Still being sore at him, I reported by telephone to the ranger station the fewest number of times required—three times a day. The telephone, in a coffin-shaped box, was nailed to the tent pole and had a crank on it. Two longs rang the ranger station, and one long and a short was my call, but nobody called me from the station. There was one woman on a distant lookout and her call was two longs and a short, and I am sure the rest of us lookouts often stood poised ready to ring two longs and a short, but never did. Instead we looked at her mountain and thought it looked different from other mountains, and we took off our telephone receivers and listened to her voice when it was her turn to report to the station. She was married and talked every night to her husband in Kooskia, but we did not listen to avoid feeling sorry for ourselves.

After a few days of resting and not mending the tent, I started to feel tough again. I knew I had been sent up here as punishment. I was expected to sit still and watch mountains and long for company and something to do, like playing cribbage, I suppose. I was going to have to watch mountains for sure, that was my job, but I would not be without company. I already knew that mountains live and move. Long ago when I had had a child sickness and nobody could tell what it was or how to treat it, my mother put me outside in a bed with mosquito netting over it, and I lay there watching mountains until they made me well. I knew that, when needed, mountains would move for me.

About the same time, I began to have another feeling, although one related to the feeling that I wasn't going to let Bill punish me by making me watch mountains. Somewhere along here I first became conscious of the feeling I talked about earlier—the feeling that comes when you first notice your life turning into a story. I began to sense the difference between what I would feel if I were just nearing the end of a summer's work or were just beginning a story. If what were coming was going to be like life as it had been, a summer's job would be over soon and I would go home and tell my pals about the big fire and packing my .32-20 on the fire line and the dynamite. Looking down from Grave Peak, though, I was no longer sure that the big fire was of any importance in what was starting to happen to me. It was becoming more important that I didn't like the damn cook, who was nobody, not even a good or bad cook, and could do nothing well except shuffle cards. Faintly but nevertheless truly I was becoming part of a plot and being made the opponent of my hero, Bill Bell, in fact, mysteriously making myself his opponent. The cook began to look like the mysterious bad guy; even I became mysterious to myself—I was going to show a ranger and a cook that I couldn't be defeated by being made to watch mountains, which were childhood friends of mine.

It doesn't take much in the way of body and mind to be a lookout. It's mostly soul. It is surprising how much our souls are alike, at least in the presence of mountains. For all of us, mountains turn into images after a short time and the images turn true. Gold-tossed waves change into the purple backs of monsters, and so forth. Always something out of the moving deep, and nearly always oceanic. Never a lake, never the sky. But no matter what images I began with, when I watched long enough the mountains turned into dreams, and still do, and it works the other way around—often, waking from dreams, I know I have been in the mountains, and I know they have been moving—sometimes advancing threateningly, sometimes creeping hesitantly, sometimes receding endlessly. Both mountains and dreams.

In the late afternoon, of course, the mountains meant all business for the lookouts. The big winds were veering from the valleys toward the peaks, and smoke from little fires that had been secretly burning for several days might show up for the first time. New fires sprang out of thunder before it sounded. By three-thirty or four, the lightning would be flexing itself on the distant ridges like a fancy prizefighter, skipping sideways, ducking, showing off but not hitting anything. By four-thirty or five, it was another game. You could feel the difference in the air that had become hard to breathe. The lightning now came walking into you, delivering short smashing punches. With an alidade, you marked a line on the map toward where it struck and started counting, "Thousand-one, thousand-two," and so on, putting in the "thousand" to slow your count to a second each time. If the thunder reached you at "thousand-five," you figured the lightning had struck about a mile away. The punches became shorter and the count closer and you knew you were going to take punishment. Then the lightning and thunder struck together. There was no count.

But what I remember best is crawling out of the tent on summer nights when on high mountains autumn is always approaching. To a boy, it is something new and beautiful to piss among the stars. Not under the stars but among them. Even at night great winds seem always to blow on great mountains, and tops of trees bend, but, as the boy stands there with nothing to do but to watch, seemingly the sky itself bends and the stars blow down through the trees until the Milky Way becomes lost in some distant forest. As the cosmos brushes by the boy and disappears among the trees, the sky is continually replenished with stars. There would be stars enough to brush by him all night, but by now the boy is getting cold.

Then the shivering organic speck of steam itself disappears.

By figuring backward, I knew it was the twenty-fifth of August when an unusually hot electrical storm crashed into the peak and was followed by an unusually high wind. The wind kept up all night and the next day, and I tightened all the ropes on my tent. Cold rode in with the wind. The next night after I went to bed it began to snow. It was August 27, and the stuff was damp and heavy and came down by the pound. Most of it went through the tear in my tent but there was enough left over so that by morning you could track elk in the snow.

I didn't think much of the immediate prospects of building a fire and cooking breakfast, so first I climbed to the top of the peak. When I looked, I knew I might never again see so much of the earth so beautiful, the beautiful being something you know added to something you see, in a whole that is different from the sum of its parts. What I saw might have been just another winter scene, although an impressive one. But what I knew was that the earth underneath was alive and that by tomorrow, certainly by the day after, it would be all green again. So what I saw because of what I knew was a kind of death with the marvelous promise of less than a three-day resurrection. From where I stood to the Bitterroot wall, which could have been the end of the world, was all windrows of momentary white. Beyond the wall, it seemed likely, eternity went on in windrows of Bitterroot Mountains and summer snow.

Even before I got back to camp it had begun to melt. Hundreds of shrubs had been bent over like set snares, and now they sprang up in the air throwing small puffs of white as if hundreds of snowshoe rabbits were being caught at the same instant.

While I was making breakfast, I heard the ticktock of a clock repeating, "It's time to quit; it's time to quit." I heard it almost as soon as it began, and almost that soon I agreed. I said to myself, "You fought a big fire and packed a big gun," and I said, "You slit waxy sticks of dynamite and stuck detonation caps in them and jumped back to watch them sizzle," and then I said, "You helped Bill pack and you watched mountains by yourself. That's a summer's work. Get your time and quit." I said these things several times to impress them on myself. I knew, in addition, that the fire season was over; in fact, the last thing the ranger had told me was to come in if it snowed. So I rang two longs for the ranger station; I rang two longs until I almost pulled the crank off the telephone, but in my heart I knew that the storm had probably blown twenty trees across the line between the peak and the station. Finally, I told myself to stay there until tomorrow when most of the snow would be gone and then to walk to the station and get my time and start over the hill to Hamilton.

What I neglected to tell myself is that it is almost impossible to quit a ranger who is sore because you do not like his cook, or to quit a story once you have become a character in it. The rest of the day I straightened up the camp, finally mended the tent, and listened to the ticktock get louder. I put the boxes of tin cans in trees where the grizzly bear couldn't get them. I had seen him split them open with one snap to a can.

It was nearly ten o'clock the next morning before I started for the ranger station. There was no use starting until the sun had done some more melting. Besides, I had decided to take along the tree-climbing outfit with the faint hope that maybe the storm had blown only two or three trees across the telephone line, so in addition to my ax and my own little odds and ends, I was walking bow-legged with climbing spurs and climbing belt and was carrying insulators and number nine telephone wire. I doubt if I had dropped more than a thousand feet of altitude before I was out of the snow. Also, by then I had chopped two trees that had fallen across the line and had made one splice in the wire. I should have known from the count that I would never clean out twelve miles of telephone line in a day, but now that I was going to quit I developed a pious feeling, wishing to end in the act of conscientiously performing my duty, so I kept the climbing spurs on and followed the telephone right-of-way, watching the line dip from tree to tree. When you are following line this way you lose all sense of the earth, and all that exists is this extended pencil line in your eye. I wouldn't have seen a rattlesnake unless he had wings and was flying south for the winter. As far as I was concerned, there were no rattlesnakes in Elk Summit district, and, if there were any, they would be holed up because it was late in the season and had just snowed. You could have examined my thoughts clear to the bottom of the heap and never found a snake track.

I don't need to tell you how a rattlesnake sounds—you can't mistake one. Sometimes you can think that a big winged grasshopper is a rattlesnake, but you can never think that a rattlesnake is anything else. I stayed in the air long enough to observe him streaking for the brush, an ugly bastard, short, not like a plains rattler, and much thicker behind his head.

I don't know how far I jumped, but I was mad when I lit—mad at myself for jumping so high. I took off my climbing spurs, picked up my ax, and started into the brush after him. I remembered about the crazy sheepherder in the valley who had been bitten that summer by a rattler and, instead of taking it easy and caring for the bite, had chased the rattler until he killed him—and himself. I also remembered the crew talking about it and saying that, even for a sheepherder, he must have been crazy. I must have been crazier, because after remembering I went into the brush after him. I went in too fast and couldn't find him.

We talk nowadays about a "happening," which is a good term to describe the next section of my life. In my mind it didn't occur successively and can't be separated: the snake was coiled about four feet in front of me I stuck the ax down between him and me he hit the ax handle the ax handle rang like a bell that had been struck and there was no punctuation between any of this. Then time started again because it was after this happening that I felt my hands sting from holding the ax handle the way your hands sting when you are a kid holding a baseball bat and not paying any attention and another kid with a bat comes sneaking up and hits yours with his.

The snake lay there as if he had never left his coil. He whirred and watched. He just barely left the next move up to me, and I made it fast. I almost set a record for a standing backward jump. It was getting so that I was doing most of my thinking in the air. I decided if I got to the ground again that I would try to take some of the sting out of my hands by chopping a few more fallen trees but instead when I lit I stood frozen trying to picture the snake as he struck because part of the picture was missing. All I could recall was about a foot and a half of his tail end lying on the ground. His head and all his upper part weren't in the picture. Where they should have been was just a vertical glaze. As I backed off farther, I came to the conclusion that about a foot and a half of him stayed on the ground as a platform to strike from and what struck was too fast to see. The bastard still whirred, so I backed off even farther before I strapped on my climbing spurs. This time when I started to follow the line, I kept one eye and a good part of another on where I was putting my feet.

If you have ever strung much wire, you know there is an important difference between the climbers used on telephone poles and on trees. Tree spurs are about two inches longer, because when you are climbing trees your spurs first have to penetrate the bark before they can start getting any hold in the wood, which is all fine and dandy as long as the trees have bark. But pretty soon the line crossed an old fire burn, maybe one of those 1910 burns, and the only trees standing were long dead and had no bark on them—and were as hard as ebony. I could get only about half an inch of spur in them and so I rocked around on the tips of my spurs and prayed the half inch would hold. The higher I climbed these petrified trees, the more I prayed. Before long, the line crossed a gulch 250 yards or more wide, and it was natural but tough luck that the line on one side of the gulch was down. A span of 250 yards of number nine line is a hell of a lot of weight for a dead tree to hold up in a storm, and one of the trees, rotted at the roots, had come down. I chopped out the line that had got wound around the tree when it fell and I spliced the line and added a few feet to it and picked a new tree to hang it on. Then I almost left the line lying there and started for the ranger station, because I didn't want to climb a dead tree while carrying that weight of line, but whenever I started to duck out like that the ranger was sure to be watching. So I put the wire over my climbing belt and the belt around the tree, and started up with my rear end sticking straight out to punch as much spur into that calcified tree as possible. You've seen linemen at work and know it's a job for rear ends that stick out and you should know why, even if you've never had climbers on. And when you're hanging line on trees instead of poles, you have an extra hazard to overcome—you have to lean even farther back on your rear end and swing a little ax to chop off the limbs as you go up, because your belt is around that tree and it has to go up if you are. Also going up with you are at least 250 yards of number nine wire, getting heavier and tauter every time you stick half an inch of spur into this totem pole of Carborundum. Below on the tree are the sharp stubs of branches you have chopped.

Less than half way up, the line had become so taut it would have pulled me out of the tree if I hadn't been strapped to it by the belt. The half inch of spur became less and less. Then I heard the splinter. Maybe I would have felt better if I had had no belt and the wire had just flipped me over the cliff into the gulch. Anyway, with my spurs torn out of the totem pole I came down about ten or twelve feet, and then my belt caught on something, and I dangled there and smelled smoke from the front of my shirt, my belly having passed over ten feet of the snag ends of chopped branches. I worked the belt loose and fell ten or twelve feet more, and so on. I never could push far enough away from the tree to jab my spurs into it again, and when I finally reached the ground I felt as if an Indian had started a fire by rubbing two sticks together, using me for one of the sticks.

I was afraid to look at my lower quarters to see what was still with me. Instead, I studied the snags of those branches to see which of my private parts were to hang there forever and slowly turn to stone. Finally, I could tell by the total distribution of pain that all of me was still on the same nervous system.

I was suddenly destitute of piety, and knew that I had done all the telephone repair work that I was going to do that day. I tried to tie my outfit into one pack, but all I was thinking about was how thick that mountain rattler was behind his head. And how warm I was in front.

It was downhill to the ranger station, and I arrived there late in the afternoon, still not altogether cooled off. As I expected, Bill was in the warehouse, and he didn't look up when I came in. He said, "Why did you leave the peak?" He knew damn well why I came in—he had told me to come in if it snowed. I said, "There are rattlers up there." He grinned and seemed pleased with himself and the snake. I didn't mention anything about tree climbing, although the front of my shirt was torn.

from The Journey Home
by Edward Abbey

Edward Abbey (1927–1989) figured working

as a fire lookout was the ideal role for an ama-

teur philosopher like himself.

July 12, Glacier National Park

We've been here ten days before I overcome initial inertia sufficient to begin this record. And keeping a record is one of the things the Park Service is paying us to do up here. The other, of course, is to keep our eyeballs peeled, alert for smoke. We are being paid a generous wage (about $3.25 an hour) to stay awake for at least eight hours a day. Some people might think that sounds like a pretty easy job. And they're right, it is an easy job, for some people. But not for all. When I mentioned to one young fellow down at park headquarters, a couple of weeks ago, that I was spending the summer on this fire lookout he shuddered with horror. "I'd go nuts in a place like that," he said, thinking of solitary confinement. I didn't tell him I was cheating, taking my wife along. But that can be risky too; many a good marriage has been shattered on the rock of isolation.

Renée and I walked up here on July 2, packs on our backs, two hours ahead of the packer with his string of mules. The mules carried the heavier gear, such as our bedrolls, enough food and water for the first two weeks, seven volumes of Marcel Proust, and Robert Burton's

Anatomy of Melancholy. Light summer reading. Renée had never worked a fire lookout before, but I had, and I knew that if I was ever going to get through the classics of world lit it could only be on a mountain top, far above the trashy plains of *Rolling Stone, Playboy,* the *New York Times,* and *Mizz* magazine.

The trail is about six miles long from Bowman Lake and climbs 3,000 feet. We made good time, much better time than we wished because we were hustled along, all the way, by hordes of bloodthirsty mosquitoes. We had prepared ourselves, of course, with a heavy treatment of government-issue insect repellent on our faces, necks, arms, but that did not prevent the mosquitoes from whining in our ears and hovering close to eye, nostril, and mouth.

We also had the grizzly on our mind. Fresh bear scat on the trail, unpleasant crashing noises back in the dark of the woods and brush, reminded us that we were intruding, uninvited, into the territory of *Ursus horribilis,* known locally as G-bear or simply (always in caps) as GRIZ. It was in Glacier, of course, only a few years ago, that two young women had been killed on the same night by grizzlies. We clattered our tin cups now and then, as advised, to warn the bears we were coming. I was naturally eager to see a GRIZ in the wild, something I'd never done, but not while climbing up a mountain with a pack on my back, tired, sweaty, and bedeviled by bugs. Such an encounter, in such condition, could only mean a good-natured surrender on my part; I wasn't *about* to climb a tree.

Bear stories. My friend Doug Peacock was soaking one time in a hot spring in Yellowstone's back country. Surprised by a grizzly sow and her two cubs, he scrambled naked as a newt up the nearest pine; the bear kept him there, freezing in the breeze, for two hours. Another: Riley McClelland, former park naturalist at Glacier, and a friend were treed by a GRIZ. Remembering that he had an opened sardine can in his pack, Riley watched with sinking heart as the bear sniffed at it. Disdaining the sardine lure, however, the bear tore up the other man's pack to get at a pair of old tennis shoes.

Sacrifice, that may be the key to coexistence with the GRIZ. If we surprise one on the trail, I'll offer up first my sweat-soaked hat. If that won't do, then cheese and salami out of the pack. And if that's not enough, well, then nothing else to do, I guess, but push my wife his way. *Droit du seigneur à la montagne*, etc.

We reach the lookout without fulfilling any fantasies. The lookout is a two-room, two-story wood frame cabin at timberline, 7,000 feet above sea level. On the north, east, and southeast stand great peaks— Reuter, Kintla, Numa, Chapman, Rainbow, Vulture. Northwest we can see a bit of the Canadian Rockies. West and southwest lie the North Fork of the Flathead River, a vast expanse of Flathead National Forest, and on the horizon the Whitefish Range. Nice view: 360 degrees of snow-capped scenic splendor, lakes, forest, river, fearsome peaks, and sheltering sky.

We remove the wooden shutters from the lookout windows, shovel snow from the stairway, unlock the doors. The pack string arrives. The packer and I unload the mules, the packer departs, Renée and I unpack our goods and move in. Except for a golden-mantled ground squirrel watching us from the rocks, a few Clark's nutcrackers in the subalpine firs, we seem to be absolutely alone.

July 14 (Bastille Day!)
The Great Revolution was a failure, they say. All revolutions have been failures, they say. To which I reply: All the more reason to make another one. Knocking off "work" at five o'clock (the transition from work to nonwork being here discernible by a subtle reshading in the colors of the rock on Rainbow Peak), my wife and I honor this day by uncorking a bottle of genuine Beaujolais. With Renée's home-baked crusty French bread and some real longhorn cheese from the country store down at the hamlet of Polebridge, it makes a fitting celebration.

A golden eagle soars by *below us*, pursued by—a sparrow hawk? My wife the bird-watcher is uncertain; but it must have been. Looking unhurried but pursuing a straight course, the eagle disappears into the vast glacial cirque above Akakola Lake, followed steadily, slightly above, by the smaller bird. More Clark's nutcrackers. Chipping sparrows.

Mountain chickadees. Oregon juncoes. Clouds of mosquitoes whining at the windows, greedy for blood. A doe, a fawn, a yearling buck with velvet horns jostling one another at our salt deposits on the rocks outside. The doe is dominant; the young buck retreats. Women's Lib has reached out even here, for God's sake, all the way from Washington Square to Numa Ridge. Depressing thought. Striving to uphold the natural superiority of the male, I have beaten my wife—at chess—five games straight. Now she refuses to play with me. You can't win.

What *do* people do on a lookout tower when, as now, the season is wet and there are no fires? Aside from the obvious, and reading Proust and *The Anatomy of Melancholy*, we spend hours just gazing at the world through binoculars. For example, I enjoy climbing the local mountains, scaling the most hideous bare rock pitches step by step, hand by hand, without aids, without rope or partners, clinging to fragments of loose shale, a clump of bear grass, the edge of an overhanging snow cornice, above a nightmarish abyss, picking a route toward even higher and more precarious perches—through these U.S. Navy 7 x 50 lenses. The effortless, angelic, and supine approach to danger.

It's not all dreaming. There are some daily chores. Ever since arrival I've been packing snow to the lookout from a big drift a hundred yards below, carrying it up in buckets, dumping it into steel garbage cans, letting it melt in the sun. Now we've got 120 gallons of snow water in addition to the drinking water brought up by muleback. Then there's firewood. Although we have a propane stove for cooking, the only heat in the lookout comes from an old cast-iron cookstove. And with the kind of rainy, windy weather we've been having, heat is a necessity. Even in July. So a couple of times a week I go down the trail with ax and saw, fell one of the many dead trees in the area—fir, whitebark pine—buck the log into eighteen-inch lengths, tote it up the hill armload by armload.

Three times a day we take weather observations—wind speed and direction, temperature, relative humidity—or my wife does, since she is the scientist in this family. We wash windows, occasionally. We patch and repair things. We listen to the Park Service radio and the Forest

Service radio, ready to relay messages if necessary. I entertain the deer and the squirrels with my flute. Renée bakes things, studies the maps, memorizes the terrain. But mostly we sit quietly out on the catwalk, reading about aristocratic life in *fin-de-siècle* Paris and looking at north-western Montana in the summer of '75.

This is a remote place indeed, far from the center of the world, far away from all that's going on. Or is it? Who says so? Wherever two human beings are alive, together, and happy, there is the center of the world. You out there, brother, sister, you too live in the center of the world, no matter where or what you think you are.

July 16

Heavy cloud buildup in northwest. Lightning likely, fire danger rising, humidity dropping. The haze lies heavy over yonder Whitefish Range, obscuring the farther peaks. Looks like smog, but is only water vapor, dust, the smoke from many campfires along the North Fork. They tell us.

One longs for a nice little forest fire. We need some excitement around this joint. Nothing healthier for the forests than a good brisk fire now and then to clear out the undergrowth, give the moose and bear some living room. Besides we need the overtime pay. If that idiot Smokey the Bear (the noted ursine bore) had *his* way all us fire fighters would starve to death.

We see a Townsend's solitaire, abundant here. Hermit thrush. Swallowtail butterflies. Little spiders hanging on threads from the attic trap-door. A six-legged spider (war veteran) on the outside of the windowpane chewing on a mosquito. Good show! mate. One snowshoe hare loping into the brush.

Gordon the Garbage Man, one of the park's seasonal employees, comes up the mountain for a visit, leaves us two big Dolly Vardens fresh from the lake. Fried by my frau, filleted and anointed with lemon, they make a delicately delicious supper. If I weren't so corrupt and lazy, I'd take hook and line myself, drop down to Lake Akakola 1,200 feet below, and catch a similar supper every evening. According to the old logbooks here, at least some of the previous lookouts used to do that.

Officially, all measurements at Glacier National Park are now given in meters. All road and trail signs, all park maps, show distances and heights in meters and kilometers, without their Anglo-American equivalents. The Park Service, no doubt at the instigation of the Commerce Department, is trying to jam the metric system down our throats whether we want it or not. We can be sure this is merely the foot in the door, the bare beginning of a concerted effort by Big Business—Big Government (the two being largely the same these days) to force the metric system upon the American people. Why? Obviously for the convenience of world trade, technicians, and technology, to impose on the entire planet a common system of order. All men must march to the beat of the same drum, like it or not.

July 17
Still no real fires, aside from a few trivial lightning-storm flare-ups in the forest across the river, soon drowned by rain. But we are ready. Perhaps I should describe the equipment and operations of a lookout.

We live and work in the second story of the cabin. The ground-floor room, dark and dank, is used only for storage. Our room is light, airy, and bright, with windows running the length of all four walls. Closable louvred vents above each window admit fresh air while keeping out rain. In the center of this twelve-foot by twelve-foot room, oriented squarely with the four directions, stands the chest-high fire finder. The Osborne Fire Finder consists essentially of a rotating metal ring about two feet in diameter with a handle to turn it by and a pair of sights, analogous to the front and rear sights of a rifle, mounted upright on opposite sides. When the lookout spots a fire, he aims this device at the base and center of the smoke (or flame, if discovered at night) and obtains an azimuth reading from the fixed base of the fire finder, which is marked off into 360 degrees. By use of the vernier scale attached to the rotating ring, the lookout can get a reading not only in degrees but precisely to the nearest minute, or one-sixtieth of a degree.

Having determined the compass direction of the fire from his own location, the lookout must still establish the location of the fire. To do that he must be able to recognize and identify the place where the fire is burning and to report its distance from his lookout station. A metal tape stretched between front and rear sights of the fire finder, across a circular map inside the rotating ring, gives the distance in kilometers. Another aid is the sliding peep sight on the rear sight, by means of which the lookout can obtain a vertical angle on his fire. Through a bit of basic trigonometry the vertical angle can be translated into distance. Or if another lookout, at a different station, can see the same fire, the line of his azimuth reading extended across a map of the area intersects the line of the first lookout's reading to give the exact point of the fire. Assuming both lookouts are awake, fairly competent, and on duty at the same time.

If these procedures sound complicated, that is an illusion. The technical aspects of a lookout's job can be mastered by any literate anthropoid with an IQ of not less than seventy in about two hours. It's the attitude that's difficult: Unless you have an indolent, melancholy nature, as I do, you will not be happy as an official United States government fire lookout.

Anyway, having determined the location of his fire, and being reasonably certain it is a fire and not a smoking garbage dump, a controlled slash burn, a busy campground, floating vapors, or traffic dust rising from a dirt road, the lookout picks up his radio microphone or telephone and reports his discovery to fire-control headquarters. After that his main task becomes one of assisting the smoke-chasers in finding the fire, relaying messages, looking for new and better fires.

July 20

Bear claw scratches on the wooden walls of the ground-floor storage room. Last thing before retiring each night I set the bear barrier in place on the stairway leading to our quarters. The bear barrier is a wooden panel with many nails driven through it, the points all sticking out. Supposed to discourage *Ursus stairiensis* from climbing up to our catwalk balcony. In a previous lookout's log we had read this entry:

Woke up this morning to see a big black bear staring at me thru window, about six inches from my face. Chased him off with a Pulaski.

The Pulaski is a fire-fighting tool, a combination ax and pickax. I keep one handy too, right under the bed where I can reach it easy. I'd keep it under the pillow if my old lady would let me.

Thinking about GRIZ. Almost every day, on the park or forest radio, we hear some ranger report a bear sighting, sometimes of grizzly. Campers molested, packs destroyed by hungry and questing bears. Somebody was recently attacked and mauled by a GRIZ north of the line, in Waterton Lakes. Bear jams on the park highway, though not so common here as they used to be in Yellowstone, before so many of Yellowstone's bears mysteriously disappeared, do occur in Glacier from time to time.

No doubt about it, the presence of bear, especially grizzly bear, adds a spicy titillation to a stroll in the woods. My bear-loving friend Peacock goes so far as to define wilderness as a place and only a place where one enjoys the opportunity of being attacked by a dangerous wild animal. Any place that lacks GRIZ, or lions or tigers, or a rhino or two, is not, in his opinion, worthy of the name "wilderness." A good definition, worthy of serious consideration. A wild place without dangers is an absurdity, although I realize that danger creates administrative problems for park and forest managers. But we must not allow our national parks and national forests to be degraded to the status of mere public playgrounds. Open to all, yes of course. But— *enter at your own risk.*

Enter Glacier National Park and you enter the homeland of the grizzly bear. We are uninvited guests here, intruders, the bear our reluctant host. If he chooses, now and then, to chase somebody up a tree, or all the way to the hospital, that is the bear's prerogative. Those who prefer, quite reasonably, not to take such chances should stick to Disneyland in all its many forms and guises.

• • •

July 22

Bowman Lake 3,000 feet below looks more like clear Pennzoil than water. A milky turquoise green color, strange to my eyes. The North Fork even more so. The cause is not man-made pollution of any sort, but what is called "glacier milk," a solution of powdered rock washed down from under the bellies of the glaciers hanging all around us under the high peaks.

Toy boats glide up and down the lake, trailing languorous wakes that spread across the oil-smooth water in slow-subsiding ripples. Anglers at work. The fishing is poor this summer, they say; weather too wet, too much insect life in the air and floating down the streams.

Too wet? You can say that again. This is the foggiest, boggiest, bug-giest country I have ever seen in my life. Everywhere I look, below timberline, the land is clothed in solid unbroken greenery. Damp, humid green all over the place—gives the country an unhealthy look. I guess I really am a desert rat. The sound of all these verdant leafy things breathing and sweating and photosynthesizing around me all the time makes me nervous. Trees, I believe (in the ardor of my prejudice), like men, should be well spaced off from one another, not more than one to a square mile. Space and scarcity give us dignity. And liberty. And thereby beauty.

Oyster stew for lunch. Out of tin can. Had buckwheat cakes for breakfast, with wild huckleberry syrup by Eva Gates, Bigfork, Montana.

Enormous clouds with evil black bottoms floating in from the Pacific, great sailing cities of cumulo-nimbus. Lightning plays among their massy depths. Will it bring us fire? God, one hopes so. What are we up here for, perched like condors on this mighty mountain, if not to conjure up a storm? The children need shoes. All those fire fighters down at headquarters need overtime. The forest needs a rebirth, a renascence, a weeding out.

July 23

Down the mountain I go, returning same day with mail, wine, cheese, other essentials. I sing, as I march along, songs I hope will warn the

GRIZ of my approach. But what kind of music does the GRIZ like? Suppose he hates old cowboy songs? Or Puccini?

All the way up the mountain, under a dark and grumbling sky, a personal cloud of hungry mosquitoes envelopes my head. I am relieved and glad when the first lightning strikes begin to bounce off the crags above. Am less glad when I reach the open ridge at timberline with jagged high-voltage bolts crashing all around. No place to hide now; I, keep going for the relative safety of the lookout cabin and reach it just as the storm bursts out in all its awful grandeur.

We cower inside in the dark, Renée and I, trying to stay away from all metal objects, as instructed. But, of course, the lookout is crowded with metallic objects—iron stoves, fire finder, steel cots, water cans, buckets, ax, dishpan. We can feel the next charge building up, we stand on the negative terminal of a high-powered electrical system, the positive pole directly overhead. Our skin prickles, our hair stands up. We hear a fizzing noise above us, on the roof of the cabin where the lightning rod sticks up. A crackling sound, like a burning fuse. I know what's coming now, and an instant later it comes, a flash that fills the room with blue-white light, accompanied simultaneously by a jarring crash, as if the entire cabin had been dropped from the sky upon our rocky ridge. No harm done. The building is thoroughly grounded, top and sides, and Thor's hammer blow passes on safely into the heart of the mountain. Lightning strikes many times in the same place. As every lookout learns.

That evening we spot a couple of small flare-ups across the river in the national forest. But both are soon drowned out by rain and never go anywhere.

July 27

The bird list grows slowly. Add barn swallow, cliff swallow, water pipit, raven, blue grouse, white-tailed ptarmigan, rufous hummingbird, brown creeper, gray jay, evening grosbeak, red-shafted flicker, loon. Loon!—heard from the lake far below—that wild, lorn, romantic cry, one of the most thrilling sounds in all North America. Sound of the ancient wilderness, lakes, forest, moonlight, birchbark canoes.

We have also seen two cow moose, one with calf, romping through the fields below the lookout, and a badger, several black bear (but no GRIZ yet), elk droppings, mountain goat tracks, least chipmunks, ground squirrels, pikas, hoary marmots, many deer. And there's a big wood rat living downstairs among the water cans, firewood, tools, and boxes. Met him the other day.

The flowers have been blooming, on and off, ever since we got here. We've identified the following so far: purple-eyed mariposa, false asphodel, valerium, harebell, blue penstemon, arnica, fleabane, mountain penstemon, bear grass, sulfur flower, stonecrop, Indian paintbrush, alum root, glacier lily, prince's pine, mountain gentian, forget-me-not, bluebonnet, alpine buttercup, yellow columbine, elephant head, blanket flower, alpine aster, swamp laurel, fireweed.

The bear grass, with its showy panicle of flowers on a two- or three-foot stalk, is the most striking flower in Glacier. It reminds me of pictures of the giant lobelia on the slopes of Mount Kilimanjaro. The deer eat the flower stalks.

Bear sighting reported on park radio: A ranger reports one grizzly sow with two cubs in "Moose Country," along the Going-to-the-Sun Highway. The bear, he says, is reared up on her hind legs, roaring and waving her arms at tourists as they surround her, their cameras clicking. He breaks it up. Nobody hurt. This time.

The park radio is our chief amusement. Over a million people visited the park last summer, most of them driving through by way of the Going-to-the-Sun. Many traffic problems every day, much police work.

Exempli gratia 1: 1961 converted schoolbus at Logan Pass, brakes burned out, driver thinks he can bring bus down mountain by driving in low gear, requests ranger escort. Not allowed. Tow truck dispatched.

E.g. 2: Ranger reports distraught wife and children at Lake McDonald campground. "Woman is very upset," he says. Cause? Her husband, the children's father, went off on a hike with a fifteen-year-old baby-sitter, been gone for hours. (Family is reunited later in evening.)

E.g. 3: Rookie ranger reports five bikers camping under highway bridge and smoking a controlled substance. "I think they're smoking dope," he says, "although, of course, I don't know what dope smells like."

Our friend Gus Chambers up on Swiftcurrent Lookout in the center of the park spots the first genuine park fire of the season. (And the only one, as it turns out.) He gives his azimuth reading, the UTM (Universal Transverse Mercator) coordinates, locates it one kilometer south-southeast of Redhorn Lake. No one can see the fire but Gus; we other lookouts are sick with envy and rage. One snag burning in a small valley, remote from any trail; too windy for smoke jumpers, fire fighters are flown to scene by helicopter.

Fire caused by lightning. When Smokey Bear says that only *You* can prevent forest fires, Smokey is speaking an untruth. A falsehood. Ninety percent of the fires in the American West are lightning-caused, as they have been for the last 20,000 years, or ever since the glaciers retreated. Yet the forests survived. And thrived. Hard to explain this to some old-time foresters, who often feel the same passionate hatred for fire that sheepmen feel for coyotes. Now, after fifty years of arduous fire-suppression effort, the useful role of natural fire in the forest ecosystem is becoming recognized among foresters. But the public, indoctrinated for so long in the Smokey Bear ethic, may not be easy to reeducate.

No one disputes the fact that it will always be necessary to quell forest fires that threaten lives, homes, business establishments, or valuable stands of timber scheduled for logging.

July 30

Renée bakes a prune pie. An experiment. I read Burton on "Heroical Love." The days sail by with alarming speed; why this headlong descent into *oblivion?* What's the rush? Sinking comfortably into the sloth and decay of my middle middle age, I am brought up short nevertheless, now and then, by the alarming realization that all men, so far, have proved mortal. Me too? Each day seems more beautiful than the last. Every moment becomes precious. Thus are we driven to the solitary pleasures of philosophy, the furtive consolations of thought.

Gus's fire is out. Burnt only five acres. Snow slides in Logan Pass again, traffic halted. Hiker killed on Snyder Lake trail, trying to climb cliff. Child lost and found. Woman, sixty-seven, lost for three hours near Bowman Lake. Found. GRIZ trees three hikers at Trout Lake.

More bugs. Mosquitoes as numerous as ever, soon to be augmented by swarms of flying ants. And now another enemy, the moose fly, appears, the bloodsucking *Muscas horribilis sangria*. Mean, vicious Draculas with wings. About the size of bats. We stay inside when the wind dies and all these flying plagues come forth together.

I read the old lookout logs. First of all Numa Ridge lookouts was Scotty Beaton, who worked here twenty-two summers, beginning in 1928. Unlike all succeeding lookouts, whose logbook entries tend (like mine) to rant and ramble, Scotty kept his notations terse, laconic, to the point. Viz.:

Aug. 2, 1945: hot & dry done my usual chores

July 28, 1946: Very warm—Hugh Buchanan the ranger came up with a Paper to have me Pledge I wouldn't overthrow the government that never entered my mind in the fifty five years I been in this country

July 5, 1948: Moved up today the bears had moved into the lower part of the Lookout & took a few bites out of the upper story. The lower part a hell of a mess.

July 22, 1949: Done usual chores

Sept. 11, 1950: Found mud in bottom of water barrel put there by youngster from McFarland's dude ranch. Same kid who broke crosshairs on firefinder, tramped down nails in bear board and set my binoculars on the hot stove.

According to the logbooks, every lookout since Scotty found Numa Ridge a delightful place—but only one of the twenty-four (including many couples) came back for a second season, and the second was enough for him. In the fire lookout's vocation many are called, few chosen. The isolation is too much for most. This is my seventh summer as a lookout; I guess I like it.

Down on Loneman Peak in the southern part of Glacier sits Leonard Stittman. This is his fourteenth summer on Loneman. In all those summers he has had a total of eight visitors, all of them rangers.

We've had a ranger-visitor too—Art Sedlack, the man who shot the snowmobile.

It happened one night in December 1974. Sedlack, on duty at Walton Ranger Station in Glacier, caught a snowmobiler buzzing around in an area where snowmobiles are not supposed to be. This sort of thing had been going on for a long time, and the operator of this particular snowmobile was a repeat offender. Suddenly inspired, Sedlack drew his trusty .38 Ranger Special and shot the snowmobile right through the head. "One snowmobile, immobilized," he reported by radio. Sensation! For a while Sedlack's rear end was in a sling as the owner of the slain snowmobile and other local motorized recreationists demanded blood, a head for a head. Sedlack might have lost his job but for an outpouring of public support, phone calls and letters from all over west Montana. Reconsidering, the park administration suspended him for one week without pay, then sent him to the service's police-training school in Washington, D.C. Now he is back in Glacier, an unrepentant and even better ranger.

Art talks about the bear problem in the national parks. Really a human problem. Too many humans crowding the roads and trails, conflict inevitable. Solution: Reduce population. Which population? Ah yes, indeed, that is the question.

A bear, when caught in mischief, is tranquilized and tagged on the ear. Caught again, it is tagged on the other ear. A bear with both ears tagged is in trouble. It may be transported to a locality remote from human activity, but this is not a solution. There are no vacant areas in nature. The newcomer bear is not welcome among established inhabitants, is harried, fought, driven out by native bears, becomes a loner, an outlaw, a rogue doomed. If caught in trouble a third time he or she will likely be "taken away" for good. That is, shot dead.

August 2

Fog and rain. Foul is fair and fair is foul. Cut more wood, keeping bin full. When I go down the hill to the john in the morning I find the mosquitoes huddled inside, waiting for me as usual. As usual I light up a Roi-Tan, a good cheap workingman's cigar, and the mosquitoes flee, choking and swearing. I sit there and contemplate, through the smoke, the dim shapes of fir tree and mule deer through the mists. On clear mornings, sunshine on my lap, I can look right down on the pearly, oily, iridescent surface of Bowman Lake in all its incredible rich blueness. I think, if I think at all, about simplicity, convenience, the advantages of what I call Positive Poverty.

There is of course no flush toilet on a fire lookout. But the pit toilet is a perfectly adequate, comfortable and even pleasant substitute for the elaborate bathrooms of the modern home. A little lime or wood ashes keep down the odors, discourage flies. In cold weather one kerosene or Coleman lamp keeps the outhouse warm enough. What more does one need? And no freezing pipes, no water pump, no septic tank to worry about, no awful plumber's bills. And the basic good sense of it: Instead of flushing our bodily wastes into the public water supply, we plant them back in the good earth where they belong. Where our bodies must go as well, in due course, if we are to keep the good earth productive.

Nor is there running water up here. Or electricity. I carry the water by the bucketful up from the barrels in the cellar. We heat the water on the wood stove, wash and scald-rinse the dishes in a pair of dishpans, bathe (when we feel like it) in a small galvanized tub set on the floor or out on the catwalk when the sun is shining. Before the big drifts melted, Renée and I sometimes scrubbed ourselves with handfuls of snow, standing naked on the dazzling snowbanks, in the heat of the sun.

Hauling water, cutting firewood, using a pit toilet seem like only normalcy to me, raised as I was on a backwoods Pennsylvania farm. For

Renée, a city girl, these methods are new, but she adapts at once, without difficulty, to such minor deprivations. No problem at all. Most of what we call modern conveniences are no more than that at best. They are far from being necessities. And what a terrible price most of us have to pay for our tract homes, our fancy plumbing, our automobiles, our "labor-saving" appliances, the luxuriously packaged ersatz food in the supermarkets, all that mountain of metal junk and plastic garbage under which our lives are smothered. Men *and* women trapped in the drudgery and tedium of meaningless jobs (see Studs Terkel's *Working* if you don't believe me), and the despoliation of a continent, the gray skies, the ruined rivers, the ravaged hills, the clear-cut forests, the industrialized farms, all to keep that Gross National Product growing ever grosser. Madness and folly. Untouched by human hands. Unguided by human minds.

Not that technology and industrialism are evil in themselves. The problem is to get them down to human scale, to keep them under human control, to prevent them from ever again becoming the self-perpetuating, ever-expanding monsters we have allowed them to become. What we need is an optimum industrialism, neither too much nor too little, a truly sophisticated, unobtrusive, below-ground technology. For certainly science, technology, industrialism have given us a number of good things. Not many, but some. My list begins with the steel ax. Matches. Nails, hammer, handsaw. Writing paper and pen and ink. The birth-control pill. Or the condom. (Forget-me-not.) Galvanized bucket—no, strike that item; the old oaken bucket is good enough. The cast-iron stove. Electricity. And solar heating. Windmills and suction pumps. Candles, Aladdin lamps, pianos, and platinum flutes. The coal-burning locomotive, transcontinental train service, the horse collar, the pneumatic-tired wagon, bicycles, the rocket-powered spaceship. But not automobiles. (What? Spaceships! Yes. Why not? I believe space exploration is a worthy human adventure.) Radios and record players, but not television. Anesthetics and aspirin, but not BHT, sodium nitrite, monosodium glutamate, or artificial coloring. The democratic rifle and the egalitarian revolver, but not the authoritarian B-52. And so on.

But we cannot pick and choose this way, some technophiles may insist—it's the entire package, plagues and all, or nothing. To which one must reply: If that is true then we have indeed lost control and had better dismantle the whole structure. But it is not true: We *can* pick and choose, we can learn to select this and reject that. Discrimination is a basic function of the human intelligence. Are we to be masters or slaves of the techno-industrial machine?

My cigar has gone out. The mosquitoes come sneaking back. They whine around my ears like the sirens of commerce, like bill collectors, like the National Association of Manufacturers. The sound of greed.

Time to sharpen the old ax. A chill wind is blowing and the fog rolls in again. Dark birds flap through the mist, croaking for blood.

August 3
Done usual lookout chores.

August 4
Done usual lookout chores. To wit: woke, ate, answered radio check, looked, chopped wood, carried water, read Burton ("Of all causes of this affliction," he writes, meaning romantic love, "the most remote are the stars"), looked, releveled fire finder, washed dishes, played chess then flute, watched sun go down, went to bed.

In the evening after sundown an owl flies round and round the lookout, swooping silent as a moth through the fog and gloom, checking out our chipmunks. Barred owl? Short-eared owl? Hard to tell in this darkness. A spooky bird of ill import.

August 5
My wife looks prettier every day. By God, a man begins to get ideas in a place like this.

August 7
High winds all day, clear sky, scudding clouds. The surface of the lake below, stirred by the wind, looks like brushed aluminum, has the color

of my knife blade. The peaks round about stand forth in startling, blazing, preternatural brilliance. A cold, immaculate clarity. Shall we climb Rainbow Peak one of these days? Ever see Goat Haunt? Belly River? Mount Despair? Loneman? Gunsight Pass? Rising Wolf Mountain? Spirit Lake? Two Medicine Mountain? Almost A Dog Mountain? Vulture Peak?

August 11
Storms. Fog and drizzle, brief blaze of sun—a rainbow floats in the fog below.

Lightning again, flashing through the mist; the thunder rumbles in at a thousand feet per second. Pink lightning. Heaven and earth link nerves in illuminated ecstasy—or is it pain? Once, in another place, I saw lightning score a direct hit on a juniper tree. The tree exploded in a burst of flame.

Now comes another direct hit on our lookout. First the buzzing sound, the eerie *hiss* and *fizz* directly overhead. That sinister touch, God's fingertip upon our roof. Light, deadly, an almost dainty touch, you might say. Followed by the flash of light and the *crack!* of a great whip. The building vibrates.

When the hard winds blow the cabin creaks and groans, tugging at the cables that keep it anchored to the rock. On our east side the ridge drops off at fifty degrees down a treeless slope to the bottom of the cirque 600 feet blow.

In the evening things settle down a bit. We go for a walk down the trail, down through the drifting fog. The huckleberries are ripening now, but it looks like a poor crop. The bears will be roaming and irritable. Mushrooms bulge through the damp duff under the pines—fat, brown, speckled domes of fungoid flesh. Delicacies for the deer. The mushrooms remind me of bitter days at another lookout post, 2,000 miles away and a decade in the past. I was enduring the agonies of unrequited love, exactly as Burton describes them, and in my misery I contemplated with interest some of the mushrooms growing all about the tower of that other lookout; the rosy hoods of *Amanita muscaria* suggested the possibility of flight beyond the sorrows of this sublunar sphere. But I refrained, not from fear of hallucination or death, but because I was becoming accustomed to the realization that I enjoyed my sufferings more. So the girl I loved had betrayed me by running off with her husband. What of it? I survived.

Men have died and worms have eaten them, but not for love.

August 15

Been gone three days, leaving Renée to man the lookout on her own. She was willing and ready and is in fact a better fire lookout than I. Much more conscientious, not so corrupted by subversive notions of fire ecology, etc.

Down from Numa Ridge, the first thing I did was go to Logan Pass, hike the Highline Trail to Granite Park and up Swiftcurrent Peak to visit Gus at his fire lookout. Late in the evening I returned to Logan Pass. Nineteen miles round trip. On the way I had passed a group of mountain goats, six of them, grazing not fifty feet from the trail, indifferent to my presence. Returning at twilight, I encountered five bighorn rams bunched up right on the trail, blocking my way. They showed no inclination to move and I wasn't going to climb around them. I approached to within twenty feet, waved my arms and whistled; grudgingly they got up and let me through. That's the way it is in the Peaceable Kingdom, the wildlife so accustomed to hikers they won't even get out of your way.

I had timed my walk badly. The dark settled in while I was still five miles from Logan Pass, the road, and my car. The trail wound through thickets of alder brush, with a cliff on my left and a drop-off on my right. A cloudy, starless night. Hard to see more than ten, fifteen feet ahead. Odd noises off in the thickets. I began to think about GRIZ again. What to do if I met one now? No climbable trees in sight and my only weapon a pocketknife. Words of wisdom, often heard at Glacier, whispered through my brain: "Anyone who hikes alone, after dark, is asking for trouble." Bears are omnivorous, have no pride at all, will eat anything, even authors. Even if the GRIZ hears me coming, I realized, he will have difficulty getting out of my way on this mountain trail. We'd have to sidle past one another, smiling apologetically, like strangers in a narrow doorway. I walked on, singing loudly, feeling foolish, half amused by my own fear. Yes, I did want to meet a grizzly in the wild—but not just yet. Nothing happened that night. I saw nothing but shadows, heard nothing but the wind and those obscure crashing sounds, now and then, below the trail.

August 16

Old magazines on the shelves under the fire finder, left here by former lookouts. I leaf through *Field and Stream, Outdoor Life, Hook & Bullet News.* Here's an interesting item:

> *Stock taking.* California has a new procedure for scattering the trout it stocks in streams in an attempt to foil hatchery-truck chasers. The fish are not released until dusk or after dark and are placed in one spot rather than in several. Wardens report that the fish are well scattered by daylight and the night stocking stymies the truck followers.

And another:

> *Pump Priming.* In an effort to stimulate the lagging fishing and subsequent business decline caused by the ban on keeping fish caught in Lake St. Clair, the Michigan Marine and Snowmobile Dealers Association is trying to raise $50,000 to $100,000 to finance the tagging of thousands of fish that would be worth anywhere from $100 to $10,000 apiece to the anglers catching them. The ban resulted from mercury contamination tests run on some of the lake's fish.

So it goes, sportsmen.

Reflections on hunting. My father was a hunter. During the Great Depression and the war years, he killed dozens of deer, hundreds of cottontail rabbits, in order to put meat on the table for his hungry family. My mother would can the extra rabbit, putting it up in jars. During the fifties and sixties, as the times got better, my father gradually gave up hunting. Never in his life has he killed another living thing for sport. Except, that is, during his boyhood. Before he grew up. Hunters, he would explain, never kill for sport.

All those red-coated men we see out in the field during deer season—what are they up to? Well, some of them are hunters, engaged in the ancient, honorable, and serious business of providing meat for kith and kin. The majority, however, outnumbering the hunters and the deer as well by ninety-nine to one, are not hunters but merely gunners. Sportsmen.

The sportsman's pursuit of game is incidental to his primary purposes, which can be defined as follows, in descending order of importance:

1. Get away from wife and kids for a few days
2. Get drunk and play poker with cronies by the light of a Coleman lamp in tent, lodge, or Winnebago
3. Swap lies with same
4. Maybe shoot some legal game
5. Failing that, shoot some illegal game—cow, horse, chicken, game warden, etc.
6. Failing that, shoot *something*—side of barn, road sign, his own foot, whatever's handy.

How do I know about this? Because I was there. I too was once a sportsman. But I grew up. In that one respect anyhow. Like my old man, Paul, who beat me to it.

August 18

Somebody falls into McDonald Falls again. "Bring the wagon," radios ranger. The hurry-up wagon. Happens every year. As at North Rim, Grand Canyon, where somebody disappears every summer.

Whole family mauled by a grizzly on Grinnel Glacier trail. Father, mother, two children. Apparently the children had been walking far ahead of their parents, got between a sow and her cub. Children attacked. Their screams bring father running to the scene, who attempts to fight off the GRIZ with his bare hands. Reinforced by mother, the bear knocks them both about, then wanders off. Entire family hospitalized with serious injuries. Rangers close trail to further hiking for time being.

Might be hard to explain to those people why the grizzly bear is a vital part of the Glacier wilderness. But it is. The parks are for people? Certainly. And for bears also? Absolutely. How do we resolve the inevitable conflict? Are we going to ration the wilderness experience? Probably; that process has already begun at Glacier National Park, where back-country camping is restricted to certain sites, requiring written permits and advance reservations. A sad and ominous but unavoidable expedient.

One calamity after another. One mishap after another. A ranger's work is never done. And more and more, in every national park, that work consists largely of police work. The urbanization of our national parks. All through the summer bumper-to-bumper auto traffic crawls up and down the Going-to-the-Sun Highway. I've said it before and I'll say it again, we've got to close the parks to private cars if we want to keep them as parks. The parks are for people, not machines. Let the machines find their own parks. Most of America has been surrendered to them already, anyway. New Jersey, for example. Southern California.

On the forest radio, the weather report concludes as usual with the daily fire-fighting capability report: "We have available in Missoula today fifty-two smoke jumpers, two B-16s, one Neptune, two twin Beechcraft, two helicopters, four DC-7s, etc." All on standby, in readiness.

There used to be ten active fire-lookout stations in Glacier. Now there are only four. My old lookout tower on North Rim was deactivated five years ago. More and more lookouts are superseded by aircraft patrols. Part of the national industrializing pattern, human beings put out of work by machines. Labor-intensive jobs (so to speak) made obsolete by capital-intensive substitutes. One hour of an airplane's time costs more than two or three days' pay for a human lookout on a mountaintop. But no doubt it is, as they say, more efficient. And what happens to all the displaced fire lookouts? They swell the ranks of the unemployed. They wander the streets of small western towns, kicking beer cans around, getting in trouble.

Who cares? Most fire lookouts are crazy anyhow. Once from a peak in southern Arizona, at sundown, with the western sky full of smoke, dust, and clouds, I looked straight at the sun with my lookout's binoculars. I knew it was a foolish thing to do. Could have ruined my eyes forever. At the very least might have impaired my night vision. But the haze seemed so extremely dense, the sun so blood-red behind it, that I thought it might be safe, just this once. All I wanted was one quick glimpse of those plasmic bonfires 10,000 miles high leaping into space from the rim of the roaring sun. So I looked. And I saw them. It was a sublime and terrifying spectacle, which I can never forget. And my eyes survived, apparently unharmed, although a few years later I began to have trouble reading the numbers in a phone book, and my arms seemed too short to hold a newspaper far enough away from my eyes to make it readable.

"You need glasses," the eye doctor said. "You're farsighted."

"Why?"

"Middle age."

I told him about the time I stared at the sun face to face.

"You were lucky," he said.

August 22

Renée takes off for a three- or four-day tour of the park, leaving me here alone with my dirty dishes and the unswept floor. Two old-time park naturalists arrive, sit around drinking my coffee and telling what they call North Dakota jokes.

"Why won't a North Dakotan eat pickles?"

"Can't get his head in the jar."

"What does it say on the bottom of Coke bottles in North Dakota?"

"Open other end."

Etc. They do all the laughing.

Fog and rain, rain and fog. The fire season is shot to hell. Word from headquarters is that we're to be "terminated" (without prejudice) on September 5. Lookout completely socked in. Black bear with two cubs seen near Moose Wallow during my evening walk. Huckleberries, whortleberries, raspberries all ripening, but few of them.

The short-eared owl comes back at dusk, circling my glass-walled home. Perhaps it is me that silent bird is looking for. All my superstitions rise to the surface. At midnight under the full moon, dip your hand in the punky water of a hollow stump if you want to rid it of warts. Etc.

Cut and stack wood, refilling bin. Install new stovepipe. Caulk window frames. Repair broken shutters. Won't be here much longer.

One young punk showed up at nine-thirty this morning, jogging up the trail. Gasping for breath, before he even said hello he asked what time it was. So he could time his hike. A goggle-eyed bore with hairy legs, wearing track shorts and tennis shoes. Outward Bound type. He hung around for a few minutes, saw little of interest in me or the lookout, and trotted down the trail again, vanishing into the clouds below.

Days now getting perceptibly shorter. Full moon rising over Rainbow Peak. Grand, gorgeous, shocking-pink sunset. Feel of autumn in the air. In August! Two golden eagles hovering on the sky, high above my cabin. God Bless America—Let's Save Some of It. Long live the weeds and the wilderness yet.

August 23

Rain, wind, rain, and fog. When the storm clears I see fresh snow on Kintla, Rainbow, and Reuter peaks, down to the 8,000-foot line. Temperature was 34° F this morning at 0630. Everything wet and slimy. Expect to see snails and other Mollusca crawling up the windowpanes. Horny octopi. . . .

• • •

August 24

Awoke this morning, after a long cold night, to find two inches of snow on the catwalk railing, on the pines, on everything in sight. Wet, fat snow, clinging to every twig and needle.

Renée returns, but only briefly. Has to leave at once for Vancouver. Her grandfather's dying. I am alone for the final week on this cold, dismal, rain- and snow-soaked mountain. I get so lonesome I wash the dishes for diversion. Loneliness. Mount Despair. Wintertime in August.

August 26

Termination date has now been advanced to August 28.

I go for long walks in the evening, hoping for one clear sight of GRIZ. The silence of the woods. No birds speak except one woodpecker, far below, hammering on a snag. But 1,000 feet below, under the snow-line, the weather is late summer. Tufts of moss, like scalp locks, dangle from the branches of the lodgepole pine, the larch, the spruce. This is the forest primeval. Elaborate spiderwebs hang face-high across the trail, each with a tiny golden spider waiting at the center. Damp smells of fern and pine bark, the distant drumming of the woodpecker. Sounds like Red Norvo at the vibraphone. Bluebells still in bloom down here, wild roses covered with dew. Running water across the stones of the trail. I pause on the way back up to drink a handful; the sweet, cold, piney flavor reminds me of boyhood, the Allegheny Mountains back in old Pennsylvania. Lost at twilight in the green depths of the Big Woods.

Back to the cold darkness of the lookout cabin. I build a fire in the stove, sit with my feet on the open oven door and play the flute. The deer outside lift their heads to listen for a moment, then resume their feeding. Down in Arizona I used to rouse the coyotes at dawn, playing certain high notes on this silver-plated instrument. I'd play our tune and wait and after a few moments their wild cries came floating back to me across the desert, mimicking my song.

• • •

August 27

Last full day on the mountain. Sun shining for a change. Many deer hang about, fighting over my various urine-supplied salt deposits. Obvious pecking order among them: One old battle-scarred six-point buck is clearly dominant; the others keep their distance from him but jostle one another roughly.

Always looking and listening, these deer. Even the fawns have that wary look. Danger everywhere. Nor do they look well-fed, even now in late summer. Gaunt and ganted, lean and bony deer, how will they ever get through the coming winter? A tough life. Always hard times for deer. The struggle for existence. All their energy goes into survival—and reproduction. The only point of it all—to go on. On and on and on. What else is there? Sometimes I am appalled by the brutality, the horror of this planetary spawning and scheming and striving and dying. One no longer searches for any ulterior significance in all this; as in the finest music, the meaning is in the music itself, not in anything beyond it. All we have, it seems to me, is the beauty of art and nature and life, and the love which that beauty inspires.

Smell of cooking rubber. I withdraw my booted feet from the oven.

August 28

Raining again. Storm predicted. The packer with his mules is coming up the mountain this morning. I clean the lookout, put everything away, bolt the shutters back on the windows, pack our baggage, sign off on the radios. "This is Numa Ridge Fire Lookout going ten-seven [out of service] for about ten months. Have a good winter, everybody."

The packer arrives. Followed by the wind. We load the mules in a driving rain and start down the mountain.

A Reporter at Large: Fire
by Thomas Hackett

Thomas Hackett (born 1964) was a mes-
senger at The New Yorker *when he took a*
month off to visit fire fighting teams in Yellow-
stone National Park during the summer of
1988. Fire had burned 190,000 acres by the
time he arrived.

Whenlightning ignited a fire in the Lamar Valley, in the northeastern part of Yellowstone National Park, on May 24, 1988, nobody thought anything of it. "All fires start small," firefighters often say, and this one, like most, stayed small. Rain fell that day. For the past sixteen years, Yellowstone administrators had been following a "prescribed-natural-burn" policy, which allowed certain lightning-caused fires to burn unhindered. This policy was based on the idea that burning could bring an old and ailing forest back to life. But most of the time, when lightning struck, nothing happened. From 1982 through 1984, for instance, the staff at Yellowstone's fire cache—the headquarters of Yellowstone's resident fire-fighting teams—reported twenty-eight lightning-caused fires and ten fires credited to people, and in those three summers not a single acre burned. Many people thought that in Yellowstone—where winters are long and severe, summers short and often rainy—you couldn't start a forest fire if you tried. So on June 23, 1988, when, after an especially wet spring, lightning struck again and ignited another fire, this time in the woods near Shoshone Lake, in the southwest corner of the park, the park superintendent, Robert Barbee, didn't think much of it, either. The Shoshone fire was allowed to burn. "Normally, if you get a hundred acres out of a fire in Yellowstone it's something to get excited about," Barbee told me a few weeks later. "I just thought, Well, it's moving into the green stuff, and you've got a couple of meadows down there, so no big deal. A couple of days go by, and then all of a sudden—*kapow!*— you've got a sixty-mile-an-hour wind knocking trees down, and the fire has taken off."

Two days after the Shoshone started, the Fan fire—named after Fan Creek—started, in the park's northwest corner. In the next couple of weeks, fires called the Red, which joined with the Shoshone; the Lava, to the south of the park's administrative headquarters, at Mammoth, in the northwest corner of the park; and the Mist and the Clover, which eventually joined together in the northeastern corner, were burning. All were lightning fires, and all were allowed to burn. On July 21st, by which time seventeen thousand acres (twenty-seven square miles) had burned, the park suspended its natural-burn policy. Donald Hodel, then the Secretary of the Interior, paid a visit to Yellowstone on July 27th and confirmed the suspension, declaring that for the rest of the year all fires would be fought. Yet, in spite of Hodel's decision, a hundred and twenty thousand acres (a hundred and eighty-eight square miles) had burned by the end of July—some five and a half per cent of the park's two million two hundred thousand acres.

"You have to remember, we didn't anticipate that it would go on like this," Barbee remarked a few weeks later. Throughout the fire season, Barbee, who has worked for the National Park Service for thirty-one years, was the park's front man. He didn't manage the blazes; Yellowstone's fire cache has only limited resources to fight fires, so park rangers usually call on the regional Forest Service office, in Missoula, Montana, to manage their fires—and sometimes, as in 1988, use the nationwide resources coördinated by the Boise Interagency Fire Center, in Idaho. Nevertheless, he put in eighteen-hour days, seven days a week, for about three months over the summer, meeting with congressmen, Presidential candidates, reporters, citizens of surrounding communities, the Secretaries of the Interior, of Agriculture, and of Defense, the director of the National Park Service, and the men who actually called the tactical shots on the fires—the incident commanders, who are otherwise known as fire bosses. All that time, he kept hoping that the weather would break. "We've nervously waited for the fronts to come in, and they have come, except they're dry fronts—cold, dry fronts, with lightning and no rain," he told me. "All we need is just a little bit of rain. We'd settle for half an inch— one of those days you always have in the northern Rockies, where it's gray and cruddy and everybody bitches and moans about the weather. That's all we want."

On the day I arrived at Yellowstone, August 9th—about a hundred and ninety thousand acres (two hundred and ninety-seven square miles) had burned by then—the fires still did not seem terribly threatening. I had come from Redding, California, accompanying a group of firefighters called the Redding Hot Shots—one of fifty-one well-trained Hot Shot crews that the Forest Service maintains across the country— who had been called upon late the night before by an incident commander, through the Boise Interagency network, to come to Yellowstone. Three hours after meeting up with the Hot Shots, I was in the park, assigned to the North Fork fire. We were briefed at the North Fork's fire camp, a temporary headquarters, which made use of one of the park's service yards near Old Faithful; it was at such camps all over the park that firefighters ate and slept, and morning and evening briefings were held. By that time, the North Fork fire—named, as all forest fires are, for a geographical feature near the point of origin, which in this case was a tributary of Split Creek, just west of the park—had burned thirty-two thousand acres. That was already more than had been burned by the largest fire in the park's history. (An eight-hundred-and-forty-acre fire would wipe out Central Park, and a fourteen-thousand-acre fire would destroy Manhattan.) But in a park as large as Yellowstone, which occupies the northwestern corner of Wyoming and spills over into Montana and Idaho, the North Fork fire appeared as a small splatter of ink on the maps posted at the North Fork's camp.

In 1988, forty-nine fires began in Yellowstone or just outside it. Blame for the North Fork fell on a woodcutter who had tossed a cigarette on the ground a few hundred feet west of the park, in Idaho's Targhee National Forest, six miles south of the Idaho-Montana-Wyoming junction. That was on July 22nd, a hot, dry, windy Friday afternoon, and, with optimum burning conditions, the fire quickly crossed into Yellowstone. The woodcutter, a man named Leland Owens, was one of four partners who had received permits to cut firewood for their private use but in fact made a business of selling the wood during the winter. The woodcutters left behind empty beer and soda cans and cigarette butts after a day's work. One cigarette, traced to Owens by a saliva test, ignited the duff at the bottom of a wooded draw that faced the southwest wind and the hot afternoon sun. Within an hour, seventy-five acres had burned.

The area where the North Fork fire originated is about ten miles west of Old Faithful, the park's biggest attraction. Just about everybody who visits Yellowstone visits Old Faithful. The geyser itself was, of course, not endangered by fire, but the Old Faithful Inn, which is eighty-five years old, was. It is the largest and, some say, the handsomest log building in the world. The threat to it became immediate national news, yet after an initial attack by the firefighters (and in contravention of the policy change) a Forest Service spokesman assigned to the fire at the time said, "Basically, we've decided to allow nature to take its course."

"That's preposterous," Barbee said when I mentioned this statement. "The decision to pull the crews off has been interpreted as 'Oh, well, they're going to let it go.' But that's not the case at all. We went to Area Command"—a temporary outfit at the airport in West Yellowstone, Montana, that the regional Forest Service office set up after the number of fires multiplied and the acreage for each enlarged, to oversee all the fires in the region—"and they gave us three options. One was just to let it burn and take it at Old Faithful. Another was to try to put a line around the whole thing, and that would cost x million dollars. The last was to secure the south and east flanks, to keep the fire out of Old Faithful, and to let it free-burn to the north and hope that it would rain, but if it didn't we could tie it off at the Madison River. They told us that if we tried to circle the fire with a bunch of crews working in front, and we got a big wind, we were likely to kill a bunch of people. So you rule that one out. And then you rule out the option of 'Well, we're just going to sit back and watch this thing.' And I thought it made the most sense to pursue the option where you secured the south and east flanks and let it free-burn to the north. If we got rain, then we could go in and attack it; otherwise, we'd let it burn to the Firehole and Madison Rivers, and we'd tie it off there."

So Barbee's stated objective was to contain (though not control) the North Fork fire, which had climbed the western slopes of the roadless Madison Plateau—isolated, untravelled country. Driven by the winds, the front of the North Fork fire had aimed straight for the bluffs at Madison Junction, where the plateau ends abruptly with a three-hundred-foot drop at the confluence of the Madison, Firehole, and Gibbon Rivers. Crews constructed fuel breaks, or fire lines, along the south and east flanks of the fire, and also along the park's western boundary, and then positioned themselves near the fire's head, checking its progress with occasional backfires. But a drizzle dampened the fire on July 28th, and Area Command declared the Old Faithful area out of danger and kept only six hundred and eighty-five firefighters there. A team of experts in fire-behavior analysis ("the best this country has to offer," Barbee said) had by that time completed a long-term prognosis, which said that, given normal weather—the usual August rainstorms—the fire, if it went unfought, would not reach the northwest edge of the plateau, at a confluence of rivers and roads at Madison Junction, before the end of the summer. And even if it did, as Barbee pointed out, fire would have difficulty crossing the Madison River, to the north, and the Firehole River, to the east.

• • •

You hear a lot of military humor on the fire lines, and the remark that fire crews use most is "Hurry up and wait." I went out with the Redding Hot Shots on August 11th, and we did nothing all morning but lie around in a staging area, a matted short-grass meadow on the east bank of the Firehole River. A makeshift heliport had been set up there, between a service road and the river, and three Chinook helicopters sat idle in the grass: smoke from the previous day's burning, to the west, pressed down on the flats and choked the sky, keeping them grounded.

The Redding Hot Shots were one twenty-man crew in what was at the time a six-hundred-and-forty-five-man militia—eighteen crews, most with some twenty firefighters—that had been called to the North Fork. At the heliport that morning, I talked to crews from the Sento Domingo Indian reservation, in New Mexico; the Fort Hall Indian reservation, in Idaho; Greybull, Wyoming; Silver City, New Mexico; Lake Tahoe, California; and the Utah State Prison. (The men in the prison crew called themselves the Flame-in-gos; a few nights later, one of them raped a female firefighter in camp, and the crew was sent back to prison.) Most fire crews are made up of athletic college-age boys, but the Redding Hot Shots were men and women, mostly in their thirties and married, with full-time careers in the Forest Service or the Bureau of Indian Affairs. They took their orders from an incident-command team: the fire bosses—the generals—who had done their time in the ground-crew ranks and were now, in most cases, career Forest Service employees free-lancing each summer in what they call the fire game. Not far away from the meadow where the crew was awaiting its orders, a herd of elk grazed and mingled with a herd of buffalo. The crew members read, played cards, batted at gnats, or slept.

By one that afternoon, the sun had forced its way through the haze, and the helicopters whined, wound up, squealed, and thumped into the air. We flew west over burned-out patches on the Madison Plateau and landed in Buffalo Meadow, or Helispot 12. The maps in the fire camp showed the meadow to be within the fire's perimeter and included it in the total burned acreage, but in fact the meadow hadn't been burned; it was just a dry, bleached-out brown—evidence that, as

Yellowstone's public-affairs office maintained, the figures for the burned acreage were overstated. Wind-driven fire skips and dashes and runs in elongated finger patterns across the landscape, and within burned perimeters patches the size of several city blocks may remain untouched. A detailed fire map would be as craggy and intricate as a map of the Maine coastline. We stood for a while, tools in hand, hard hats and gloves on, ready to work. The crew leader, Elizabeth Little—a tall, imposing woman—stood on a knoll studying a map and waiting for our orders to come over her walkie-talkie. They didn't come right away, so we lounged around, ate our lunches, and got some sun. Then the helicopters returned, and we got back on. "Hurry up and wait," someone said.

This time we flew into a smoky war zone. As we bounded out of the helicopter and gathered equipment, I asked one of the men in the Redding crew if he knew where we were. He said, "Are you serious?" and repeated my question to the rest of the crew. Someone explained that we were back in the place where we had spent the whole morning—at the heliport along the Firehole River. But in the hour we were gone the landscape, though so far unscathed, had been smothered under a low cloud of black smoke, and now only the buffalo and the elk were immediately recognizable. The meadow lay under a sombre pall reminiscent of a solar eclipse. Certain colors caught a strange light, and our fluorescent-orange hard hats stood out vibrantly against the charcoal-gray backdrop. Between the helicopters' taking off and landing, I could hear, perhaps a mile away, a deep rumble, like the sound of the ocean, but the smoke was too thick for me to tell whether the fire was nearby or far away.

We marched about a mile down the service road, and then snaked, single file, through a stand of lodgepole pines to the grassy riverside. Beth Little decided to begin the fire line in an area of blackened, burned grass. A man called Tank, second-in-charge of the crew, said that from there we would work through the sparse timber, cutting a line, parallel to the river, that was supposed to halt the fire before it reached a highly flammable pine stand loaded with dead and downed trees near and beyond the service road. Then we went to work. The sawyers, in the lead, buzzed away with chain saws; the swampers, whose job is to clear away any possible fuel for the fire—slash, sage-brush, loose branches, old logs, and just-cut timber—began making a lane; the rest of us began cutting a line, hacking and digging and raking through the hard topsoil to the mineral soil. One person chopped at the ground with a Pulaski (a combination axe and hoe named for a heroic Forest Service ranger); a second person took a further dig at the loosened earth with a shovel; a third scraped a line with a heavy-duty rake-and-hoe combination called a McLeod. In this way, we began cutting a foot-wide firebreak that was meant to slow the advancing front coming down off the eastern slopes of the Madison Plateau.

And for an hour, with the heat bearing down and the smoke often unbearable, we cut perhaps a quarter of a mile of line through the pines. The line seemed to me a mere scratch in the dirt, and I had a hard time understanding what good it could do against a fire that could leap the river. The plan, someone said later, was to tie in with a line that a crew ahead of us was cutting, and then, as the flames came closer, to ignite backfires and rob the inferno of fuel. But as the fire jumped over the river we could feel its wind whirling and whipping. Three-hundred-foot flames—rising three times as high as the tallest trees—lashed at the sky. Firebrands ignited small fires, called spots, beyond our line. A fallen tree caught an ember in its tangled, exposed roots, and before anybody could throw water or dirt on it the log was consumed by flames. A snag—a tree that is standing but dead—burned like a candle for a few moments, and then all its brittle branches fired up like a torch. A woman behind me kept yelling, "Bump up! Bump up! Let's go! Let's work!" I was winded, though, and, because I was swinging a Pulaski, was also having trouble keeping my safety glasses on. The smoke seared and scalded my mouth and throat; my eyes teared and my nose ran uncontrollably. The roar of flame grew so loud that I could hardly hear a warning that someone called when a snag crashed less than ten feet away.

Even with all the advances in firefighting—the use of aerial retardants, of helicopters for waterdrops and helitorching, of explosives, of improved backfiring techniques, and of mechanisms to induce rain—there is almost nothing that can be done to contain, let alone extinguish, the kind of fire we faced while we were digging the fire line. Within five minutes, the blaze had coalesced into a firestorm—the kind that has been studied in the interests of knowing what would happen in the first hour or so of a nuclear war—and as the twisting winds sucked the surrounding air and drafted upward in a tight convection column the fire seemed to gather still more energy and power. It was as if we were standing on the fringes of a hot tornado.

The intensity of the flames soon forced the crew to abandon the line, and we turned our attention to pouncing on as many small spots as we could. An unnoticed spot could quickly crown, or jump, into the upper canopy, spreading rapidly from one treetop to the next, and move toward the main front, trapping us. If that had happened, we could have opened our fire shelters—aluminum-foil-and-fibreglass cloths shaped like pup tents and able to withstand heat up to 1,400 degrees Fahrenheit—and climbed in, lain on the ground, and waited for the flames to pass. We could have also, if possible, retreated "into the black"—into the charred wake, where the burning was complete. But, of course, neither of these options was without risk.

Amid the riot of falling trees, a woman called Christie shouted to me, and she and I slipped through the fire and into the black. I know that's what we did, but even an hour later it still seemed unreal. I remember being sure to walk—not panic and run—down the fire line with Christie toward our anchor point, keeping my head up, watching for falling snags, and being blinded by smoke. And I remember gasping for breath in the scorched open space where we had begun the line. Over a walkie-talkie Christie heard from Beth Little that she and the rest of the crew had retreated from the fire and were near the service road. We waited a minute or so in the pall of smoke, trying to catch our breath, and then, when the wind seemed to abate, we trudged back up the line to where we'd left off. But we hadn't been there more than a minute before somebody—somebody flying over in a helicopter—got

Beth on the walkie-talkie, and she pulled us off the line. Quickly, we beat it out of the woods—back to the service road and out into the meadow, where we could breathe.

As the crew members set to sharpening their chain saws and their Pulaskis, a red pickup truck arrived. A short, burly man got out and said to all of us, "This is the most radical fire behavior I've ever seen."

I asked him to elaborate.

"You were out there jamming line—you could see for yourself that it looks bad," he said. He was Joseph Carvelho, who was the operations chief of the North Fork—the commander of the forces. "I've been doing this for twenty-three years, and this is just the ultimate. So O.K., it crossed the Firehole River—it's going big-time! But there are things for us to do. If it wants to come across the meadow, let it. But we've got to hold it at the highway now."

By three o'clock, the fire had raced out of control, burning thirteen thousand acres by the end of the day. That afternoon, Bob Barbee put in a call to Area Command for one of the Forest Service's Type One Incident Command teams, and that night, in the fire camp, Carvelho had to brief his replacements. There are only sixteen Type One teams in the country, and they are not called upon unless a fire threatens lives or valuable property or requires the management of hundreds— sometimes thousands—of firefighters, and dozens of helicopters, airplanes, and engines. The team that Carvelho belonged to, a Type Two team, which typically deals with smaller, quieter, more manageable fires, had been called out about a week before, when the drizzle temporarily tamed the North Fork. The new team, led by a longtime Forest Service employee named David Poncin, had just finished two weeks of fighting the Red-Shoshone fires—also called the Snake River complex. The team had more or less let the fire do what it wanted (in accordance with the park's natural-burn policy), but had protected the buildings—especially a resort at Grant Village, on the southeast shore of Yellowstone Lake. Poncin left that fire with a "positive feeling," he said later, that he and his team had accomplished their job. But the fires hadn't actually been put out, and a few weeks later the Red-Shoshone got back on its feet, and Grant Village was forced to close for the summer.

On the North Fork, Poncin's group again had the job of looking out for campgrounds and a few buildings, including the Old Faithful Inn, but they were also told to contain the fire, to keep it from moving east toward Old Faithful, north toward Madison Junction, and west toward the Targhee National Forest boundary. The fire would be allowed to burn within certain limits—burning the pockets of unburned fuel on the plateau, if it wanted—but not beyond them.

After a transitional briefing in which Carvelho and (on behalf of the superintendent's office) Joseph Evans, one of the park's four district rangers, outlined these objectives, I talked to Poncin in the fire camp's mess tent. Poncin, who is fifty-two, is tall and has the loose but slightly creaky swagger and slump of an old athlete. In his younger days with the Forest Service, he had been a smoke jumper—a firefighter who specializes in parachuting into remote, often dense forests and starting an initial attack on a fire. When he's not battling forest fires as an incident commander, Poncin is the fire, recreation, and lands staff officer in the Nez Perce National Forest, in Idaho. As we talked, buses of fire crews rumbled in after an evening of mopping up spot fires. Sooty, bleary-eyed firefighters lined up for pork chops and stuffing and ate slowly and quietly, hunched over their plates. It was after ten—late for the fire camp—and by now cold, so Poncin and I had a cup of coffee to stay warm.

I brought up the park's natural-burn policy, and asked Poncin what he thought of the job he had to do here.

"As a Type One team, we seldom get called out on anything less than a million-dollar fire, and this one has cost right around four million already," he said. "But then, these Yellowstone fires are different. We've spent eighty years putting fires out, developing the Smokey Bear thing, and saying fire is just plain bad. And, sure, if you're into logging, of course fire is a villain. But in a wilderness area like Yellowstone, where you're trying to keep something natural, you can't do without fire. If this fire were being suppressed—and by that I mean 'Let's put this baby out, let's do the job'—they'd have been flanking it all along, and then, as soon as we got the chance, we'd be able to head it off. But in this case, fine—the Park Service needs to take advantage of the opportunity of the burning."

We finished our coffee and got up from the table, walking past empty Ryder moving vans, which served as offices for the business of managing the forest fire—keeping track of finances, personnel, resources, and supplies. At a service garage, where photocopying, mapping, and briefings took place, Poncin and his team were gathering for a quick closed meeting. He told me that he and the six section chiefs and their deputies in his incident-command team (for finance, logistics, safety supply, air support, planning, and fire-behavior analysis, and two for operations) liked to meet once a day to compliment and criticize one another, a practice that they feel strengthens the unity of the team. Among the less personal items on the agenda was a plan to move the fire camp, which was half an hour's drive away (much too far) from the head of the fire. Things were pretty quiet now—some of the firefighters sat by glowing heaters called salamanders, but most had gone to sleep—and while we still had a minute Poncin and I stood in the warm light of the garage and went on talking.

"The problem is with a philosophy of natural management in a *near*-natural environment," Poncin said. "You've got a park that's two million two hundred thousand acres, but you've also got something like forty thousand visitors coming through those gates each day. In my estimation, that takes the park out of a natural-management philosophy altogether. I'm not saying the park isn't doing what it should be doing, but I am saying that, like most fire teams, we're suppressionists—we feel that unless we put the fire out we haven't done our job."

If you enter Yellowstone from the park's north gate, just outside the honky-tonk town of Gardiner, Montana, and drive up dry, grassy slopes that in late summer turn pink and purple just before sunset, you'll pass through the Roosevelt Memorial Arch, which has the inscription "For the Benefit and Enjoyment of the People." Whenever the purpose of the park is disputed, as it was in the summer of 1988, the inscription invariably comes to mind as hard evidence in favor of the argument that the first priority of the park is the enjoyment of the people who visit it. Yellowstone, the world's first national park, wasn't conceived as what Barbee calls "a repository of naturalness." In fact, some of the founders, who spoke of its "wild, weird beauty," hoped that it would someday become America's Riviera. In 1870, a Montanan named Nathaniel Pitt Langford organized the first successful government-endorsed expedition into this part of the country, which had long remained terra incognita, and, after seeing the upper and lower falls of the Yellowstone River, Yellowstone Lake, and the geyser basin around Old Faithful, a member of the expedition, Cornelius Hedges, had an idea that "the whole of it ought to be set aside as a great National Park." Langford, agreeing, predicted that "the march of civil improvements will reclaim this delightful solitude, and garnish it with all the attractions of cultivated taste and refinement." Though Langford soon became a tireless campaigner for the world's first national park—and he was its first superintendent, from 1872 to 1877—wildlife conservation as we think of it today was not what he had in mind: hunting big game was seen as one of the park's main attractions, and in order to persuade Congress that preserving the land wouldn't be wasteful he had teamed up and lobbied with the Northern Pacific Railroad, which hoped to run tracks into the park and someday make a killing from tourism.

It might have been better if Yellowstone hadn't been called a park— if it had been called, say, a preserve—for this parcel of land is larger than Delaware and Rhode Island put together. Although two and a half million tourists visit Yellowstone each year, the park is also the habitat of buffalo, black and grizzly bears, deer, elk, moose, bighorn sheep, and transient wolves, among other species. Indians, who had traditionally avoided the geysers because they thought spirits inhabited them, described Yellowstone as unfinished. Even now, there is something primordial about the park. It sits on one of the hottest spots on earth, with intense volcanic activity stewing below, and with more geysers, hot springs, mud pots, and steam vents than exist in all the rest of the world. An ill-defined caldera, or giant crater, that pocks the heart of the park has been following a cycle of heating and bulging and exploding every six hundred thousand years. It has been estimated that the most recent eruption—about six hundred thousand years ago—released more than a thousand times the explosive power of the Mount Saint Helens blast, covered much of the United States in ash, and blotted out the sun for about a year. The caldera is puckering again, and scientists suspect that it is due to erupt soon—perhaps within the next few hundred thousand years.

Before Congress approved plans for the park, in 1872, it had to be convinced that Yellowstone, however wondrous, was essentially worthless, unprofitable land. (If geothermal power had been thought practical then, chances are that Yellowstone wouldn't be a park today.) A few decades later, even in the midst of almost unstoppable land grabbing throughout the West, the idea that nature and wilderness had value in and of themselves began to seep into the American consciousness. In 1916, the National Park Service Act officially declared the need to "conserve the scenery and the natural and historic objects and the wild life therein and to provide for the enjoyment of the same in such manner and by such means as will leave them unimpaired for the enjoyment of future generations." What may strike us as a conflict today—between providing "for the enjoyment" and "conserv[ing] the scenery and the natural and historic objects and the wild life"—perhaps didn't seem so in 1916, when tourism was light. Still, the legislation was confusing; many people have speculated about, for instance, exactly what the lawmakers meant by "unimpaired." Does a hotel or a road impair a park? How about a hydroelectric dam? Or forest fires? "What is the agreed-to manifesto, the list of sovereign principles that guides all parks?" Bob Barbee has said. "Have you read the National Park Service Act? What does it mean?"

Most people seem to think of Yellowstone not as a place in which to commune quietly with nature but as a vacation mecca. Still, the park is also the largest wildlife preserve in the continental United States; the largest preserve in a temperate climate anywhere in the world, cited by the United Nations Educational, Scientific, and Cultural Organization for the "global value of its ecosystem and gene pool"; and the only place in the world where herds of buffalo still range freely. In Yellowstone, you can follow a grizzly bear's tracks in the ash after a fire. Or you can stop your car in the middle of the highway at five in the morning to take a picture of a few hundred grazing elk, and you may just then hear the howl of a wolf down the road. In Yellowstone, where you feel the immediacy of wilderness, where you make sure not to bring food into your tent for fear of hungry bears, wonderful and dangerous encounters with nature are possible.

A lot of people have come to the conclusion, by various routes, that such experiences are what Yellowstone is all about. Bob Barbee may sometimes wind up a discussion by saying, "Naturalness—that's what Yellowstone is all about." Then he may pause and say, "Yellowstone is a social concept of land use which tries to preserve and conserve naturalness to the greatest extent possible." But he may add, "Yellowstone is here only because of people. Its only contribution to society has to do with its relevance to humanity." A minute later, he may throw up his hands and say, "To say it's all about any one thing begins to fall apart. I say naturalness, but really it's all about all those things we say it's all about."

About fifty years ago, guided by the idea that a place like Yellowstone is all about wilderness, the national parks stopped killing predators such as wolves and cougars (but not before they were pretty much eliminated). In Yellowstone, rangers and ecologists no longer feed bears or elk, no longer reseed the range, no longer kill buffalo or elk when it is thought that their population has expanded beyond the carrying capacity of the range. All the same, wildlife managers have been reluctant to let nature manage itself. "We think, My God, how did nature get along without us?" Barbee says. The Leopold Report—a 1963 Department of the Interior report from the Advisory Board on Wildlife Management, headed by the University of California—

Berkeley zoologist A. Starker Leopold—traced some of the rudimentary fault lines of the park system and broke trail toward natural regulation. The parks were refuges, the report said, not zoos, resorts, hunting grounds, or playgrounds. Though the report conceded that it was necessary to manage the habitat, it concluded that "above all other policies, the maintenance of naturalness should prevail." While not yet giving nature full license to manage itself (Leopold and his colleagues encouraged herd cropping and favored prescribed burning over natural fires), man had loosened his grip. Not long after the report came out, natural regulation emerged with the idealistic conceit that, although the parks might never again be completely natural, one such as Yellowstone could be managed—or, rather, not managed—to allow the wild setting to act as it would under primitive conditions. And that meant, of course, that fires would have to be tolerated.

In Barbee's opinion, fires serve as "a catalyst" to raise probing questions about the role of parks and wilderness in American life. "What do the American people want of these places?" he asks. "Are the national parks going to be tree museums or big rustic fun farms or jumbo safari parks where things are artificial and contrived? Are they going to be dipped in formaldehyde? Or are they going to be relatively wild places, where wildlife lives, and processes like fire can play themselves out? Is scenery greenery?"

It was in 1943 that fire was first advocated as a way to rejuvenate forests in the national parks—by George McDougall, an assistant park naturalist, who was known for having said, "Nature doesn't get enough respect." Although ample evidence indicated that fire was beneficial, and even necessary, to a wilderness setting, and although ancient cultures, American Indians, and early settlers had no compunction about making use of fire for farming or hunting, the Park Service, like the Forest Service and the country at large, associated such practices with "bad habits and loose morals," in the words of Bernhard Fernow, a nineteenth-century forester. During the Second World War, posters of an Uncle-Sam-like forest ranger proclaimed that fire control was tantamount to our national defense, and a religious zealot named H. N. Wheeler equated fire control with devotion to God. Walt Disney's "Bambi," in which the fawn and his father are chased almost to their demise by a raging forest fire, inspired Smokey Bear after the war. And Smokey Bear, saying, in a deep, sonorous voice, "Remember, only you can prevent forest fires," became one of the most successful advertising campaigns of all time. By the nineteen-sixties, when more and more forest ecologists had begun to challenge the largely undisputed notion that fire was inherently evil, Smokey Bear was considered the most popular symbol in the country, according to a national advertising-research report, and, like Santa Claus, he had his own Zip Code.

Although today you can still see roadside placards of Smokey across the country, you won't see him campaigning in Yellowstone or any other national park. Yellowstone's natural-burn-management program—known officially as the Wildlife Fire Management Plan—began in 1972, and permitted lightning-caused fires to burn unhindered in certain prescribed areas. Park ecologists claimed that, in the absence of active forestry practices such as logging, fuel reduction, and reseeding, periodic wildfires were needed to resuscitate an old and dying forest. In the policy's first trial summer, four lightning starts burned a total of one acre. The next year, two such fires burned two acres. Though some people still regarded any leniency toward forest fires as scandalous, in Yellowstone and a few other national parks natural-burn regulation, in its initial run, was a critical, if not a popular, success among ecologists.

The prescribed-natural-burn plan is also known, particularly to its critics, as the let-burn policy—terminology that annoys Yellowstone's administrators, rangers, and ecologists, because they feel that it suggests they are lazy and delinquent wildlife managers. But those who support the natural-burn approach point out that fire was a part of the Yellowstone ecosystem long before man claimed it; that a forest is designed to facilitate fire; that "fire's as natural as the sun coming up in the morning"; that "putting all fires out is like saying, 'Let's stop it from raining' "; and that burned and unburned "mosaic" patterns create a more varied and thus healthier habitat. By preventing and suppressing a lot of small and large wildfires for so many years, say those whose definition of parks agrees with Bob Barbee's, Yellowstone lost—or, at least, endangered—the very thing it had been set aside to preserve: its naturalness.

A calm spell with seasonable humidity (it even drizzled for a few minutes one afternoon) and slack winds gave Poncin's crew a couple of slow days to replace a few branch directors and division supervisors; to install showers, hand-washers, and computer systems; and to begin another long-term forecast on the fire. Although the North Fork fire and the others kept spreading, none flared up strongly for a few days. The Fan fire, in the park's northwest corner, was perhaps the most volatile. While thirteen hundred firefighters were battling that fire, members of the Church Universal Triumphant chanted incantations at the blaze to repel it from their sacred grounds, just outside the park. The Red-Shoshone fire, in the south, squirmed around Grant Village but was obstructed by Yellowstone Lake. The Clover-Mist, the park's largest fire at the time, soon ran up and over the Absaroka Range, along the park's eastern boundary, spread into a commercial timber stand in the Shoshone National Forest, and came within a few miles of the towns of Cooke City and Silver Gate, Montana, outside the park.

Every so often, I drove around in a truck with John Krebs, the fire-behavior analyst for the new incident-command team, whose job was to look over the North Fork and try to guess when and where it might make its next major run. Since the fire was amoebalike in shape (flying around the perimeter in a helicopter took an hour), it could move in any direction. Now and then, Krebs would pull the truck over, roll down his window, and take a snapshot of, say, a bull elk grazing by the road. On August 14th, we headed up the Grand Loop Road—the main highway through the park—toward the head of the North Fork fire, near Madison Junction. Krebs pointed out several acres of strewn uprooted trees—what is called a blowdown—and said, "See that there? This is just waiting for fire." Four years before, he went on, gale-force winds had torn through the park, knocking down old lodgepole-pine stands as though they were jackstraws. Most of those stands had already been dying, from an infestation of the mountain-pine beetle. Now the blowdowns were virtually explosive, he said. When it gets as dry as it had been—when the humidity drops below fifteen per cent, when downed timber has a lower moisture content (it was then about seven per cent) than kiln-dried lumber (which is about twelve per cent)—the front of the fire can be a mile or more away, yet a blowdown can suddenly, inexplicably ignite. The Yellowstone fires spread in this way, spotting from one dry or dead patch to another; as the spots grew and moved toward one another, the gathering conflagration was apt to burn the healthier stands in between. Usually, though, it appeared that the fire had methodically skipped from one old and vulnerable stand to another. All that was needed was for one tiny ember aloft in the whirling, convective winds to fall into one of these enormous potential bonfires. A firebrand could be stamped out in a second if you happened to notice it, but on dry and windy days there were just too many spots to keep up with.

"The normal tendency of fire is to be influenced by topography—to move uphill more easily than down, and finger into the drainages with the up-canyon winds," Krebs said as we drove along. "But we're finding that this thing is influenced more than anything else by the fuels— the type of timber. It's pretty gentle terrain, so when the fire hits a blowdown or a decaying old stand she's gone. When the fire puts up a column of smoke, the convection picks up little cones and branches— I've seen convection columns that actually picked up the tops of trees, fifteen or twenty feet long, and six or eight inches on the butt end, and gave them a shake—and anything that's on a tree will come flying off. Those pieces of bark, or what have you, are like sails—they have the air-foil necessary to be carried long distances. But there's just no way this fuel is going to be reduced except through the fire process."

Blowdowns aside, in most healthy lodgepole stands there are just as many trees that are dying or already dead and are congesting the forest floor. "Erect they stand," one park enthusiast once wrote of the park's ubiquitous lodgepoles, "bristling with fierce determination,

while prone beneath their feet lie their uprooted brethren in tangled dis-
order and various degrees of decay." Ecologists say that this is the park's
natural state; a mature healthy forest is one that is half dead. While in
another climate—that of New York, say, or the Pacific Northwest—the
dead and downed timber might decompose much more rapidly, at a
pace commensurate with new growth, the climate in Yellowstone "is just
too dang high, too dry for there to be natural decomposition," Krebs
said. Natural decomposition is essentially extremely slow, unnoticeable
fire. The consequences of decomposition and fire are the same: all the
nutrients locked up in the old wood are released. In most timberlands,
fire is necessary; in dry climates, especially, such as Yellowstone's, fire is
needed to restore the nutrients to the soil, so that new growth can begin.
Otherwise, all of the forest slowly dies.

In "Fire in America," an exhaustive survey of the fire history of the
United States, Stephen Pyne writes, "The most stubborn fires burn in
fuel complexes most in need of decomposition; the fires most readily
extinguished are, in terms of the ecosystem's energy requirements,
the least important." He goes on to say, "The whole process is self-
reinforcing. The type of growth that occurs on a burn helps to determine the nature of the fuel complex, and the resulting fuel complex
determines the intensity and frequency of fires and . . . future biological effects." It is not merely that the lodgepole-pine forests in
Yellowstone have tolerated fire; they are a product of it. The forests
have evolved through a pattern of mass fires occurring at intervals of
between two and four hundred years. The saving grace for many
lodgepole pines is their serotinous cones, which normally are closed
tightly and are as hard as rocks, but open up when they are subjected
to intense heat, such as fire, and sow seeds in the ashy, fertilized soil
after a burn.

Krebs was of the opinion that fires are an inevitable consequence of
natural happenings. He said that it might be nice to put the Yellowstone fire out, but that that would be impossible unless nature decided
to do it—unless it rained. "When we first arrived in the park, to fight
the Red-Shoshone, we could look down in the valleys and they were

green," he said. "We could look under the trees and the grass was green. After two weeks, we began to notice a change of color." Blame for the fire, according to Krebs, shouldn't be focussed on the park for its natural-burn policy but, more than anything else, on a drought of several years in the northern Rockies (the past few summers in Yellowstone had been rainy, but little snow had fallen in the winters), which was now being topped off by the driest summer on record the hottest year ever, worldwide. Krebs thought that if the conditions had been any different the fires would not now be burning, regardless of policy. But beetles had killed trees; winds had piled those trees up like kindling; and more trees were dying all the time. What's more, it hadn't rained in weeks; the winds were gusting; the humidity was low. The North Fork fire was bound to happen—not by policy, indecision, or incompetence but by the forces of nature. In fact, the park fires may have been long overdue.

We got off the Grand Loop Road and went down a lush canyon drive along the Firehole River, which forms the eastern outline of the plateau. Shaded from the sun, the area was dark and green and mossy, and, though the day was clear, smoke and fog had settled in on the river. Krebs stopped the truck and got out, and after a while he said, "When is it going to happen? Where is it going to take off on us again?" A pickup truck with a family of five crammed into the cab pulled over. The father rolled down his window, swore, and said that the problem would be solved easily enough if park managers knew enough to use bulldozers. Krebs didn't say much—only that he wasn't so sure himself. The family drove on.

Krebs shook his head and said, "You don't want to argue with the public. But how do you explain to folks that a dozer just ain't going to do the trick? Sometimes you think you can stop a fire with a hand line, and other times you say you can use a bulldozer and make a twelve-foot-wide line. See, the reason you use a dozer is that it's faster, but the principle is still the same: you're stopping the forward spread of the fire *on the ground*. And that's about all you *can* do. But these have been crown fires. They've carried through every lodgepole-pine type, young and old, in their travels. Lately, they've burned through the meadows, too, though most often they've gone around or spotted across. Now, a meadow is essentially a firebreak—like a dozer line. But when you have a meadow that is maybe half a mile wide, and the flame spots a mile ahead, then the meadow is plain ineffective. So you know a dozer line isn't going to be any more help. But the main thing is, folks just hate to see the park change. They think it's being ruined. People have a tendency to want things as they are, but in nature nothing stays as it is. Once, all those blowdowns were standing—ten or fifteen years ago, or even five years ago—and now they're not. Now you've got all the deadfall, and nature is hollering, 'I'm getting ready to start over!' We'd like to shout, 'No! Not now! We're not ready for you!' But that ain't the way it works, folks."

That afternoon, Krebs and I drove north a few miles, to a rise above the Gibbon River, just past Madison Junction. If the fire had suddenly died that day—if it had snowed, as sometimes happens during the summer—the average tourist taking a drive north along the Grand Loop Road, from Old Faithful to the Norris Geyser Basin, say, might not have had any idea that this particular fire had burned, to date, sixty thousand acres. Other fires, such as the Red-Shoshone, were more visible. The early fire projections anticipated that if the fire went unfought it would not reach Madison Junction by the end of the summer. But in the past week, while Poncin's team waited for the fire to reach the rim of the plateau, you could see black smoke roll nearer to the bluffs each afternoon. Except for the point of origin, where the fire had at least been small—if not tame—the bluffs at Madison Junction were the one place where the firefighters stood a decent chance of impeding the North Fork fire. Here they had a natural barrier: a three-hundred-foot falloff, a river, a road, and meadows—a fuel break more nearly impervious than the foot-wide line a fire crew will cut, or even than a twelve-foot-wide dozer line. "We're necking the whole thing down," Krebs said as we drove in the shadow of the plateau and then up the Gibbon River, past Madison Junction. "It looks so docile—almost looks as if it were out, just lazying around up there. But I'd bet more than a beer that under the circumstances you couldn't put it out. What we need to do is buy time. It's coming right at us, and it's inevitable that it's going to come down off the plateau—but preferably under more moderate conditions. That would be the best thing in the world. If it ties off at those bluffs, without really spotting, then it's pretty secure: you can bring in another team; you can reduce your forces; we can go home. However, if it comes across, then we're in another ballgame."

For the rest of the afternoon, parked up on a rise, Krebs and I watched a column of smoke on the plateau a mile to the southwest of us switch back and forth with the wind. An hour passed. Krebs concentrated on the elements—heat, humidity, wind—and we hardly talked. At four-thirty, Krebs said he was no longer wondering whether the fire would cross the Firehole River but when. He said he hoped it wouldn't hit the edge of the plateau until late in the day, when the sun would be going down and the temperature would be lower and the humidity higher. Then we heard over the walkie-talkie that the fire had hit the bluffs and was throwing spots a mile ahead of the front. Sometime after five o'clock, we saw flames flashing out through the smoke.

In the hour or so before the fire reached the edge of the plateau, Krebs and the two operations chiefs in charge of the actual fighting tactics, Robert Meuchel and Jake Jacobsen, gave some thought to undertaking a helitorch operation—igniting a "burnout," to consume the fuel ahead of the fire, by means of a helicopter—along the Firehole River, down the snug lee side, opposite where Krebs and I had stopped only a few hours before. I hadn't imagined then that the canyon would be devastated, too, but fire makes no aesthetic discriminations. Though some fires would creep down the canyon, hit the river, and go no farther, diffidence hadn't been the character of the North Fork fire. Krebs, Meuchel, and Jacobsen agreed that with a low but rising humidity, the setting sun, and a steep, wooded ravine that would draft the fire nicely into the main fire, they could take advantage and fight fire with fire.

In a windy meadow along the Firehole River, Meuchel swatted at gnats while the helitack crew rigged a light helicopter with a helitorch—a barrel that hangs from the helicopter and drips a gasoline gel, which ignites as it hits the ground. Although Meuchel had conferred with Jacobsen and had consulted Krebs on the weather and on burning conditions, the helitorch operation was his call to make. Meuchel calls his job "the art of knowing when to do what." He isn't the kind of fastidious operations chief who works things out with pencil and paper or with a calculator designed to predict various aspects of fire behavior, such as intensity and rate of spread. He seldom looks at a map. He doesn't take notes. He makes decisions quickly and undramatically. He just says, as he had said to Krebs over the walkie-talkie half an hour earlier, "O.K., yeah, why don't we light that ridge and see what happens?"

Meuchel smoked a cigarette while he waited; smoking is a habit he picks up as soon as he's called to a fire and drops as soon as he's called off. A man named Gary Glotfelty, who, as one of the fire's two branch directors, served as supervisor of the fire crews, pulled up in a truck and got out. He suggested that they hold off on the helitorch, and wait until the fire backed down the slope of the canyon, where they could line the river with a few dozen fire engine crews.

"I don't think that would do 'er," Meuchel said. "There's a lot of unburned fuel back there, and you know me. I love a clean, black line."

"Well, that's the only kind of line to have," Glotfelty said. "You hate to go home and read in the paper five days later that the fire took off again. But I'm afraid this thing is going to spot and kill us."

"It'll spot, but it's short-range spotting—only across the road," Meuchel said. "If we can strip it out even and get it started on the bank, backing down, we should be in good shape. We'll be burning against topography, so we'll have a backing fire. You could line it and two days later have a spot in there you can't catch. This way, we'll know."

"Look at this wind now—right in our faces," Glotfelty said. "We might want to wait until morning."

Meuchel smiled and said, "I was just thinking of trying—just starting something, to see if it will burn. That sort of thing. Nothing dangerous."

"Because of that wind. Boy! And this is a critical point, too. If you don't hold the river, you're talking about it moving way out on those flats. You might be able to catch it all—"

Meuchel interrupted Glotfelty with a sharp laugh. "If it comes off the plateau and goes over the highway, we'll just let 'er go. We'll protect what we can—the structures—but we won't be able to stop it. There's just no way." They were quiet for a minute, and then, as the helicopter began to whine and throb, Meuchel stubbed out his cigarette, put it in his pants pocket, and said, "So I guess we can go start a fire."

Flames were snapping out from the crest of the plateau by the time I hitched a ride back to Firehole Canyon, ten miles up the river from the heliport. I joined Jacobsen, three other section chiefs, and a couple of park rangers, all of whom had heard about and had come up to see the helitorch operation. A dozen or more engine crews stood guard along the drive, which ran next to the river. In a few minutes, two helicopters emerged from the black smoke over the plateau and swooped along the river. On their first pass, Meuchel, who was flying in the lead helicopter, explained by radio to the pilot flying behind him where he wanted to ignite the fire. On their next pass, the second helicopter descended to treetop level, and a thin stream of the gel (about thirty-five gallons) trickled from the barrel onto the trees. In an instant, the riverbank was consumed by fire. With a deafening roar, flames raced from the ground up trunks and through branches, and made a final pirouette three hundred feet in the air.

Over a walkie-talkie Meuchel said to Jacobsen, "Burned a little more than I planned."

"Yeah, you did," Jacobsen said. "It's cooking nicely."

Krebs, who continued to watch from the rise above the Gibbon River, said over the walkie-talkie, "You can see 'er cranking now. It's snorting right along."

Firefighters chased after spot fires that began kindling on our side of the river. A giant, twin-propeller helicopter called a Vertol appeared and, from a suspended thousand-gallon bucket the size of a small room, dropped water on a cluster of torching pines. Some of the spectators rolled down their sleeves, pulled up their bandannas bandit style, grabbed shovels or Pulaskis, and went after the smaller spots in the undergrowth. The timing on the helitorch had been good, though: the wind was flagging, and the temperature was falling, and already the fire was losing energy. In an hour, the fire would smolder quietly in the cool night air. I saw an ember float across the drive and land in the duff on the other side, and, remembering that all fires start small, I walked over and stamped it out.

"We'll get in here tomorrow and kick the crap out of it," Jacobsen said. He got in his truck, and since he was heading back to camp I asked him for a ride.

Smoke pressed in low and seemed to smother the North Fork fire the next day, August 15th. Early in the afternoon, Dave Poncin and I drove to Madison Junction in a Dodge Caravan, with the headlights on. As the incident commander, Poncin was not actually engaged in the tactical business of positioning and maneuvering fire crews, calling in waterdrops, and helitorching hillsides; he went out that day, as I did, merely to see what would happen. "We've got a long afternoon," he said. "I think before the day's over it's going to get about as heavy as it ever gets. The fire is going to come over the top in an hour or so, when the winds come up and the humidity drops, and it's liable to spot down at the junction and burn up the Gibbon River flats. It'll probably clear the grass and the river, and all we can do is be there when that happens."

We drove around for about an hour: through the closed and evacuated Madison campground; above the Gibbon, to say hello to Krebs at his post; and down the Madison River, where through the smoke we could see the silhouettes of grazing elk. Driving back to Madison Junction, we saw a spot fire burning in the grass near the bridge that crossed the Gibbon River. Given the size of the North Fork fire, the spot seemed nothing to bother about, but Poncin pulled over anyway, flagged down a passing fire engine, and borrowed a couple of shovels. We slapped at the flames with the shovels, and beat the fire out in a couple of minutes. This was so satisfying that when I noticed a log in flames lying near a lodgepole stand we went for it without discussion. We had some trouble there, though, until an obliging helicopter helped out with a waterdrop.

We left the log to smolder and walked up the highway and across the bridge, into a dense tumult of smoke. From a distance—from the town of West Yellowstone, Montana, say, fifteen miles away—such billowing smoke might look something like the plume of an atomic explosion. We were not more than a mile from what would have been ground zero, and the smoke overwhelmed us. I could feel the fire as it sucked in toward the junction, but I couldn't see anything. At the bridge, an engine crew tried to fell a snag that hung dangerously over the road. Poncin led the way up a slope until we couldn't see or breathe and began tripping over fallen snags. If a snag above us had fallen just then, we couldn't have heard it over the roar or seen it through the smoke. Poncin yelled (though I was standing less than a yard away, in order not to lose sight of him), "Do you really want to do this?" and we walked back across the bridge. A few minutes later, we tried driving through the smoke, but we couldn't see the hood ornament on the van, and we turned around again.

Farther down the Madison River, we escaped the thick smoke and found some relatively fresh air. (Both of us had the headache and faint nausea symptomatic of carbon-monoxide inhalation.) A few minutes later, someone on the walkie-talkie reported a spot fire just past the Gibbon Bridge. When a crew member said his crew couldn't get to it, Poncin said, "O.K. Sounds like a job for America's finest." We got back in the van.

Beyond the confluence of the rivers, a few hundred yards from the highway and down a wooded slope, a spot fire had kindled in grass, shrubs, and juniper bushes and beneath a fir log. Each of us took a side of the spot, which covered about a quarter of an acre, and began to dig and throw dirt and slap at the burning grass with our shovels. We could do nothing about putting out the flames that consumed the log, however, and could only hope to keep the spot from spreading. After a while, I couldn't see Poncin anymore. I clambered up the slope to catch my breath. I felt lost. I told myself that the woods were thin and there was not a lot to burn, so the fire wouldn't take off, but that if it did I could jump into the river or beat it to the highway, where the van was, with the keys in the ignition. My adrenaline level was high, though, and I decided to keep working. Trimming along the edges of the spot, I was hardly subduing the flames, but I made my way almost around the perimeter. Then I saw Poncin working toward me. He looked up, took off his hard hat, wiped his brow, and stepped back. "Operations, this is the I.C.," he said on the walkie-talkie. "We're down here on that spot by the bridge, and we could sure use a hand."

Meuchel came on and said not to bother. He said there were uncontrolled spots crowning and running miles ahead of us—a long way up the river flat already. "You might as well get out of there," he said.

Jacobsen, who had been listening in, said, "Kind of took it in the shorts. So much for our objectives."

After that, Poncin and I and, it seemed, everybody else stopped fighting fire. Barbee told me later that when he heard that the fire had crossed the river at the junction he knew there was nothing anybody could do to stop it. Poncin didn't say anything then, but he, too, later admitted that at that moment he had lost hope of beating it. It was only three o'clock, but it was clear that nothing short of rain or snow would stop the North Fork fire.

And whatever success yesterday's helitorch operation had had along the Firehole River didn't matter much now: under the gathering winds, the spot fires that hadn't been entirely quenched the day before picked up, and the fire swept over the river, across the road, and up into the woods. We had to wait awhile, standing around with an engine crew, before we ventured over the bridge and, again driving blind through smoke, made our way back down the highway to the canyon. Only half a mile or so down the road, more fallen snags made driving impossible so we got out and walked. The canyon had a creepy, desolate feeling. A pale liquid half-light washed over Poncin's face. Small fires smoldered here and there, and bluish smoke danced on stumps, but almost nothing was left to burn. Where trees had stood there were now only shiny charcoal sticks and on the ground were the ashy ghostlike after-images of logs that had burned to nothingness. We came to what remained of a power line and followed it away from the Firehole River into the ravaged woods. The hot ash underfoot melted the rubber soles on my boots. Trees had been uprooted and the ones that hadn't already fallen teetered and creaked. On the rises, the smoke wasn't too bad, but in the troughs it scraped at our throats and blinded us. We had to turn around once again.

As we hiked back to the van, Poncin said, "You know, I've always been enthusiastic about this job. I've always figured that it could never get too tough. But I'm beginning to face mortality now, and it does get tough. The ground gets harder to sleep on—I guess that's O.K. But days like today . . . You don't look good when you lose a lot of acres, and the fire's getting to be just plain big. It's the failure that gets to you."

Thirteen thousand acres burned on August 15th. In the six days since I arrived, thirty-four thousand acres had burned; that is, the fire had more than doubled in size. And for the next week the head of the fire ran unchecked, at about two miles a day, over the flats along the Gibbon River toward Norris Junction and beyond. Because the fire was moving so quickly and impulsively, a frontal assault was not even considered. Crews dug fuel breaks up the remote west flank, continued mop-up operations on what at the time was considered the quiet east side, near Old Faithful, and were sent ahead to prepare various evacuated structural enclaves, such as the Norris Geyser Museum and, later, Canyon Village, by thinning out the surrounding woods, carting the dead timber and slash away, and dousing the buildings with a soapy fire retardant that looked like snow. Crews would get dropped off by helicopter in the morning on the remote backcountry flanks; hike for an hour (lugging chain saws, gas cans packs, Pulaskis, shovels, McLeods, and water bags); cut two or three miles of line during the day; hike back to a bivouac at their drop-off point; eat a lukewarm dinner; sleep; get up at 5 a.m. for a lukewarm breakfast; and do the same thing all over again. They would live like this for three or four days at a stretch and then maybe they would get to come in to the fire camp for a night, to shower and perhaps to make a phone call. The next morning, they would be back on the lines. Most crews had been on the lines, seldom working less than fourteen hours a day, with only one or two days off, since early June. Across the country, over fifteen thousand firefighters were now employed—more than three thousand of them in Yellowstone, and a thousand on the North Fork alone. Toward the end of August, the Army sent two battalions of six hundred soldiers each to the park from Fort Lewis, Washington, and in September almost three thousand military personnel were in the park. From the time the fires began until they were officially declared out, in November, nearly ten thousand people were engaged in fighting the Yellowstone fires.

I lost touch with the Redding Hot Shots after a week. Later I heard from a crewman called Mary, who fought fire six months of every year and travelled the world the rest of the time, that the Hot Shots had been sent to Smoke Jumper Hot Springs, on the east edge of the fire. They were supposed to cut and hold a line up the northeast flank there to keep the fire from barrelling at Old Faithful, but in addition to cutting line they spent much of their time trying to keep up with and contain hundreds of spot fires, many larger than an acre. The Hot Shots stayed out five days, and because an impenetrable smoke inversion held the smoke close to the ground and prevented helicopters from getting to them they were not supplied for the last three days. Luckily, they had plenty of water.

I hung around the fire camp, which had been moved to the campground at Madison Junction—after the fire skirted by—and complained about the smoke, and ate well. Some days, I drove around with Meuchel and Jacobsen or flew the fire by helicopter as they continued to direct crews and to attempt backfires, burnouts, and helitorchings. Over the next four days, the weather kept getting hotter and drier, and the winds kept blowing, and the fire kept rolling deeper into the heart of the park. John Krebs, pointing out that the woods could get only so dry, said, "They're not going to spontaneously combust, you know." One good thing, Poncin said, was that the days were getting shorter; and he felt certain that it would eventually rain.

In the meantime, there may have been some consolation in the claim of just about everybody, including the firefighters themselves, that 1988 would go into the record books as the worst fire season in American history. In terms of acreage burned, the summer of 1988 was not yet quite as bad as what is generally thought of as the worst year ever—1910, when five million acres burned in the northern Rockies (but not in Yellowstone), and seventy-nine firefighters were killed. But in 1988 Southern California's toughest month was still ahead; the previous September, fire had ravaged eight hundred thousand acres in Northern California and the Central Sierra Nevada and killed ten people. (Nobody was killed in Yellowstone in 1988, but one person, struck by a falling snag, was killed just outside the park.) By late August, about three and a half million acres had burned nationwide, and, though that figure included fires that burned two million acres in Alaska, the fires that burned in and around the northwest corner of Wyoming, in the world's first and best known national park, were the ones that attracted media attention. Many of the stories only exacerbated the let-burn controversy. A story in *Time* bore the headline "WE COULD HAVE STOPPED THIS"—quoting a firefighter, who added, "They won't let us." Whether or not the assessment of one firefighter obscured the facts, the natural-burn controversy made good copy, dovetailing nicely with stories about the drought, global warming trends, the greenhouse effect, and refuse washing up on Eastern shores.

Among the fire bosses, the general attitude seemed to be that, in Bob Barbee's words, "no matter who did what when, Yellowstone would have burned." A fifteen-minute downpour could have accomplished what millions of dollars and thousands of men and women could not. But among the firefighters it remained a popular notion that the devastation was the park management's doing. "See, the Park Service, they don't let you put the fire out," a firefighter told me in a confidential tone at dinner one night. "If they didn't say protect the ground, the trees, and all this dead shit—as if that was the forest—we'd have gone in with heavy retardant, a lot of dozers, a lot of hand crews, and this fire would have been out in a week. They tried to nurse this critter along, but I'd say they got a tiger by the tail now." Citizens of the town of West Yellowstone echoed this sentiment, telling reporters that the crews complained when they were in town that they weren't allowed to do everything they could to put the fires out. Politicians, among them Senator Max Baucus, of Montana, assumed a knowledge of fire management, and reiterated their constituents' and the fire-fighters' general disgruntlement. On August 19th, Senator Baucus told local reporters, "I flew over the entire North Fork fire and frankly I'm not convinced that if enough men and equipment were utilized that fire couldn't be stopped."

Although Barbee later said he thought that media control could be more effective than fire control, the park administrators' initial optimism about the fire, and the miraculous ecological boon that would ensue, had caused a public-relations problem. Most environmental groups, such as the Audubon Society, the Wilderness Society, and the Greater Yellowstone Coalition, supported natural-burn management, but Ed Lewis, the executive director of the Coalition, remarked, "[The park] tried to make the fire a totally positive thing." Although Barbee rejected any suggestion that the park officials had been indecisive, he realized that the situation had seemed to send out a garbled signal. "Here we are, on the one hand, in a massive firefighting effort—massive—spending a hundred and twenty million dollars trying to put the damn things out, and then, on the other hand, trying to dispel the anxiety about the world's first national park being on fire," he said to me late in August. "We're not Nero here—we're not promoting holocausts. But ecologically this is not a disaster. The bottom line is that it's a plus." To someone who feared for the park, however, or whose vacation plans had been ruined, or who had been awakened early in the morning and told that he and his family would have to leave the park, Barbee's statement that "fire is a stimulant and as important to the ecosystem as sunshine and rain" was probably little consolation.

Nor had the enthusiasm of park administrators and ecologists impressed the citizens of West Yellowstone. They met in the town's convention hall before noon on Saturday, August 20th—almost a month after the North Fork fire started—to express their indignation to Barbee and the managers of the fires. Immediately adjacent to the park's western entrance, West Yellowstone draws fifteen million dollars' worth of business from park visitors in a good year. The town is often the subject of derision—some people find it amazingly ugly—but, whatever it looks like, its eight hundred or so year-round residents have a lot of civic pride. Although the fire was nine miles distant, and the southwesterly winds seemed to be pushing the blaze away from the town, it was hard for anybody who lived there not to feel menaced by a thirty-five-thousand-foot-high cloud of brown smoke blotting out the eastern sky each afternoon. But more than that, the citizens' outrage stemmed from the feeling that their worries as a community, as businesspeople, had been utterly ignored in the park managers' fever for fire. At the meeting, they demanded to know why, if man-caused fires were supposed to be put out, the North Fork fire hadn't been. And a man who was concerned about the tourism that supported three hotels and four restaurants he owned in town asked if there was any way the fire managers could preserve what he called a greenbelt of unburned trees along the highways, to create an illusion of scenery. A man sitting behind me said that instead of any more talk about trying to contain the fires he wanted to hear some more about putting them out. A woman on the other side of the room asked if it wasn't possible "to use those big water bombers and just come in and supersaturate everything," and added, "They do that in other parts of the country, you know."

Poncin, Krebs, Barbee, and John Varley, the head of the park's research department, answered the questions, telling the people of West Yellowstone that "the absolute objective from Day One was to get the fire controlled, contained, suppressed, or whatever"; that the firefighters had had "precious few breaks"; that until the firefighters did get a break they themselves couldn't talk realistically about extinguishing the fire; that they would take the idea of a greenbelt into consideration; that bulldozers weren't as effective as everybody would like to think; that the animals were not terribly bothered by the fires, but that a lot of elk and buffalo could die over the winter, more because of the drought than because of the fires; that the questions were excellent ones; and, finally, that "this is not going to last forever."

At one o'clock that afternoon, as the town meeting adjourned, the winds were blowing at thirty miles an hour, with gusts up to seventy. I watched Bob Barbee step out into a blast of hot, dry air, look at his wife, and let out a sigh that said, "Oh, God!" A hundred and sixty-five thousand acres in Yellowstone burned that day—more than had burned in the entire history of the park. It was the single worst day in the history of firefighting, and it became known in the newspapers as Black Saturday.

About a week after Black Saturday, when I heard that Dave Poncin's team was being replaced, after twenty-one days on the job, I decided to leave, too. By then, the North Fork fire had grown so huge and ungainly that it had a second name: the southern half was still the North Fork fire, but the northern half was now referred to as the Wolf Lake fire and was being managed as a separate fire by a second incident-command team. The night before I left, Bob Meuchel told me that this had been the most frustrating fire he had ever fought, and that he had never felt completely defeated before, as he did now; he spoke vaguely about getting out of firefighting. A lot of firefighters surely understood Meuchel's despair, whether they said anything or not. A day like Black Saturday obliterated weeks of work, and made it easier for the public and the politicians to hold the park administrators and their policies in contempt for having allowed the fires to burn in the first place. In the end, almost a million acres had burned in Yellowstone Park itself, and about a million and a quarter acres in the greater Yellowstone area.

Long before the fires were out, park ecologists and administrators had begun to worry that the natural-burn policy would be abandoned. With Wyoming's Senators Malcolm Wallop and Alan Simpson calling for the resignation of the director of the Park Service (Wallop also called for Barbee's), the ecologists realized that a revision of some sort was inevitable. "There are going to be people who will want to chuck the whole thing," Roy Renkin, a field researcher in the park, had told me before I left. "Then there will be middle-of-the-road people, who want to keep the policy except in drought years. And that's probably how it will be revised. But that's a death knell to the natural-fire plan, because we get fires of any consequence only with the infrequent occurrence of dry conditions. So if they change it they're still keeping these biologically significant events from happening."

On September 13th, after Secretary of the Interior Hodel, Secretary of Agriculture Richard Lyng, and Deputy Secretary of Defense William Taft briefed him on the damage, President Reagan intimated in a meeting with reporters that the natural-burn plan would be amended. The next day, Hodel announced that the National Park Service would change its practices and, he implied, revert to a more grudging, impatient relationship with nature. He promised that reforestation and revegetation of some burned-out areas, as well as feeding wildlife, would take place after the fires were out. Although Hodel said that natural regulation would not be overturned completely, Barbee and the park's ecologists had to cringe. After official review teams surveyed the fires and took stock of the damage, a Greater Yellowstone Postfire Assessment, prepared and issued this spring by the Park Service and the Forest Service, hailed the virtues of fire, saying, for instance, of the wildlife, that "individual losses can be considered to be relatively minor when compared to the magnitude of long-term fire-related benefits." But, like most Park Service documents, the announcement was ambiguous; "what Yellowstone is all about" was still uncertain. And, as Renkin had predicted, even fires that meet the prescribed-natural-burn criteria will be very closely monitored in dry years, and probably put out. In addition, the parks were actively encouraged to set occasional small prescribed fires to clean up the accumulated fuel loads and stave off future holocausts. The government also decided that through the 1989 fire season, across the country, all fires in national parks would be fought, and, accordingly, it tripled the firefighting budget. But then this summer was typical in Yellowstone—twenty-three fires started, the largest of which burned less than five acres.

In Yellowstone, the controversy persists. The concern is not only whether nature should have its way but also whether the park, a public trust, should be a stage where nature performs. But if not Yellowstone, where? Park ecologists continue to believe that natural regulation works, but most people, Barbee says, are made uneasy by the fact that nature regulates more strenuously than human beings might. It seems that we want nature but don't want it to be entirely natural—we want wilderness to behave. More than most natural occurrences, I think—more than, say, an earthquake or a volcanic eruption—forest fires touch off a basic frustration with nature. Man believes that he has taken possession of fire and therefore controls it, but then a wildfire that lasts for months and burns almost a million acres snatches that authority away. More than twenty-five million dollars was spent on the attempt to put the North Fork fire out—a hundred and twenty million dollars on all the Yellowstone fires—but ultimately, according to the Postfire Assessment, the largest fire effort in the history of the United States "probably did not significantly reduce the acreage burned."

Yellowstone will survive the fires of 1988. By the fall, spears of grass were poking through the blackened soil, and this spring a riot of wildflowers erupted, as usual. In a typical burned acre, where perhaps three hundred and fifty old lodgepoles once stood, perhaps a hundred thousand pine seeds were scattered; most of those seeds will be food for squirrels and deer mice, and most of those that aren't eaten won't take root, but within five years some six thousand saplings will rise from the forest floor. And, so long as the trees that survive are not cut down, in two or three or four hundred years— someday, anyway—when conditions have conspired once more, when it is dry and hot and windy, probably toward the end of a prolonged drought, those trees will burn, too.

from Yellowstone's Red Summer
by Alan Carey and
Sandy Carey

*Alan Carey and Sandy Carey collected images
and stories about the 1988 Yellowstone fires
for their book* Yellowstone's Red Summer. *Here hiker Tom Shorten recalls his attempts to
find shelter from the inferno.*

On the morning of August 20, Tom Shorten of Billings, Montana; his German shepherd dog Chico; and three companions set out from Lulu Pass into the Absaroka-Beartooth Wilderness Area just north of Yellowstone for a three-day backpacking trip. Hiking cross-country to Anvil Lake, they made camp, and then Tom decided to take his compass and his dog and explore on his own.

"I had been hiking for quite a while when I noticed that it was becoming very smoky; the denseness of the smoke increased rapidly. I began to be a little anxious, and realized that I might be somewhere that I didn't want to be. As I was trying to get my bearings, a fire blew over the ridge. The heat, the wind, and the fire—it was amazing. Grabbing my dog, I ran blindly toward a nearby creek.

"Fortunately, I found a place where two large rocks had fallen together and made a cavelike space across the water; there was a small opening at the top where the rocks met. We dove in under this shelter and lay in about two feet of water—because of the drought, it wasn't very deep anywhere in that area. We lay there looking out; at that point, I wondered if we would make it. It became desperately hot and bright even though we were as far under the rocks as we were able to get. There was so much debris flying through the air and falling through the opening above us that my hair and clothes kept catching on fire.

"The wind created by the fire was unbelievable—I saw it take an apparently healthy eight-inch pine tree right out of the ground. That roaring wind sucked everything up. Then came the flames; they passed over us with the sound of a jetliner and moved down the creek. By then we had been in the water about forty-five minutes. The smoke was so heavy and thick that it was difficult to breathe; I was able to filter out some of the smoke by breathing through my shirttail, which I'd pulled up over my face, but my dog kept passing out.

"Although it was nighttime, it was as bright as day, and I watched the fire continue to burn down the creek and then cross the next ridge. As the brightness dimmed, I began to relax, then noticed that the roar of the fire was getting louder rather than more faint. The fire was coming back, and the sky began to lighten again . . . I was shocked, and felt that we might not survive this attack. Then, like a miracle, it hit a spot that had been burned earlier and shot off in another direction.

"We had been in the water for about three hours by this time, and finally the cold drove us out. We were both shaking violently, and although everything was still on fire and burning around us, we climbed on a rock in the water near a burning log and tried to get warm. We sat on that rock until daylight.

"When it was light enough to see, we started to head south through what seemed like miles and miles of devastation. There was nothing green in sight, and I was walking in six to eight inches of ash. I had to carry my dog most of the way—his feet were badly burned—and as a result, had to stop frequently to rest; we travelled this way for seven or eight miles, dodging falling trees. The knowledge that one could fall on us was almost as bad as being in the creek and watching the fire come back. By the time we reached Lulu Pass and my car, my shoes were just about burned off, my shirt was in tatters, and I was black from head to foot, but grateful to be alive.

"During the whole ordeal, I did a lot of praying, because I really didn't believe that I was going to make it. And I believe that I wouldn't be here now if it weren't for answered prayers. This happening turned into a personal kind of tragedy-triumph for me and I thank the Lord."

from Seasonal: A Life Outside
by Ed Engle

Ed Engle spent 12 years as a seasonal employee of the U.S. Forest Service. This essay from his 1989 book about that experience recalls the California fires of 1987.

The pictures were all over the national TV news. There was a squad of Forest Service firefighters standing in front of a house somewhere in southern California. The brush for as far as the camera panned was blacked down into piles of smouldering ash. They had saved the house. They grinned into the camera and the ecstatic homeowners hugged and kissed them. Dan Rather smiled.

I noticed that one of the firefighters clutched a small note pad in his hand. It was the standard issue three-by-five-inch tablet. The pages are gridded in blue quarter-inch squares. There are 216 squares on a page and the top is perforated so each page can be neatly torn off if required. The acquisition clerks would know that this is the 1300-18a(3-66). To most of us it is simply known as the Idea book. This comes from the message emblazoned fully across the cover:

> *I*nnovate
> *D*evelop
> *E*ncourage
> *A*ctivate
> *S*uggest

It is a simple acronym meant to guide us along our way. In the upper right hand corner of the cover are the italicized words "Work Safely Don't Get Hurt!"

I know why that firefighter was holding so tightly to his Idea book. From the second he had received the fire call from wherever he was stationed he had been keeping track of his fire time. He had carefully noted his regular hours and the quarter time hazard pay he would get until the fire was declared controlled. There was another column showing his overtime pay that would go time and a half plus hazard pay. There might be a column for night differential.

Time and three-quarters is what can make a grunt's day on the fireline. At any given moment that firefighter who was standing out in the ash and smoke could probably give you an exact figure in dollars and cents of how much money he had coming. It helps *E*ncourage him to *A*ctivate when he is dirty, tired, thirsty, and bored.

I don't know what makes Dan Rather smile, but I do know what makes firefighters smile.

Most seasonal forest fire fighters get started on their home districts. At the beginning of the season there is an orientation that explains how the district is operated. A couple of days is usually devoted to fire training. Firefighters learn how to size up "smokes" and hopefully put them out. The basic notion in most wildfire suppression is that the fire must be deprived of fuel by cutting a fireline around the burning area.

There are hundreds of refinements to fireline theory, but it always works down to clearing away anything that might burn from the fire's path. This means a "line" dug down to mineral soil all the way around the fire. It might be two feet wide or the width of six or seven D-9 cat blades depending on the size of the fire. Other options include taking the heat from the fire by cooling it with water, if water is available. Still, the mainstay is always the fireline. This is sacred.

The tools that a firefighter uses are basic. A shovel to scrape and dig fireline and throw soil on hotspots to cool them and the Pulaski, which is a combination ax and grubbing hoe, to break up the soil and cut small trees and brush. Other more specialized tools like chainsaws, brush hooks, and the rake-like McCleod sometimes come into play, particularly on the larger fire crews.

The working organization of a fire suppression crew is similar whether it is a two- or three-man "initial attack" crew or a standard twenty-man hand crew. The firefighters line out with Pulaskis in the lead and "brush" out the fireline and break up the sod or duff. The shovels follow and scrape the line down to mineral soil. Sometimes a chainsaw man will lead off if there are trees or a lot of brush that needs to come out. Brush hooks may also work along with the Pulaskis. McCleods may be used in conjunction with the shovels.

The idea, particularly in the larger twenty-man crews, is for each fire-fighter to give the line a "lick or two" then move on and let the next guy do the same. If the crew is "well oiled," they will have built a per-fect fireline, down to mineral soil, by the time the twentieth man puts his licks in. If it isn't, either the firefighters up front will do all the work or the ones in the back will. A good crew can build a lot of line quickly because, theoretically, no one firefighter gets too tired.

The entire fire organization is set up to deal with a much broader spectrum of eventualities. The direction is mostly oriented toward the very big, or project, fires. These fires often employ thousands of indi-vidual firefighters and an array of equipment.

On a big fire the twenty-man crews might be organized into divisions and sectors. Some of those crews might be hotshot or interregional fire-fighting crews whose main function is wildfire suppression—sort of the Green Berets of firefighters. Specialized engine crews lay hose, supply water, and protect structures that might be threatened. Fixed-wing air-craft might be used to drop slurry. Helitack crews utilize helicopters to transport firefighters, scout out the fire, and drop buckets of water on hotspots. There may be overhead teams, Dozer bosses, tree felling bosses, supply bosses, transport bosses, information officers, reconnaissance teams, field observers, planners, tacticians. . . . It has all the beauty of a war except nobody's shooting at you. Actually, it's amazing that as few people get hurt or killed as do on the big fires.

Despite the technology of it all the bottom line still comes down to the basic fact that everyone, either directly or indirectly, is trying to remove the fuel or the heat or maybe even the oxygen from the wildfire. And it could be that the wildfire, on some weird level, is a life itself. Something to be called by name. Sometimes, "Sir."

Most firefighters don't get their start on the big ones. It's seldom the kind of blazing inferno that makes its way to the nightly news. Most often, at least in the Rockies, it is a lightning strike that has managed to nail a single pitchy snag. One burning tree can puff up a lot of smoke and the district will dispatch a couple of firefighters out to the area. Although the smoke is easy to see from the air or maybe from a fire tower posted off on some distant ridge, it can be a different story when you are looking for it on the ground in the jumble of the forest.

Smoke does funny things when it is gliding across the land. If it's early in the morning when the wind is coming down the draws, smoke can carry miles from the source and layer into a hollow of cold air. When you are new at it you will think things are quite simple when you see a concentration of smoke like that and dive off a ridge and follow it. Maybe after searching for an hour or two you learn a first lesson—where there's smoke there isn't always fire.

I remember a burning snag on the Pikes Peak ranger district in Colorado. The fire tower had spotted it late in the evening and they called us up and told us to be ready to go after it first thing the next morning. There was a new forester on the district and he was going along. He was straight out of college and had all the course work in fire management. His skills on the ground were limited, but the Forest Service figured this was a good way for him to learn—they made him the boss.

We gathered at the office at dawn and headed out. The night before we'd pulled the air photos of the area and found a road that would get us close. It took about an hour to wind our way up out of town and into the area. When we got out of the truck and had a look we saw a small draw about half a mile off that was filled with smoke as far down it as we could see.

This is when we learned that the forester had apparently had some leadership training, too. He took the show over in a character-istic military sort of way. This isn't unusual on a fire because a para-military type chain of command and mode of action is well suited when you have to move lots of firefighters and equipment as quickly and efficiently as possible. On these smaller smoke chasing deals we usually would forego some of the formalities, but we figured this guy was green.

He barked some orders out, we grabbed our tools, and busted double time over to the draw. We didn't talk it over when we got into the smoke and headed down the draw. I knew where the fire was and so did the other grunts with me, but we followed. After about forty minutes we were working hard not to giggle when we left the chainsaw and some hand tools leaning up against a tree. The forester didn't even notice as he raced around searching for the fire.

Finally, we broke out laughing when he asked us where the hell our tools were. We told him they were up the draw toward the fire and his pupils began to dilate. Sweat was pouring out from under his hard hat. We pointed all the way back up the draw. A single ponderosa pine was puffing smoke on a ridge not more than a thousand feet from our truck. He took it well and even choked out a muffled laugh as we headed back. It has happened to all of us and we never told anyone in the office about it.

Fighting district wildfires is the best kind of apprenticeship for a fire-fighter. Sometimes they turn out to just be a snag, but in other cases it could be three or four acres or maybe upwards of twenty. We learned how to size each smoke up and decide what to do about it. Sometimes if the fire was just crawling along in the duff we took our time digging line around it.

If the fire was hotter and walking or even trotting a little we often decided to hotline it, which meant we went right to where the fire was moving the fastest and tried to get a line around that area. If things worked out it meant that we stopped the advance of the fire at the head and then could take our time finishing the fireline out around the areas that had already burned or weren't burning very hot.

It was good training in the basics of how to safely carry the tools over rugged terrain and pace ourselves for the long haul when we used them. We picked up tricks from other more experienced firefighters, like how to push the shovel with a knee while scraping line and conserve our strength. We learned how to anchor the fireline into a creek or rocks or roads so that we knew the fire wouldn't get behind us.

The details were critical, like making sure to throw any twig or branch that had burned in toward the fire but anything that was totally green outside the fireline. This prevented the possibility that even an ember might get outside the line and start up some trouble. The saying went, "green to green and black to black."

When there was a line around the entire fire, the dirty, boring, and absolutely crucial mop up work began. On the smaller fires this meant going to every log, every stump, every ember, and every pine needle that had any fire in it and putting it dead out. Most of the time we did it by "dry-mopping," which meant we chopped the embers off logs, then mixed dirt with them and spread them until we could hold a hand to them and feel no heat. We did the same for anything else that held any heat. They called it "cold trailing."

Sometimes we carried five-gallon backpack pumps with water that we used to cool the embers and duff down before we stirred and spread. The backpack pumps, or "piss bags," were miserable and heavy to carry but greatly speeded up the process. We used the same mop-up techniques—it was just quicker with the water. The rule of thumb was that if you didn't know how to dry-mop, then you couldn't wet-mop, either. Just spraying water on a hotspot won't put it out—it needs to be broken up, stirred, fiddled with.

Most importantly we learned that fires and firefighters keep some odd hours. We learned about telephone calls in the middle of the night and sticking with things even though we were going to have to work through the entire night following the light from our headlamps. We learned that you could be more tired than you ever thought was possible and keep digging fireline. We learned how to take care of ourselves and watch out for the occasional fire that the wind would throw into the crowns of the trees where it could take off into an uncontrollable run. We learned that you don't always stop them and that the little fires can get big in a hurry. And that sometimes people get hurt.

All of it prepared us for the big fires, the project fires, where the call might come at two in the morning and before you knew it you were on an airplane heading out to some monster fire in California, Idaho, Montana, Wyoming, Nevada, Virginia . . . a fire that would have camps with hundreds, even thousands of tired firefighters sprawled out, sleeping on the ground or trying to get to a telephone to let someone know where they were. It can get into your blood.

I would like the project fires for no other reason than the going. Aside from the adventure of it all and the mystery of where you might end up and what you might see and the money you might make I would settle for the simple pleasure of being constantly in motion. During the fire season most firefighters have a packed bag standing by the door or in the trunk of their cars. It's an everyday reminder that at any moment a call might come and you will be on the road.

It is travel stripped bare. There are no photo stops, no educational sidesteps, no chance to get a feel for anything other than the wind over a truck's windshield or an airplane's wing. The idea is to just get there. Your meals are covered. You throw a sleeping bag out wherever you end up when you can't continue. You catnap. You keep moving. I was born with a feel for it.

The fire crews that mobilized for the great California fires in the fall of 1987 did it so well that the Army came by and asked how it was that they could get five or ten thousand people and their equipment on the road and headed out in just a day or two. They'd been trying to find the answer for years. The Israeli and the Swiss armies and apparently the American firefighters know the answer. It's simple enough—they have all their gear at home, ready to go, actually just waiting, almost hoping to go. The Army tends to draw the line at M-16s stashed in every soldier's home.

I was called to the California fires that year and in a lot of ways they were like most of the other big project fires I've worked on. There was one exception, though. We drove a strike team of five fire engines from

Colorado to California. It seemed like most of the engines in California were the big jobs and the need for the small, mobile, four-wheel-drive type of initial attack "pumpers" that we use in the Rockies was recognized. We left Durango, Colorado, at two in the morning, two firefighters to a truck, one driving and one wedged in that dreamy zone this side of unconsciousness—the place where the little green men live—and we drove for thirty hours with a three-hour nap in Ely, Nevada.

I know fatigue much better than I know the other phantoms in my life and I can thank firefighting for the friendship. The rulebook says they can work you for the first 24 hours straight when you get the fire call and after that you're entitled to 12 hours on duty and 12 hours off. It seldom works that way, at least in the early stages of a big fire. Figure some stretches at 18 or 20 hours a day, figure 100 maybe 120-hour work weeks if things get ugly. Figure on no relief. Figure on making exhaustion a friend rather than the enemy. Make it a give and take relationship and hope that you're "on" if things get hot. The little green guys dancing across the road, or the fireline, or in the mess line are all right, but draw the line at the little blue guys.

I was working night shift on a big fire near Fairplay, Colorado. My job was simple—just make sure that a Pacific Marine pump located by a small stream kept the water coming to the firefighters up on the line. There wasn't much to do other than gas it up every few hours and listen for any break in the mechanical hum that might mean things were going wrong. After three or four days of it I got to where I could doze next to the pump and wake up instantly when it started to sputter for lack of gas. Sleeping off shift, during the day, wasn't going well. The fire camp was noisy and too bright. We were getting three or four hours a day.

One night I figured to break up the boredom and walked over to talk to another firefighter that I'd noticed rummaging around in the back of a nearby pickup. It turned out that all that was there was a broom, stuck up in the bed of the truck by its handle. I don't think I talked to it for very long before I realized. . . .

The language conveys something of a chromatic scale—tired, dog-tired, fatigued, bushed, beat, worn out, weary, exhausted, goneness, dead tired, spent—but these are only the notes in a fugue. You can come to understand the orchestra, the composer, and even the performance.

They put us up in a motel when we pulled into Redding, California. It wasn't part of the plan. The dispatcher had figured to head us straight up to the fireline, at least, until our strike team leader told him that the crew wasn't going to move a goddamn inch until they got some sleep. We'd been seeing the little blue guys.

At four the next morning we left for the fire. We made the district ranger station in Hayfork, California, at dawn, just in time for chow at a fire camp that had been set up nearby. The place was chaotic. A huge storm full of lightning, but no rain, had torched eighty percent of the district. They didn't even know how many fires they actually had burning. They dispatched us to another fire camp farther to the west. Smoke filled all the valleys.

The fire camp had been up in the mountains, but when we arrived they were in the process of moving it to a huge field near Hyampom, California, which they figured would be big enough to hold the expected two or three thousand firefighters who were on the way. We grabbed the best campsite we could find in the new fire camp and set up shop. Word was that we would be pulling night shift. We left for work at six that evening.

At first it was easy duty. We'd been charged with protecting a fireline that had been backfired on the previous night shift. Backfiring is a form of wildfire control that you see a lot of on the bigger fires. Generally a fireline is dug, or in our case a road is located that is in a position ahead of the direction that the wildfire is moving. Controllable fires are deliberately set at the fireline with the intention of burning out the fuel ahead of the fire. When the wildfire meets with the backfired area it is deprived of fuel and theoretically stopped. It's a way of creating the *very* wide firelines necessary to hold huge wildfires that can jump over any line dug by firefighters or bulldozers.

A lot can go wrong with a backfire. If the wind changes and it gets out of hand it can jump your fireline and you're right back where you started. If things go right the backfire can eliminate the fuel from the oncoming fire and even change the direction or force of the fire's convection column and turn it back into itself. Most backfiring is done on the night shifts when the humidity is a little higher and conditions don't favor the kind of blowups that can occur during the day shifts.

They like having pumper trucks like the ones we'd brought from Colorado to follow the firefighters who are lighting the backfires. If the thing gets out of hand and spots over the fireline, the water is available immediately to put it out. Spot fires are the firefighter's enemy. If they get out of control not only do they mean that all the work put into the fireline is worthless but that you may end up having wildfire on both sides of you. This isn't considered sporting.

The section of line we were patrolling was in good shape. The backfire had gone as planned and there were just a few hotspots, here and there, that we figured were too close to the line and put out. It looked like an easy shift that held the potential for a catnap. An experienced firefighter will always sleep when he can, because he knows that at any minute he may be called on to go full out at one hundred percent if something blows up. We laid back.

It didn't last. Around one in the morning they dispatched us to a couple of spot fires that had jumped the line on another part of the fire. From the beginning it was what firefighters call a watch-out situation. In fire training they give you a little book with a skull and crossbones on it. The title is *Fire Situations that Shout Watch Out.* There are thirteen of them. What they are trying to get across is that if you don't watch out you may get your ass burned.

As axioms for survival go they are pretty simple. Take number seven—"You are in country you haven't seen in the daylight"; number ten—"You are getting frequent spot fires over your line"; number eight—"You are in an area where you are unfamiliar with local factors influencing fire behavior"; number one—"You are building a fireline downhill toward a fire." I like number thirteen—

"You feel like taking a little nap near the fireline." All of these and a few more applied. There was that wonderful jolt of adrenaline that watch out situations can provide. The kind that can get you through an entire night shift. We checked for our fire shelters.

Yes, the Fire Shelters. They are the neatly packaged outfits that look like an aluminum pup tent when deployed. The idea is that a firefighter who has run out of options can find a spot relatively clear of fuel, hopefully a purposely created wide spot in the fireline called a safe zone, set up his fire shelter, and get into it with his feet pointed toward the oncoming wildfire. The aluminum and fiberglass lined fire shelter will reflect the intense heat of the fire away from him while he breathes the cooler air an inch or two above the ground. He can crawl around in the shelter to get away from any unbearable heat if necessary. He must hold the shelter down tightly when the fire and its accompanying cyclone of winds goes over him. The shelters are proven and there are a number of firefighters alive today thanks to them, but it still doesn't keep us from calling them "Shake and Bakes."

Things *do* happen. Years before I'd been on a project fire in southern California. The fuels there are flashy to the point of being explosive. I was on a hand crew that was backfiring a section of line out. The squad doing the firing was using flare guns. The key when backfiring with flare guns is to shoot the flare in from the fireline twenty or maybe thirty yards. When it ignites the fuel the fire doesn't have enough time to get a head on it before it meets up with the preconstructed fireline and can be controlled.

This particular squad got to screwing around and was shooting the flares too far down a steep slope of heavy fuel. The fire took off and overran them. I managed to run down the fireline to safety, but some of the crew had to deploy their shelters. It was over as quick as it started and we ran up to them. Everyone was okay except for one firefighter who'd had his sleeves rolled up. The shelter, which he had to hold down with his forearms, had gotten so hot that it burned his arms. It wasn't as bad as it could have been.

Another time in southern California I was on a twenty-man crew along with four other twenty-man crews on a narrow ridge away from the main fire—a watch out situation. We were there awaiting instruction from Command. The main fire shifted and came our way. The crew leaders radioed for instructions and were told to stay put. The main fire, which was still a couple of miles off, kept coming, but we could hear it even that far away. People started getting edgy. The crew bosses called in again and were given the same instructions. The fire began to run.

That's when the crew bosses began looking for spots to deploy our shelters and came to the conclusion that the country was so steep there wasn't enough room for the 100 firefighters on that ridge to put out their shelters if they needed to. We were backed up to a steep, almost vertical slope on one side. The fire was boiling when they called Command and requested a slurry drop to try and slow the fire so they could think.

The planes came in low and made their drops. There was no talk because even us grunts knew things were getting tight. Less experienced crews might have bolted and that would have been the kiss of death. The slurry slowed the fire just a little, but it was enough for us to pull up a hose lay that was on the fireline, tie it into whatever we could find, and go hand over hand down the steep slope to safety. That's when we started the banter, yelling at the crew bosses to call in for 100 pairs of clean shorts.

Those are the exceptions. Most of the time the firefighting is boringly routine. If you are going to get hurt it's more likely to occur when you're flying, or being transported by the National Guard, or by the sudden randomness of a huge burned out snag that falls out of nowhere. The snags may be the most feared because there is absolutely nothing you can do if your time is up. It takes some getting used to.

Those spot fires when we were on the pumpers in northern California? Well, we didn't do too well. They got away from us. Another crew came up but refused to help because they thought the situation was too dangerous. We pulled back when the flames started racing into the crowns and lit backfires to try and slow it, but it was too close to morning and the sun heated things up. The whole thing blew up on us. We went back to camp after being up twenty-five or thirty hours. As they say, "That's show biz!" The pay really is the same.

Eventually, the crews did get a handle on the fires, which were collectively called the Gulch Complex. Our lives turned into an endless string of patrols and backfires—all night shifts. The smoke hung in thick and once or twice the carbon monoxide took its toll in the form of nausea and delirium, but we just figured it was fatigue. One shift it was so bad that when a division boss came to talk to one of our engine bosses he found him completely incoherent. The division boss asked, "How long have you people been out here?" We couldn't tell him. We became the walking dead.

I remember the rest of that time in California more like the two-minute sound bites you get on the nightly news. It is all in fragments and the story line is hard to find. I remember sitting around a warming fire that Frankie Maestas and I built one cold night on the fireline and talking about how we would stop at Reno if they ever let us go home. It struck us as funny and we laughed until the tears rolled down our cheeks and we slid into that deep, dark kind of fatigue that even scares the little blue guys away.

I remember getting released from one fire only to be dispatched to another. Fire camps that looked all the same in the Seiad Valley, Happy Camp, North Elk, Norcross, Forks of the Salmon . . . and endless night shifts. There was R&R for a day or two in Yreka, California, and the feeling that I would never get enough sleep. Our strike team leader was going nuts trying to get us relieved. One morning I looked over at one of the firefighters on the crew and I realized how bad it was. There was no light to be found. Her eyes were dull. I figured that we all must have the thousand-mile stare. We were sick and coughing from the smoke.

Finally after thirty-five days they sent us home. We made it to Reno, but when the leggy bargirl came over and asked what she could do for us, we just stared into space.

"Somebody say something," she said. We told her we'd been on the fires for a very long time.

The crew split up after Reno and we all drove home our separate ways. We'd had our fights and reconciliations the way all crews do on a long run, but most of it was forgotten. We were family whether we liked it or not.

I ended up driving alone for the final leg of the trip from Grand Junction to Durango. Try it after you've been with ten other firefighters day and night, good and bad, for thirty-five days. It's a new kind of aloneness. The best month in Colorado is September and it was over, but the air was clear and some of the aspen were still brilliant and yellow as I drove over Red Mountain Pass. It was nice to see mountains that I knew. It was a lot like home.

I read later that the Fire Siege of 1987 involved 22,000 firefighters in California and Oregon. In California 775,000 acres burned. Enough timber was burned to build homes for a city the size of San Francisco. Fire suppression costs in California alone were over $100 million. An interesting footnote gave the results of a study on the crews that pulled night shifts on the fires—they averaged three to four hours of sleep a day. Ten firefighters lost their lives.

And none of it, with the exception of the lost lives, would hold a candle to what was to happen in the Yellowstone National Park area in 1988.

Wildfire fighting, at least the grunt work that most of the seasonals do, is a job for young men and women. Needless to say, the hours are long, but the money *is* good although there comes a time on the big fires where even the money doesn't matter.

After twelve years of firefighting I've gotten to the point where on any project fire I go to I'll see a firefighter that I've met on some other obscure jumble of topography that was burning. In many cases it could be that the wildfire was the best thing that ever happened to the landscape. But we were there anyway, whatever the politics of nature are.

I could say that after having worked on somewhere close to a couple hundred wildfires, both large and small, that I'd had enough and it would be almost true. But there is another part of me, the part that just lives to be on the move, that is always looking for the next fire call, the next column of smoke over the next ridge, and wondering what that fire will be doing. Will it be crawling in the duff or roaring up some ridge? Will it be the kind of fire that charges me full of adrenaline and wonder? Will it be the kind of fire that has a life of its own?

I'm still no different than all the other grunts. I'm still in it for the rush and the cash.

Pride and Glory of Firefighting
Is Hard to Resist

by Louise Wagenknecht

Writer and sheep rancher Louise Wagenknecht (born 1949) has worked for the Forest Service for almost 30 years.

T he southwest winds brought waves of red smoke streaming into the valley from the fires near Boise and McCall every day last summer. A helicopter would come in overhead, and I'd hear the almost subsonic whump-whump-whump that meant a big craft.

The smoke and the morning air and the noise took me back to a mountainside, to a morning years removed, when that most reassuring of sounds hit my ears: large helicopters, flying again, after our long night of cutting fireline into the dark.

The firepack is on my back and the pulaski in my gloved hands. With a scoop of chew tucked into my lower lip, I see the river, 2,000 feet below, and the faint wisps of September fog trailing up the canyon. And cutting through it all, rising like a dragonfly off the helibase pad, Helitack 1, or 2, or 3. Whump-whump-whump. It sounds very, very good.

That's the part of firefighting that makes you just a bit cocky, just a bit proud. You feel stronger and smarter than you really are. Firefighting is a skill, a craft, a yearly dance in which roles are clearly defined and where certainties abound to compensate for the uncertainties of the enemy. It requires specialized, even arcane knowledge, and those who master some particular part of it are professionals.

Line boss, sector boss, buying unit, camp leader: Titles that often have nothing to do with our usual jobs are ours on a fire. Actual GS-ratings mean very little: GS-4s order GS-13s around.

I started "going out on a fire" because I needed the money. Bit by bit, my firepack acquired the little comforts that make 48-hour shifts more bearable. I kept a few cans of baked beans, fruit cocktail and juice stashed away in case of inadequate sack lunches. Headlamps furnished by the Forest Service were awkward and unreliable; most of us bought better ones from an industrial catalog with our own money. My pockets were full of hard candy, gum, tobacco, paperbacks (as in any military operation, much of firefighting consists of waiting) and toilet paper.

Firefighting changes your ideas about outdoor recreation. Standing on an 80 percent slope at midnight, listening warily for the ominous creaking noises that mean a giant vegetable is about to kill you, then curling up just before dawn to catch a few winks in a ditch filled with ashes and the odd scorpion, erodes the desire to go camping just for the fun of it.

Once, while mopping up in deep ash in a grove of giant, conk-ridden Douglas firs, we heard the fearful groaning of a dying tree.

Whirling 360 degrees in panic, we tried to see the assailant. Impossible. The sound was everywhere. With a final seismic thump, the tree fell. It missed everyone, but the concussion raised a blinding ash cloud that reduced visibility to zero. The crew boss shouted, and we groped our way uphill, out of the grove, and into an open area. Shaken, we all sat down.

"Lunch!" said the crew boss. We made it last until our shift was over.

In my experience, it is the common sense of crew bosses that saves lives on a fire, but it takes a strong one to refuse a hazardous order. It was a brave crew boss, for example, who refused to continue night mop-up on a nearly vertical slope with rocks the size of clothes dryers hurtling by in the dark. In the face of Al's assertion that this was dangerous and unnecessary on a 12-acre fire already plastered with retardant, the honchos down at fire camp insisted that we continue.

Al stopped arguing, but led us out of the burned area to the firelines, where we spent the night improving the trenches, out of range of rocks, while Al lied his head off on the radio.

It took a tough crew boss to categorically refuse to have our crew flown to the top of a 100-acre fire burning in heavy fuels so we could dig line downhill toward the fire.

"No," said Rick to the line boss. "We're not going to do that. We're going to start digging here, at the bottom, and you will have two crews coming up behind us, and you will have a spotter across the canyon to keep us informed, and you will get some engines down here and start pumping out of the river and putting a hose lay up behind us."

Through a long night of chain-saw work in dense, jackstrawed trees, while squirrelly winds fanned the flames and 80-foot firs crowned out above us, ours was the only line that held. If we had been up on top cutting line downhill, would we have died for the line boss's error in judgment?

Working downhill toward a fire has been a factor in many fire fatalities over the years, yet it continues to be done on uncontained fires, as happened on the fatal fire in Colorado this summer.

I stopped going on fires after the Great California Cookout of '87. I saw the plantations that we had thinned so carefully only a couple of years before go up like A-bombs as the slash ignited, torching so thoroughly that not even stumps remained.

I saw fire fronts come to a dead halt as they hit an area of old growth that had experienced an underburn a few years before. I came off the fires in October with a raging ear infection, bronchitis that swiftly became pneumonia, and the realization that firefighting, like combat, is for 20-year-olds who still believe they're immortal.

Yet, when the chopper came in that morning last summer, just for that moment, I missed the dirt and the smoke and the camaraderie of the fireline. I suddenly mourned the fact that the fire stories I have to tell are the only ones I will ever have.

When I work on fires now, it's in an air-conditioned building, and although I know I've done my bit and don't need to suck any more smoke to prove myself, the smoky winds can still send adrenaline into my blood.

As the Forest Service struggles—perhaps more than any other wildland agency—to change its attitude toward fire and reject the put-'em-all-out-now shibboleth that has landed us in this fix, Chief Jack Ward Thomas may find an unexpected barrier to true fire management: It's this love of the rush that belongs to firefighting, all the more powerful because no one talks about it.

Any threat to the status accruing to blackened, sleep-deprived, hard-hatted, snoose-dipping smoke warriors will be resisted, any suggestion that those who make a career of firefighting do so because they enjoy it will be rejected as somehow immoral.

Ending the war games will be unpalatable to many. But the games will end.

The beginning of the end came last summer when the Payette National Forest in Idaho announced that an all-out effort to extinguish the Blackwell and Corral Complexes would cost $42 million and stand only a 15 percent chance of succeeding before winter did it for free. With that, the government admitted it can no longer afford to indulge career fire managers in their hobby of battling an element which should never have been allowed to become an enemy in the first place.

It is time for the fire gods to admit that they love battle for its own sake, and for what it has brought them in the way of pride, and power, and glory. It is time for them to recognize this, and get over it, and get another life.

Those who have died deserve that from us, at least.

The Fires Next Time
by Rick Bass

When wildfires threatened land and homes in Montana's Yaak Valley in 1994, writer Rick Bass (born 1958) and other residents had to come up with an evacuation plan.

t is a windy day in mid-August 1994 here in the wet Yaak Valley, northwest Montana's greenest valley. Almost the whole valley—100 or so of us—is gathered in a little log church that doubles as a community center. We've had bake sales in this little cabin, and we've voted here. Today we are listening to a heavyset Army sergeant, all dressed up in camouflage, explain to us how to try to keep from burning to death.

There is copper-colored smoke filtering through the sunlight all around us, like fog, and it just won't go away. It feels as heavy as the lead apron that you wear during X rays. The last really good fire that came through this valley was in 1910, and it burned from Spokane to Kalispell—3 million acres. The smoke was visible in Chicago.

There's no phone service in most of this valley. We are cut off from news of the outside world—which is usually how we like it. But what we are most interested in today is a weather report, and we get one: high winds, possibly 30 to 40 miles an hour, from the west, with dry lightning—no precipitation. Already the flames are sawing their way up the logged-over slopes of the Mount Henry–McIntire country, chewing their way through dead lodgepole pine that the timber companies said they would log but didn't. (Instead they took the big green trees, spruce and larch.)

Closer to home, the flames are also sawing their way up the side of Lost Horse Mountain, leaping from clearcut to clearcut. All the fires are curiously here on the south side of the river—a function of the spectacular lightning storms that moved down the valley in late July, and again on the 14th and 15th of this month, lighting certain trees in the forest like candles, tongues of lightning flickering and splitting the heavens open with white light, each one searching for the one tree, the one dry dead tree with the itch, the specific itch, to be born again. Over two nights in mid-August, more than 160 fires were reported in the Kootenai National Forest. From that point, it was up to the wind to see if the fires would run (they almost always climb, rather than descend) and bring new life behind them, in their wake and in their ashes—or whether the old order of rot and decay would be preserved, in places, for at least another year.

At night some of us have been driving up to the top of Hensley Face, on the other side of the river—for now, the "safe" side. From the top of Hensley Face we can look down on the valley and see the lights of the fires blinking yellow through the bed of smoke, fires blinking like a thousand flashbulbs, seeming sometimes strangely synchronized as breezes blow across them. It's like a near version of the underworld— as if we are watching from a cliff, the last cliff, before the final descent.

In the meeting that day the sergeant guy—who had fought fires before, though never in this valley, which is unlike any other (part Pacific Northwest rainforest, part northern Rockies)—talked to us about the Fowler and Turner and Fish Fry fires, all of which were less than a mile from my home and, in his words, really rocking.

They had it down to a science, which was both reassuring and terrifying. They'd measure the humidities in combustible materials— *wood*—in advance of the fire, and the per-acre volume of fuel. They'd break these measurements down into size categories, too: Was the fuel composed of twigs and branches, or limbs, or, hottest burning of all, entire downed trees? It all mattered.

Evacuation orders and alternate plans were discussed; we took inventory of who wasn't there. If the roads were aflame, we'd all meet in Gail's big meadow along the river and hope helicopters could get through—though I had my doubts about that, as it seemed the smoke would pool in those places. It's the smoke that kills you usually, not the flames. We were instructed, if trapped, to lie down in the river or creek with a wet towel over our face.

The lecture was sometimes drowned out by the sound of choppers and big bombers cruising low over the woods, the helicopters carrying 1,000-gallon buckets of water dipped from the river and lakes, and the bombers roaring right over the ridges and spraying cloacal plumes of water, or smoking trails of fire retardant, onto the flames below. I wondered idly if the retardant was good for the soil—good for the watershed. That wind was coming, the sergeant said, and there was a good chance that the whole place could go, and go quick. We'd know within 24 hours. He wanted us to be ready to leave with less than five minutes' notice, if it came to that.

Some had begun leaving already, but most of us stayed. It's an incredible pull—the bond to home, the bond to your own place.

That afternoon I went up to the mercantile to get extra gas, but it was closed. That would be a real bummer, I thought, to be evacuating and run out of gas. Murphy's Law to the *n*th. A friend was sitting on the porch of the tavern drinking beer and watching the hypnotic sight of a mountain on fire—the mountain right across the river. "If we burn, we burn," he said.

I went up into the woods behind the house, up to the top of Zimmerman Hill, to peer down at the Okaga Lake fire; but I couldn't see anything for all the smoke. My wife was pregnant with our second child that stormy summer, and it occurred to me that this would be an even less opportune time than usual to get myself killed—to do something dumb—so I turned and went back down the hill, down the safe, unburned side. On my way down, I encountered a curious thing: a covey of blue grouse ground-roosting, midslope, with a covey of ruffed grouse. I'd never seen or heard of such a thing, and I wondered if the blue grouse had moved down off their usual roosts on the ridge because they knew the fire was going to come up over the ridge. I wondered if they could feel it coming, like a tingle or an itch, in the rocks beneath their feet, in the forest soil.

Down low, deer were moving around at all times of the day, looking dazed and confused; many of them were standing midstream in the little creek.

I decided to begin moving some things out of the cabin—books, family pictures. I took my old Ford Falcon down to the nearest town, Libby, while the road was still open—before it became crisscrossed with burning timbers and became a hot-air wind tunnel of flame.

In Libby I was stopped and given a citation because the old Ford had a brake light out. I argued with the officer. Ash floated down on us as we argued. He lives in town, where it's safe. I live in the country.

The fires ran out, as they always do; as they did even in 1910. The weight of their own smoke—the lack of oxygen—put them out, the ennui of their own existence. The firefighters put some of them out, and the rains that came on Labor Day put them out, the rains that always come on Labor Day. I would have liked to see everyone go home then—there were nearly 2,000 National Guardsmen and soldiers from as far away as Alabama, Arkansas, and Louisiana camping in this shy valley, a 20-fold increase in the social and cultural stress on the valley—but I have to say that for a couple of days I was glad they were there.

The whole town, pretty much the whole West, was glad to see them there. The belligerent yellow signs in a few storefront windows that claimed, "This Business Supported by Timber Dollars" were replaced by bumper stickers that read, "This Business Supported by Burning Timber Dollars." Perhaps it's the value-added industry we've been looking for. Instead of just growing big trees and sawing them down and shipping them off, we can set them on fire. We'd get paid twice that way: for putting the fires out and then for cutting them down and shipping them away. Forget all this fairy-tale talk of bookcases, cabinetmaking, toy and furniture factories, finger-joint molding and post-and-beam plants. Firefighting on the public lands dished out close to $1 billion last year—$6 billion in the last decade—even though, as we're beginning to understand intellectually if not yet emotionally, the only final way to fight fire is, as the saying goes, with fire. That which does not rot will burn, one day, and to me it seems to be the same process, simply at a different rate. In the wet forests, the dead trees have a good chance of rotting; in dry forests, or on dry aspects, they have less chance of making it all the way to rot. Everyone agrees that the more fires you put out, the bigger the next ones will be—or the next next, and so on. It's just a matter of biology—of waiting for the right conditions to combine, the right mix of heat and aridity and fuel and wind and ignition.

All over the West, scientists as well as residents are trying to figure out how to apply this most basic truth that has just popped up seemingly out of nowhere: *The forests have to burn.* Suppression only makes the forests lean more toward this truth. Many parts of the Yaak, for instance, are changing from the previous stable, fire-resistant system of predominantly larch and cedar-hemlock to a more combustible mix of fir and lodgepole pine. In the past, the thick bark of the older larch trees and the cedar's affinity for swamps have protected those two species. But now the highly flammable fir and lodge-pole, without fires to keep them in balance, are encroaching into new territory, displacing slower-growing, more fire-resistant species such as larch and cedar. Stresses on the forest beyond the cumulative stress of total fire suppression include the possibility of insect infestations of forests adjacent to clearcuts; in addition, there are diseased, blister-rusting white pines and weakened firs. All this adds to what's called, ominously and accurately, fuel loading.

In the past three decades of fire suppression in the nearby Lolo National Forest, for example, the volume of wood that has burned annually is about one-tenth of what it used to be. Additionally, most fires in the past burned "cooler," since excess fuel was kept from loading up by the frequency of fires. The cooler fires spared many trees and left behind a diverse mosaic of burned and unburned species and age classes, different for each fire. The forests must have been seething with diversity.

But more of today's fires—and we haven't seen a truly big one yet—are burning hotter.

The timber industry has an answer, of course, and it isn't shy about touting it. All last autumn, ads blared over the radio saying that if industry had been allowed to do more logging, the fires wouldn't have happened.

Never mind that most of the fires in the Kootenai were in logged areas. The industry had it figured: Cut down all the trees before they catch on fire.

Except: It is our past and present logging practices that have helped cause the very problem. Since in most logged-over areas there are not enough big dead trees left behind to rot slowly on site—to live out their cycle of rebirth—the soils on these lands are becoming impoverished at rates so startling that they often cannot even be measured. Sometimes the soil is washing away following the clearcuts, while other times it just sprouts knapweed, a noxious grass-replacing exotic weed that is completely indigestible to big game.

The forest isn't always coming back on its own—not the forest type that the land has fostered naturally. When new species of trees are planted, at great expense, they are often weaker, growing without the shade of a canopy, and hence more prone to the stresses of sun and wind. This can result in more deaths, and greater volumes of tree death—"fuel loading"—which can make a stand more susceptible to hot fires. The hot fires then do further damage to the soil, and the ashes from these hot fires often slump into the nearby streams and creeks, causing severe sedimentation.

It's big-time out of balance. We need to back off and try to reestablish order—and, certainly, to keep our hands off the roadless areas, which are the true sources of and models for forest health. But the current Congress, greedy for all the big burned sticks, won't hear of it. It's declared an "emergency." To make sure industry can go in and cut all that wood before any of it returns to the way wood has been for roughly the past 4 billion years, Congress has passed a bill—written by the timber companies—outlawing any environmental restrictions or regulations on "salvage" harvests.

Salvage in theory refers to dead trees, but it is defined in this bill as anything with the potential to burn, which basically covers any tree in the world. Bill Clinton vetoed the bill—it was a rider tacked onto the budget rescissions bill—the first veto of his presidency. The Yaak—and the West—was granted one more year of life.

The aerial photos of postfire forests tell an interesting story. The blackest areas—the fires' origins, in many instances, and places where they burned hottest—radiate from the edges of the big clearcuts and into the weakened, diminished forests. A favorite saying in the timber industry is "Clearcuts don't burn," but they do. The sun at the clearcut-forest interface scorches that area exceedingly, making it unnaturally dry, as do the strong winds that sweep across the clearcut's lunar surfaces. These winds blow down excessive snarls of weakened timber around all edges of the clearcut.

But, says industry, the clearcuts hold their snowpack longer, since they release most of their radiant heat back into the atmosphere each night, without that pesky heat-trapping overstory. And it's true, they do. And then along about the first of June, about the time the streams and rivers have finally started to clear up from normal spring runoff, all the remaining snowmelt (and sediment) goes at once, in slumps and muddy gushes, rather than trickling slowly out of the old cool cedar woods, like a tap being slowly turned on—the way nature, and springtime in the Rockies, are designed to work.

It's 1995. Are we really still debating clearcuts?

I never set out to become a pagan. It just kind of happened. It's as if, rather than my moving toward it, a whole lot of other things receded, leaving me stranded on some peninsula of paganism. More and more, it seemed, everything else around me looked dumb, or dishonest. There seemed to be an incredible wisdom in the woods, so simple that even a child could understand it. The way the old-growth forests create their own stable world and maintain it and its health far better than we could manage either our world or theirs, in terms of health. The thick bark of the oldest trees, and the way they shed their branches almost coyly, almost tempting little grass fires to catch in those brush tangles and limb tangles, keeping the forest cool and clean and nutrient rich.

All those old lichens hanging down from the oldest trees, hard earned, are not just for show. Firefighters tell me that sometimes, if floating sparks land in them, the lichens can flare up like a torch and then extinguish themselves, having used up all the surrounding oxygen available in that quick flush—leaving the old tree almost totally unscathed.

Even the timing of the fire season in the West is a thing of great beauty and great health. The way the fires come, sometimes in July but usually in August, allowing just enough time to download some fuel and recycle some nutrients, but not so much that things get out of hand. In September the rains come, turning the fires to smolder, and in October and November the snows come, extinguishing them. Even the way the larch needles fly through the air in the autumn wind seems to be full of purpose. One morning in October you wake up and there's a quarter- or half-inch mat of beautiful gold needles, and beautiful gold aspen leaves, spread all across the countryside. This golden blanket helps pin down the charred coals and ashes of August, keeps too much of the ash from blowing away or slumping into creeks, and speeds up the soil-making process—as much as that glacial pace can be helped along.

The interconnectedness of things. I'm all for prudent salvage logging, as long as it's not in roadless areas. But when some industry asks to be put above or beyond the law, I get frightened, and angry. It is not the fires of late summer I fear. I respect those—they are nature's way and can no more be controlled than the wind or the rain. They're part of the weather of the West. But going out and clear-cutting forests, or entering roadless areas, under the guise of preventing forest fires is like going into the forest with gallon watering cans during a drought. It's just not going to work. What we're dealing with is too big.

The fire season has taught me a lot, has taught me a new way of looking at the woods. Now when I go for a walk, or climb a forested mountain, I'm very conscious of the mosaic, of the microsites—those spots in the forest that could start a fire, and those that could spread it, and those that would absorb and stop it, too. I look at diversities of vertical structure, and lateral structure, in unlogged country; at species mix. In the Yaak, especially, due to the unique diversity, there are amazing bands of change on any mountain in the valley. You'll move through a forest of old lodgepole and then, 50 or 100 feet higher, into a forest of fire-buffering cedar or cedar-hemlock. Then the slope will flex more sharply, will cross to a southern aspect, and you'll be in a grove of fire-promoting ponderosa pine; and then, at the top of that ridge, fire-resistant old-growth Douglas fir.

I'm learning to look at *nature*.

Sometimes I think it is the wolves who are helping, aiding and abetting, joining in with the resurrecting fires in the West—or rather, not the wolves but the absence of them. I noticed it just the other day. I was planting some young cedars and had put gated slats and screens around them to keep the deer, elk, and moose from browsing them in winter. I'll keep the enclosures around them until they get tall enough that their branches are above the browse line.

I began planting cedars and aspens a couple of years ago. And it just hit me this spring: the before and after of it. I haven't been seeing any young aspens anywhere in the woods; just big old ones, 30 and 40 and 50 years old—trees born back in the days of predators. I noticed too that in my enclosures the aspen sprouts are doing great, but only in my enclosures. The deer herds are increasing so steadily and dramatically that they're eating all the young aspens and perhaps cedars. The cedars especially help cool the forest, which helps retain moisture—which helps buffer fires.

There are too many deer—or rather, not enough predators. They are perhaps near the edge of stripping the woods bare—changing the composition of the forest, over the past 50 years, in ways as subtle as our ways have been offensive and immense. The ways of rot versus the ways of fire.

It is not just the wolves, of course. It is everything; it is all out of balance.

It was a good snow year, this year. By April we were already watching the sky, like farmers. But the snow and rain mean little. A greenhouse-hot summer followed by a lightning storm, followed by a windy dry day—everything can change, and will change; if not this year, then next. For this reason, and so many others, we need to keep the untouched wilderness cores—the roadless areas—in each national forest. They act as buffers, absorbing and diffusing the spread of huge hot fires throughout the West. They're better at putting out fires, or diluting them, than 10,000 or 100,000 National Guardsmen—better than a billion-dollar-a-year effort. Every forest needs a big wilderness area—a chain of dedicated roadless areas, in perpetuity—come hell or high water, come war or peace, come world's end or world's beginning. Call it a place to run to when things go wrong. When the whole rest of the world goes up in conflagration.

We're just now learning new things in the West. We're always learning new things: things known by people before us, old civilizations, but now forgotten.

We scan the hot western skies in August for signs of approaching storms and try to detect the feel of electricity in the air. Any breeze at all can feel ominous. We are remembering another of nature's rules: Payback is hell.

from The Pine Barrens
by John McPhee

John McPhee's (born 1931) book on the New Jersey Pine Barrens, which cover 25% of that state, includes this explanation of how fire has affected the region's ecology and taxed its fire fighters.

Whatever else they do, men in the Pine Barrens are fire-fighters throughout their lives. There are about four hundred forest fires in the pinelands every year, and fifteen or twenty of them are major ones (more than a hundred acres). It has been theorized that the pineys are defeatists because of the constant presence of the danger of fire. They are, at any rate, extremely fire-conscious, and they know what to expect of a fire when one moves through the woods. Head fires can be as little as ten feet deep. A person overtaken by a head fire can turn, go through it, and get onto safe, burned ground. One of the first lessons in forest-fire survival is: Get onto burned ground. But this is not always easy. Head fires can also be as much as half a mile deep. Lateral fires can be only a foot deep, but they can also be a hundred feet deep. In 1936, a cousin of the fire watcher Eddie Parker was caught in the middle when a head fire and a backfire came together. He had no time to get to burned ground. The last living thing he did was to kneel, as he burned, and embrace a pine tree.

Some fires are hotter than others. What makes the difference between a standard blaze and an inferno is something called fuel continuity. This is the ladderlike arrangement of litter, understory, and overstory that naturally builds up, with time, in the forest. It begins with leaves and pine needles and other litter on the forest floor, moves up to sheep laurel and blueberries and huckleberries, on up to scrub oaks and laurel and young pines, on up to trees of intermediate age, and finally to the crowns of the tallest trees. In order to remove the lower part of this ladder, the litter and the understory may be burned under control in winter, and where this has been done the results have been dramatic. Wildfires have raced through the forest and, upon reaching control-burned areas, have stopped dead. Unfortunately, there is not manpower enough to do a really significant amount of controlled burning. As much is done in Wharton State Forest as anywhere, and of its ninety-six thousand acres only about seven thousand are control-burned each winter. Wildfires have burned more than a third of the Wharton Forest since 1954.

"I like fire. I like to fight fire," the chief Wharton forester, Sydney Walker, said to me one day. "Fire is the key down here." Equipment is, to a considerable extent, mechanical now. Hand fighting with shovels and rakes has largely been supplanted by the use of tractor-drawn plows to cut forty-eight-inch swaths through the woods, along which backfires are set with kerosene torches. The big water trucks, some of which can hold five hundred gallons, are making back tanks obsolete. Aerial techniques are improving steadily. Airdrops, from light planes, used to be made with volclay, a fine clay mixed with water. Well placed, a clay airdrop could retard a fire. Now, liquid fertilizer (nitrogen and phosphorus, one to three) has replaced volclay, and when the fertilizer hits in the right place it will smother a modest fire altogether. Airdrops require skillful and nervy flying. About a hundred and eighty gallons of mixture are laid down, necessarily from a low altitude, and the target is the head fire. Done properly, a drop will cover an area of about a half acre. Pilots with experience in combat sometimes lack whatever it is that will make a man run a slow plane in close over a crown fire. A typical report of the Forest Fire Service in such a case said, "The pilot was a retired Air Force lieutenant colonel with no previous experience in fire-bombing. Although he was repeatedly advised that it was of major importance that we get to the fire swiftly before it could build up, he took an inordinately long time in takeoff. His helmet and goggles took a long time to adjust and he appeared slower than other pilots in starting his motor. Although his pilot's reports show from fifty to one hundred feet as being the height from which he dropped his load of retardant, the ground crew in general reported that he was much higher. One warden remarked, 'He will never put out any fire dropping from that height.' And another warden said, 'He was so high he looked like a sparrow.' "

Fire in the pines is never spontaneous, and lightning sets only about one per cent. There is an area in the northeastern part of the woods where most of the lightning fires begin, probably because there is a concentration of iron deposits there. It is supposed that the Chatsworth Fire started when a cigarette was tossed away by one of a group of woodcutters who were clearing the cedar swamp where the fire began. Carelessness is the cause of many fires, but not to the overwhelming extent that one might imagine. A remarkably common cause of fire in the pines is arson. Standing in all that dry sand, the forests glisten with oils and resins that—to some people—seem to beg for flame. Oak leaves in forests that are damp and rich are different from Pine Barrens oak leaves, which have so much protective oil concentrated within them that they appear to be made of shining green leather. The ground soaks up rainfall so efficiently that the litter on its surface is, more often than not, as dry as paper. In the sand soil, there are no earthworms and few bacteria to consume the litter, and it piles up three and four inches deep. In all, the Pine Barrens respond explosively to flame, and thus they appear to be irresistible to incendiaries of many kinds. Of the thirty-seven fires that occurred in the Wharton Forest in 1966, for example, the foresters say that twenty-four were definitely set by arsonists and three others probably were. The year before that, elsewhere in the pines, one man alone set sixty-nine fires. He was, at the time, a policeman in a town on the edge of the woods. After his actions became known, he was described by surprised neighbors as "a good family man" and "a nice guy." He himself "discovered" and reported all sixty-nine fires, usually calling them in on the police radio, and when he had been placed under arrest he couldn't explain why he had felt compelled to set the woods ablaze. Another man, in recent years, stole an arm patch from a fire warden and turned up at forest fires as a participant in the fighting. Wherever he was working, spot fires would break out, until the pattern of coincidences entangled him. After a fire, men from the Forest Fire Service go through the area where the burning began, often on their hands and knees, sifting through the ashes for evidence of the cause. Sometimes they find bits of railroad flares. More often, they find the remains of an ordinary matchbook with a wire wrapped around it. Incendiaries use the wire to add weight to the matchbook so that it will carry some distance into the woods when they toss it flaming from their automobiles. That way, they don't have to get out and walk. Almost without exception, arson in the pines is committed by people who come in from the outside. Pineys *have* set grudge fires from time to time, and colliers used to set fires because charred wood was good only for charcoal and they could buy it cheaply from the owners of the burned land. Pineys also used to make "skeeter smoke" by burning a mixture of pine needles, pine cones, pine chips, and charcoal in pans on their stoves. The smoke permeated their houses, and mosquitoes stayed away. Sometimes these smudge fires jumped off the stoves, burned down houses, and expanded into forest fires. Years ago, the pineys deliberately set fires in blueberry lowlands, because wild blueberry bushes will come back strong after a fire and produce more berries than they yielded before. This practice is still carried on by gatherers of wild blueberries in Maine, Vermont, and New Hampshire, but is forbidden in the Pine Barrens, where it was once given as the cause of a tenth of all forest fires. A relatively new cause of fire in the pines is burning automobiles. Foresters make their way through the smoldering aftermath of a headlong fire and at the source they find a blackened automobile. Teen-age hoods steal cars in cities, take them into the pines, strip them, ignite them, and leave the scene.

The Forest Fire Service has indices that show when the woods are least and most vulnerable to fire. There may be fires almost any day of the spring, summer, and fall, but when the indices are high the fires tend to be big. First, there is something called the buildup index, which takes into account the ground moisture and also whether the vegetation is cured, transitional, or green. When wind velocities, barometric readings, and fuel moisture levels are added in, the result is the burning index. The scale of the burning index goes from zero to two hundred. On April 20, 1963, the day of the worst forest fire in the recorded history of the Pine Barrens, the burning index shot past two hundred into the indeterminable beyond. It was not a particularly hot day, but the vegetation was still in the cured stage, winds were blowing at about fifty miles an hour, and there was a drought. Once a fire got started, there was not much chance that it could be controlled. Actually, twelve non-contiguous major fires started on that day. The big one began after a man who was burning brush about seven miles west of Mt. Misery left his fire because he thought it was out. It was brought under control about thirty miles to the east at midnight on April 23rd, and it was finally pronounced out on May 1st. Smoke from this fire palled the air and deeply reddened the sun as far away as Princeton. The men who fought the fire made stand after stand—first at a state highway and later at county roads, sand roads, and plowed lines—only to have the flames burst over them and force them to regroup farther east. Embers went into the upper winds and advanced as much as two miles at a jump, starting new fires where they landed. Several crown fires were spread out over a six-mile front, and rolling white heat was trailed by streaks of orange flame. The fire was so hot that it caused the surfaces of macadam roads to form bubbles. Overhead, white piles of smoke went up hundreds of feet, and against this white background, now and again, appeared black twisters of smoke from pitch. Multiple airdrops were made but did not significantly help. Finally, the crews were forced back all the way to the Garden State Parkway, where, forming long lines and working with shovels and back tanks, they made a last try to control the fire. They held it there, but it had only a few miles to go anyway before it would have reached the sea. One man died. As in the Chatsworth Fire, the damage to buildings was relatively light, but only because there were so few buildings to damage. The fire crossed the Pine Barrens from one side to the other, and burned seventy-five thousand nine hundred and twenty-five acres.

A color photograph taken of a section of woods just after the 1963 fire shows about what you would expect—blackened spars above a smoldering forest floor. A photograph taken from the same spot two months later presents to the viewer a forest panoply of summer green. Of all the natural phenomena of the Pine Barrens, the most startling one is the speed with which the vegetation comes back from fire. There has been so much fire in the pines for so many centuries that, through the resulting processes of natural selection, the species that grow there are not only highly flammable but are able to tolerate fire and come back quickly. There are only three kinds of pines in the United States that respond to fires by putting forth sprouts. Two of these—the pitch pine and the shortleaf pine—predominate in the Pine Barrens. (The other, the Chihuahua pine, grows in New Mexico.) The sprouts develop from dormant buds in the trunks and larger limbs, and soon after the fire dies down, out they come. All over the woods are pine trees with splendid green crowns and trunks that are still black from old fires. Oaks that are burned usually die at the top, but they reshoot from the roots. Chestnut oaks put out so many sprouts all around their trunks that in time the shoots form palisaded enclosures resembling jails, and drunken pineys were once incarcerated in them and left there until they sobered up. Almost every woody species in the Pine Barrens has the ability to sprout after fire. The understory starts right up again, and bracken fern and sheep laurel are particularly fast. Scrub oaks put out so many acorns after a fire that they look like over-decorated Christmas trees. This helps to increase, among other things, the communities of deer and grouse.

It is because of fire that pines are predominant in the Pine Barrens. There is thought to be a progression in the development of any forest from pioneer species to climax trees. Most ecologists agree that if fire were kept out of the Pine Barrens altogether, the woods would eventually be dominated by a climax of black oaks, white oaks, chestnut oaks, scarlet oaks, and a lesser proportion of hickories and red maples. In some areas, oaks dominate now. Fire, however, has generally stopped the march of natural progression, and the resulting situation is one that might be called biological inertia—apparently endless cycles of fire and sprouting. Fire favors the pine trees because they have thick bark that provides insulation from high temperatures, and also because burned ground is just about perfect for pine seed beds. Oaks lose vigor when they are repeatedly burned. They develop heart rot, and they die. Scarlet oaks go first, then chestnut oaks, then white oaks, then black oaks. Blackjack oaks are an exception and after a fire come back strong. In an area where a fire has been extremely hot, the pines die and the blackjack oaks put out basal sprouts that grow to be the predominant trees in that section. But, for the most part, fires are not that intense, and, working in behalf of the pitch and shortleaf pines, they clear out the competition. It would be an error, however, to think of forest fires as magic wands that clean the woods. Controlled burning can have this effect, but wildfires leave an ugly trail. Oak spars and—if the fire was hot enough—pine spars stick up everywhere. There are sprouts, but for a time there is no shade. Even when pines develop new crowns, several seasons must go by before the crowns are full. The white cedars, which are the most beautiful trees in the Pine Barrens, are killed outright if they are burned, and for years—standing feathery and dead—they commemorate the wildfire that took them. Foresters can cut an old pine and read in its occasional dark rings the dates of fires that have gone through the area in which it stands; 1930, 1927, 1924, 1922, 1916, 1910, 1905, 1894, 1885, and 1872 are the dates of dark rings that can still be read in some trees. Causes differed, but fires were frequent in the pines in the eighteenth and seventeenth centuries, and before that Indians burned the woods to improve conditions for hunting and travel. Almost certainly, the role of fire in the development of the Pine Barrens has been of importance since post-Wisconsin time, when the patterns of the present vegetation began to form as the great Wisconsin ice sheet receded.

The glacier reached only about as far south as Morristown, which is fifty miles north of the pines, but the torrents that poured from it as it melted carried southward prodigious loads of gravel that mounded here and there into what are now some of the hills of the Pine Barrens. As the early vegetation developed, the climate of the area was still arctic. The Pine Barrens were then a cold desert of permafrost and tundra—a scene that I found myself imagining at one point while I was spending some time with three men from the National Park Service who were making a general survey of the pinelands area. One man had recently returned from two years in Alaska. Standing on the observation platform of the fire tower on Bear Swamp Hill, he remarked that the Pine Barrens reminded him very much of Alaska, going on to say that the evergreen species were different but that their general appearance—and the appearance of the undulating land—was much the same from that high perspective. There is a theory that the Hudson River once flowed much farther south than it does now, and that it passed through the Pine Barrens, leaving more gravels, which eventually became more hills. Helderberg limestone from the upper Hudson Valley is found in the pines. When white men first saw the region, many of the pitch and shortleaf pines were about two hundred years old and about twenty inches in diameter. The white cedars, in their swamps, were larger. Some of them were six feet thick at the base and a thousand years old. When these great trees fell, some of them sank beneath the sphagnum moss and deep into the swamps, where they were sealed away from oxygen and were also protected from fungi by the acidulous muck. They were thus preserved. The mining of ancient cedar logs was once a source of income to some people in the pines, and even today the logs are occasionally found and removed. From them come the most durable of all cedar boards and shingles. During the Second World War, wood from sunken cedar logs taken from Pine Barrens swamps was used in the hulls of patrol torpedo boats. In Lebanon State Forest, which is four miles north of Chatsworth, foresters have put on display a pair of mined cedar logs, each about four feet thick.

No one has yet determined with certainty how the dwarf forests of the eastern Pine Barrens developed, but there have been many hypotheses, and, as one after another has been shown to be unsound, the process of elimination has led back to fire. Frequent as fires are everywhere in the pines, they are more frequent in the dwarf forests than anywhere else. The dwarf forests occur in two upland areas, which do not quite touch one another. The Upper Plains and the Lower Plains, as they are called, cover about twenty thousand acres. Pitch pines predominate there, as they do elsewhere in the Pine Barrens, but instead of rising fifty or sixty feet into the air they rise five feet. A snapshot of the Plains will often seem to take in huge expanses of forest, as if the picture had been made from a low-flying airplane, unless a human being happens to have been standing in the camera's range, in which case the person's head seems almost grotesque and planetary, outlined in sky above the tops of the trees. There is aluminum in the soil of the Plains, and one prominent hypothesis was that aluminum toxicity stunts the trees. Equal amounts of aluminum have been found, however, in Pine Barrens soils where trees grow high. Another hypothesis, long in vogue among botanists and soil scientists, was that a layer of hardpan a short distance beneath the surface was stunting the vegetation. But a graduate student from Rutgers dug three hundred well-spaced holes a few years ago and concluded that there is little or no hardpan under the Plains. Because the Plains are on high ground and winds are fierce there, it has been thought that the little trees are wind-stunted. But the Plains are not on the highest ground in the Pine Barrens. Winds are at least as fierce on the higher ground elsewhere, and the trees there are of normal height. According to the Nantucket-tip-moth theory, a small creature in the Plains eats into the pine trees' terminal shoots and cuts them back, dwarfing the trees. The tip moth, however, does not eat oaks, and twenty-two per cent of the trees in the Plains are oaks and they are just as tiny as the pines. Fred Brown gave me his own explanation for the existence of the Plains when we went there one day. "This ground is so poor a pismire can't live on it," he said. "If you found a pismire here, he'd be half starved to death." Studies have shown that the soil of the Plains is about the same as the soil of the rest of the Pine Barrens. What remains is fire. Wildfires have completely swept the Plains on an average of once every seven years for centuries. Young trees there that have not yet been hit by fire are apparently normal and have taproots, but after the trees have burned they lose their taproots, and their lateral roots spread abnormally far out—from twenty to thirty feet—forming a great mat with the lateral roots of other trees, all of which are dwarfs. The correlation with fire is apparent, but no one can say how fire causes the stunting. Another curiosity apparently brought about by fire is the type of pine cone that develops in the Plains. There are two races of pitch pines. One race has open cones (these are the familiar pine cones that have gaps between their scales) and the other race has closed cones (the scales fit tightly together, and the surfaces of the cones are smooth). Open cones drop from the trees once a year, but closed cones hang on until a fire comes, or until so many years have passed that they are finally squeezed off by other cones. In either case, aloft or on the ground, closed cones remain closed until they are opened by fire. Taxonomically, the open-cone race and the closed-cone race are not distinguished. In the Pine Barrens outside the Plains, the great majority of the pitch pines are of the open-cone race. In the Plains, ninety-nine per cent of the dwarf pitch pines produce closed cones. This, again, does not indicate why the trees are stunted, but it seems to point to the exceptional frequency of fire in the Plains, where the closed-cone race has been selected. Jack McCormick, who is chairman of the Department of Ecology and Land Management at the Academy of Natural Sciences of Philadelphia, spent an afternoon with me in the Plains, where he explained these hypotheses and phenomena. His doctoral dissertation was a study of two watersheds elsewhere in the Pine Barrens, and when he was working on it he lived in a trailer in the woods for two years. He feels that the Plains are ecologically unique, and he says that they are somewhat analogous to the chaparral of southern California. He hopes that the Plains will be left as they are. "From studies made here, we can add to our fund of information about the behavior of species under the influence of fire," he said. "Heaven knows what we'll find out. The average frequency of fires—once every six or seven years—means nothing in itself. Rapid sequence of fires—say, when three occur in six years—may have something to do with dwarfism. Also, at least to my knowledge, no one has planted an open-cone pitch pine and a closed-cone pitch pine side by side to see what would happen. Nor has anyone cross-pollinated open- and closed-cone pines. We don't know which is dominant. We don't know what a hybrid would do. We don't know a God-damned thing."

Near Warren Grove, in the Lower Plains, the Navy has a target area for skip bombers and dive bombers. The planes dive soundlessly, like toys on strings, all but hitting the five-foot trees as they pull out of their dives and simultaneously drop their payloads in the target area, usually with a concerted accuracy—plane after plane after plane—that is almost unbelievable. After each plane has gone and is moving up into the sky as if it were on the inside rim of a wheel, the sound of its jet comes to a ground observer—much too late to be connected in any sensible way with its source. Three years ago, one pilot did not pull out of a dive, and his exploding plane started a major forest fire.

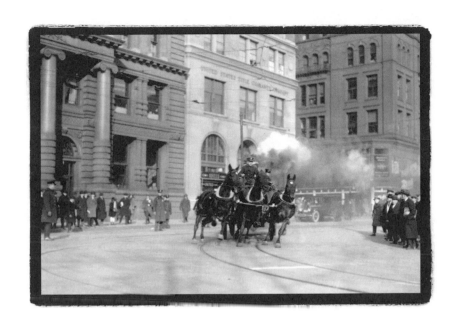

When Every One Is Panic Stricken
by Stephen Crane

*Stephen Crane's (1871–1900) 1894 portrait
of a New York City blaze reminds us that brave
and skillful fire fighters have been impressing
their fellow citizens for a long time.*

We were walking on one of the shadowy side streets, west of Sixth Avenue. The midnight silence and darkness was upon it save where at the point of intersection with the great avenue, there was a broad span of yellow light. From there came the steady monotonous jingle of streetcar bells and the weary clatter of hoofs on the cobbles. While the houses in this street turned black and mystically silent with the night, the avenue continued its eternal movement and life, a great vein that never slept nor paused. The gorgeous orange-hued lamps of a saloon flared plainly, and the figures of some loungers could be seen as they stood on the corner. Passing to and fro, the tiny black figures of people made an ornamental border on this fabric of yellow light.

The stranger was imparting to me some grim midnight reflections upon existence, and in the heavy shadows and in the great stillness pierced only by the dull thunder of the avenue, they were very impressive.

Suddenly the muffled cry of a woman came from one of those dark, impassive houses near us. There was the sound of the splinter and crash of broken glass, falling to the pavement. "What's that?" gasped the stranger. The scream contained that ominous quality, that weird timber which denotes fear of imminent death.

A policeman, huge and panting, ran past us with glitter of buttons and shield in the darkness. He flung himself upon the fire alarm box at the corner where the lamp shed a flicker of carmine tints upon the pavement. "Come on," shouted the stranger. He dragged me excitedly down the street. We came upon an old four story structure, with a long sign of a bakery over the basement windows, and the region about the quaint front door plastered with other signs. It was one of those ancient dwellings which the churning process of the city had changed into a hive of little industries.

At this time some dull gray smoke, faintly luminous in the night, writhed out from the tops of the second story windows, and from the basement there glared a deep and terrible hue of red, the color of satanic wrath, the color of murder. "Look! Look!" shouted the stranger.

It was extraordinary how the street awakened. It seemed but an instant before the pavements were studded with people. They swarmed from all directions, and from the dark mass arose countless exclamations, eager and swift.

"Where is it? Where is it?"

"No. 135."

"It's that old bakery."

"Is everybody out?"

"Look—gee—say, lookut 'er burn, would yeh?"

The windows of almost every house became crowded with people, clothed and partially clothed, many having rushed from their beds. Here were many women, and as their eyes fastened upon that terrible growing mass of red light one could hear their little cries, quavering with fear and dread. The smoke oozed in greater clouds from the spaces between the sashes of the windows, and urged by the fervor of the heat within, ascended in more rapid streaks and curves.

Upon the sidewalk there had been a woman who was fumbling mechanically with the buttons at the neck of her dress. Her features were lined in anguish; she seemed to be frantically searching her memory—her memory, that poor feeble contrivance that had deserted her at the first of the crisis, at the momentous time. She really struggled and tore hideously at some frightful mental wall that upreared between her and her senses, her very instincts. The policeman, running back from the fire alarm box, grabbed her, intending to haul her away from danger of falling things. Then something came to her like a bolt from the sky. The creature turned all gray, like an ape. A loud shriek rang out that made the spectators bend their bodies, twisting as if they were receiving sword thrusts.

"My baby! My baby! My baby!"

The policeman simply turned and plunged into the house. As the woman tossed her arms in maniacal gestures about her head, it could then be seen that she waved in one hand a little bamboo easel of the kind which people sometimes place in corners of their parlors. It appeared that she had with great difficulty saved it from the flames. Its cost should have been about thirty cents.

A long groaning sigh came from the crowd in the street, and from all the thronged windows. It was full of distress and pity, and a sort of cynical scorn for their impotency. Occasionally the woman screamed again. Another policeman was fending her off from the house, which she wished to enter in the frenzy of her motherhood, regardless of the flames. These people of the neighborhood, aroused from their beds, looked at the spectacle in a half-dazed fashion at times, as if they were contemplating the ravings of a red beast in a cage. The flames grew as if fanned by tempests, a sweeping, inexorable appetite of a thing, shining, with fierce, pitiless brilliancy, gleaming in the eyes of the crowd that were upturned to it in an ecstasy of awe, fear and, too, half-barbaric admiration. They felt the human helplessness that comes when nature breaks forth in passion, overturning the obstacles, emerging at a leap from the position of a slave to that of a master, a giant. There became audible a humming noise, the buzzing of curious machinery. It was the voices of the demons of the flame. The house, in manifest heroic indifference to the fury that raged in its entrails, maintained a stolid and imperturbable exterior, looming black and immovable against the turmoil of crimson.

Eager questions were flying to and fro in the street.

"Say, did a copper go in there?"

"Yeh! He come out again, though."

"He did not! He's in there yet!"

"Well, didn't I see 'im?"

"How long ago was the alarm sent in?"

" 'Bout a minute."

A woman leaned perilously from a window of a nearby apartment house and spoke querulously into the shadowy, jostling crowd beneath her, "Jack!"

And the voice of an unknown man in an unknown place answered her gruffly and short in the tones of a certain kind of downtrodden husband who rebels upon occasion, "What?"

"Will you come up here," cried the woman, shrilly irritable. "Supposin' this house should get afire—" It came to pass that during the progress of the conflagration these two held a terse and bitter domestic combat, infinitely commonplace in language and mental maneuvers.

The blaze had increased with a frightful vehemence and swiftness. Unconsciously, at times, the crowd dully moaned, their eyes fascinated by this exhibition of the strength of nature, their master after all, that ate them and their devices at will whenever it chose to fling down their little restrictions. The flames changed in color from crimson to lurid orange as glass was shattered by the heat, and fell crackling to the pavement. The baker, whose shop had been in the basement, was running about, weeping. A policeman had fought interminably to keep the crowd away from the front of the structure.

"Thunderation!" yelled the stranger, clutching my arm in a frenzy of excitement, "did you ever see anything burn so? Why, it's like an explosion. It's only been a matter of seconds since it started."

In the street, men had already begun to turn toward each other in that indefinite regret and sorrow, as if they were not quite sure of the reason of their mourning.

"Well, she's a goner!"

"Sure went up like a box of matches!"

"Great Scott, lookut 'er burn!"

Some individual among them furnished the inevitable grumble. "Well, these—" It was a half-coherent growling at conditions, men, fate, law.

Then, from the direction of the avenue there suddenly came a tempestuous roar, a clattering, rolling rush and thunder, as from the head-long sweep of a battery of artillery. Wild and shrill, like a clangorous noise of war, arose the voice of a gong.

One could see a sort of a delirium of excitement, of ardorous affection, go in a wave of emotion over this New York crowd, usually so stoical. Men looked at each other. "Quick work, eh?" They crushed back upon the pavements, leaving the street almost clear. All eyes were turned toward the corner, where the lights of the avenue glowed.

The roar grew and grew until it was as the sound of an army, charging. That policeman's hurried fingers sending the alarm from the box at the corner had aroused a tornado, a storm of horses, machinery, men. And now they were coming in clamor and riot of hoofs and wheels, while over all rang the piercing cry of the gong, tocsin-like, a noise of barbaric fights.

It thrilled the blood, this thunder. The stranger jerked his shoulders nervously and kept up a swift muttering. "Hear 'em come!" he said, breathlessly.

Then in an instant a fire patrol wagon, as if apparitional, flashed into view at the corner. The lights of the avenue gleamed for an instant upon the red and brass of the wagon, the helmets of the crew and the glossy sides of the galloping horses. Then it swung into the dark street and thundered down upon its journey, with but a half-view of a driver making his reins to be steel ribbons over the backs of his horses, mad from the fervor of their business.

The stranger's hand tightened convulsively upon my arm. His

enthusiasm was like the ardor of one who looks upon the pageantry of battles. "Ah, look at 'em! Look at 'em! Ain't that great? Why it hasn't been any time at all since the alarm was sent in, and now look!" As this clanging, rolling thing, drawn swiftly by the beautiful might of the horses, clamored through the street, one could feel the cheers, wild and valorous, at the very lips of these people habitually so calm, cynical, impassive. The crew tumbled from their wagon and ran toward the house. A hoarse shout arose high above the medley of noises.

Other roars, other clangings, were to be heard from all directions. It was extraordinary, the loud rumblings of wheels and the pealings of gongs aroused by a movement of the policeman's fingers.

Of a sudden, three white horses dashed down the street with their engine, a magnificent thing of silver-like glitter, that sent a storm of red sparks high into the air and smote the heart with the wail of its whistle.

A hosecart swept around the corner and into the narrow lane, whose close walls made the reverberations like the crash of infantry volleys. There was shine of lanterns, of helmets, of rubber coats, of the bright, strong trappings of the horses. The driver had been confronted by a dreadful little problem in streetcars and elevated railway pillars just as he was about to turn into the street, but there had been no pause, no hesitation. A clever dodge, a shrill grinding of the wheels in the streetcar tracks, a miss of this and an escape of that by a beautifully narrow margin, and the hosecart went on its headlong way. When the gleam-white and gold of the cart stopped in the shadowy street, it was but a moment before a stream of water, of a cold steel color, was plunging through a window into the yellow glare, into this house which was now a den of fire wolves, lashing, carousing, leaping, straining. A wet snake-like hose trailed underfoot to where the steamer was making the air pulsate with its swift vibrations.

From another direction had come another thunder that developed into a crash of sounds, as a hook-and-ladder truck, with long and graceful curves, spun around the other corner, with the horses running with steady leaps toward the place of the battle. It was always obvious that these men who drove were drivers in blood and fiber, charioteers incarnate.

When the ladders were placed against the side of the house, firemen went slowly up them, dragging their hose. They became outlined like black beetles against the red and yellow expanses of flames. A vast cloud of smoke, sprinkled thickly with sparks, went coiling heavily toward the black sky. Touched by the shine of the blaze, the smoke sometimes glowed dull red, the color of bricks. A crowd that, it seemed, had sprang from the cobbles, born at the sound of the wheels rushing through the night, thickly thronged the walks, pushed here and there by the policemen who scolded them roundly, evidently in an eternal state of injured surprise at their persistent desire to get a view of things.

As we walked to the corner we looked back and watched the red glimmer from the fire shine on the dark surging crowd over which towered at times the helmets of police. A billow of smoke swept away from the structure. Occasionally, burned out sparks, like fragments of dark tissue, fluttered in the air. At the corner a steamer was throbbing, churning, shaking in its power as if overcome with rage. A fireman was walking tranquilly about it scrutinizing the mechanism. He wore a blasé air. They all, in fact, seemed to look at fires with the calm, unexcited vision of veterans. It was only the populace with their new nerves, it seemed, who could feel the thrill and dash of these attacks, these furious charges made in the dead of night, at high noon, at any time, upon the common enemy, the loosened flame.

a c k n o w l e d g m e n t s

Many people made this anthology.

At Thunder's Mouth Press and Avalon Publishing Group:
Thanks to Ghadah Alrawi, Will Balliett, Linda Kosarin, Dan O'Connor, Neil Ortenberg, Paul Paddock, Susan Reich, David Riedy, Simon Sullivan, and Mike Walters for their support, dedication and hard work.

At The Writing Company:
Nat May did most of the research. Nate Hardcastle provided help and advice. Mark Klimek, Taylor Smith and March Truedsson took up slack on other projects.

At the Portland Public Library in Portland, Maine:
Thanks to the librarians for their assistance in finding and borrowing books and publications from around the country.

Thanks also to Sue Canavan for her design, Maria Fernandez for overseeing production and Shawneric Hachey for his generosity.

Finally, I am grateful to the writers whose work appears in this book.

"Blowup: What Went Wrong at Storm King Mountain", from *Fire* by Sebastian Junger. Copyright © 2001 by Sebastian Junger. Used by permission of W.W. Norton & Company, Inc. ✤ "Which Way Did He Run" by David Grann. Copyright © 2002 by the New York Times Co. Reprinted by permission. ✤ Excerpt from *The Fire Inside: Firefighters Talk about Their Lives* by Steve Delsohn. Copyright © 1996 by Steve Delsohn. Reprinted by permission of HarperCollins Publishers, Inc. ✤ Excerpt from *Fire Line: Summer Battles of the West* by Michael Thoele. Copyright © 1995 by Michael Thoele. Reprinted by permission of Fulcrum Publishing, Inc. ✤ Excerpt from *Working: People Talk About What They Do All Day Long and How They Feel About What They Do* by Studs Terkel. Copyright © 1974 by Studs Terkel. Reprinted by permission of Donadio & Olson, Inc. ✤ Excerpt from *Will the Circle Be Unbroken: Reflections on Death, Rebirth, and Hunger for a Faith* by Studs Terkel. Copyright © 2001 by Studs Terkel. Reprinted by permission of The New Press. (800)233-4830. ✤ Excerpt from *Report from Engine Co. 82* by Dennis Smith. Copyright © 1999 by Dennis Smith. Reprinted by permission of Warner Books, Inc. ✤ Excerpt from *On Fire* by Larry Brown. Copyright © 1993 by Larry Brown. Reprinted by permission of Algonquin Books of Chapel Hill, a division of Workman Publishing. ✤ "The Chief" by Elizabeth Kolbert. Copyright © 2001 by Elizabeth Kolbert and *The New Yorker*. Used by permission of the author. ✤ "Bound Upon a Wheel of Fire" by Sallie Tisdale. Copyright © Dec. 1989 by *Harper's Magazine*. All rights reserved. Reproduced from the January 1990 issue by special permission. ✤ Excerpt from *Young Men and Fire* by Norman Maclean. Copyright © 1992 by Norman Maclean. Used by permission of The University of Chicago Press. ✤ Excerpt from *Fire on the Rim* by Stephen J. Pyne. Copyright © 1989 by Stephen J. Pyne. Reprinted by permission of the Gerard McCauley Agency, Inc. ✤ Excerpt from "USFS 1919: The Ranger, the Cook, and a Hole in the Sky" from

b i b l i o g r a p h y

The selections used in this anthology were taken from the editions and publications listed below. In some cases, other editions may be easier to find. Hard-to-find or out-of-print titles often are available through inter-library loan services or through Internet booksellers.

Abbey, Edward. *The Journey Home*. New York: Penguin Books, 1991.

Bass, Rick. "The Fires Next Time." First appeared in *Audubon Magazine*, September-October 1995.

Brown, Larry. *On Fire*. Chapel Hill, NC: Algonquin Books of Chapel Hill, 1993.

Carey, Alan and Carey, Sandy. *Yellowstone's Red Summer*. Flagstaff, AZ: Northland Publishing Co., 1989.

Crane, Stephen. *The Complete Short Stories and Sketches of Stephen Crane*. New York: Doubleday, 1963. (For "When Every One Is Panic Stricken".)

Delsohn, Steve. *The Fire Inside: Firefighters Talk about Their Lives*. New York: HarperCollins, 1996.

Engle, Ed. *Seasonal: A Life Outside*. Boulder, CO: Pruett Publishing Co., 1989.

Grann, David. "Which Way Did He Run." First appeared in *The New York Times Magazine*, January 13, 2002.

Hackett, Thomas. "A Reporter at Large: Fire." First appeared in *The New Yorker*, October 2, 1989.

Junger, Sebastian. *Fire*. New York: W.W. Norton, 2001. (For "Blowup: What Went Wrong at Storm King Mountain".)

Kolbert, Elizabeth. "The Chief." First appeared in *The New Yorker*, October 8, 2001.

Maclean, Norman. *A River Runs Through It and Other Stories*. Chicago, IL: University of Chicago Press, 1976. (For "USFS 1919: The Ranger, the Cook, and a Hole in the Sky".)

Maclean, Norman. *Young Men and Fire*. Chicago, IL: University of Chicago Press, 1992.

McPhee, John. *The Pine Barrens*. New York: Farrar, Straus and Giroux, 1981.

Pyne, Stephen J. *Fire on the Rim* New York: Weidenfeld & Nicholson, 1989.

Smith, Dennis. *Report from Engine Co. 82*. New York: Saturday Review Press, 1972.

Terkel, Studs. *Will the Circle Be Unbroken: Reflections on Death, Rebirth, and Hunger for a Faith*. New York: The New Press, 2001.

Terkel, Studs. *Working: People Talk About What They Do All Day Long and How They Feel About What They Do*. New York: Random House, Inc., 1974.

Thoele, Michael. *Fire Line: Summer Battles of the West*. Golden, CO: Fulcrum Publishing, 1995.

Tisdale, Sallie. "Bound Upon a Wheel of Fire." First appeared in *Harper's Magazine*, January 1990.

Wagenknecht, Louise. "Pride and Glory of Firefighting is Hard to Resist." First appeared in *High Country News*, March 6, 1995.

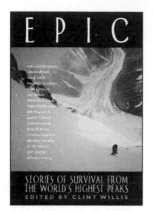

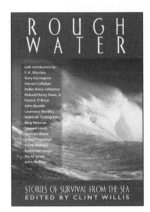
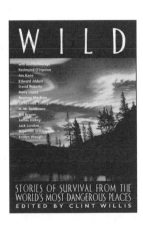
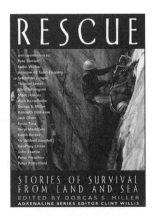

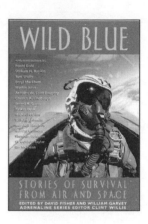

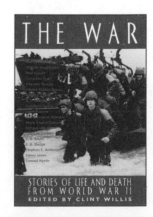